Growing Through Play

Readings for Parents & Teachers

Other Books by Robert D. Strom

Growing Together
Parent and Child Development

Parent and Child in Fiction

Growing Through Play

Readings for Parents & Teachers

Edited by
Robert D. Strom
Arizona State University

BROOKS/COLE PUBLISHING COMPANY
Monterey, California

To the teachers who have influenced me most,
Steven,
Paris,
and their mother.

Brooks/Cole Publishing Company
A Division of Wadsworth, Inc.

Printed in the United States of America

10   9   8   7   6   5   4

Library of Congress Cataloging in Publication Data
Main entry under title:

Growing through play.

1. Play. I. Strom, Robert D.
LB1137.G74   155.4'18   80-23729
ISBN O-8185-0423-4

Acquisition Editor: *Todd Lueders*
Production Editor: *John Bergez*
Interior and Cover Design: *Ruth Scott*
Cover Photo: *Stan Rice*
Interior Photos: *Shirley Strom*
Typesetting: *Nova Typesetting, Redmond, Washington*

Contributors

Dorothy Anker, Instructor of Early Childhood Education, The Erickson Institute for Early Education, Chicago

Bruno Bettelheim, Emeritus Director of the Orthogenic School and Rowley Professor of Education, University of Chicago

T. Berry Brazelton, Associate Professor of Pediatrics, Harvard Medical School, and Chief of the Child Development Unit, Boston Children's Hospital Medical Center

Jerome Bruner, Watts Professor of Psychology, Oxford University, England

James Christensen, Professor of Leisure Studies, Institute for Child Behavior and Development, University of Illinois

James S. Coleman, Professor of Sociology, University of Chicago

Rick Crandall, Professor of Leisure Studies, Institute for Child Behavior and Development, University of Illinois

Edward Devereux, Professor of Human Development and Family Studies, Cornell University

Catherine Devoney, Preschool Administrative Assistant, Montgomery County, Maryland, Association for Retarded Citizens

Jackie Foster, Head Teacher, Evanston, Illinois, Child Care Center

Mary Frank, Elementary Teacher, Home for Crippled Children, Pittsburgh

Joe L. Frost, Professor of Curriculum and Instruction, The University of Texas

C. Hugh Gardner, Assistant Professor of Educational Media, University of Georgia

Sandra Gardner, Fourth Grade Teacher at Gaines Elementary School, Athens, Georgia

Michael Guralnick, Professor of Education, The Ohio State University

Michael L. Henniger, Assistant Professor of Early Childhood Education, Southern Illinois University

Sandy Hotchkiss, Contributing Editor, *Human Behavior Magazine*

Eleanor Irwin, Clinical Assistant Professor of Child Psychiatry, Pittsburgh Child Guidance Center

Richard Louv, Contributing Editor, *Human Behavior Magazine*

Don Mack, Elementary School Teacher, Culver City, California

Rainer Martens, Professor of Physical Education, University of Illinois

Joan McLane, Head Teacher, The Free School of Evanston, Illinois

Mary Nicolaysen, Head Prekindergarten Teacher, Day School of the First Community Church, Columbus, Ohio

Mariann Pogge, Graduate Student in Legal Studies, Sangamon State University, Springfield, Illinois

Mary Ann Spencer Pulaski, Lecturer in Developmental Psychology, Hofstra University

Helen Rubin, Preschool Director, Montgomery County, Maryland, Association for Retarded Citizens

Albert J. Rutledge, Associate Professor, Department of Landscape Architecture, University of Illinois

Dorothy Singer, Professor of Child Psychology, Yale University

Jerome Singer, Professor of Child Psychology, Yale University

Joyce Sobel, Director, Evanston, Illinois, Day Nursery

Robert D. Strom, Professor of Education and Director of the Parent-Child Laboratory, Arizona State University

Brian Sutton-Smith, Professor of Education, The University of Pennsylvania

Jerry Thomas, Professor and Chairman, Department of Health, Physical and Recreation Education, Louisiana State University

Bernice Weissbourd, Educational Director, Evanston, Illinois, Child Care Center

Preface

Play is the dominant activity of children, their favorite way to spend time. Yet many parents express uncertainty about the value of play, and few teachers understand play well enough to defend its place in the school curriculum. For these reasons, it is appropriate to present a review of what is known about the relationship between play and child development.

The articles reproduced in this book present the results of recent research on a number of relevant questions. In particular, what are the unique benefits of peer play, parent-child play, dominion play, and solitary play? How can adults utilize play as a medium for teaching? What kinds of learning do children derive from experience with toys and games? What do handicapped and nonhandicapped youngsters stand to gain from playing with each other? How are children's sex roles influenced by play? How does the experience of participating in youth sports organized by adults compare with the experience of participating in sports organized by children themselves? In what ways are children affected by different types of playgrounds? What is the overall influence of play during the growing-up years? How can we prepare youngsters to thrive as grownups in a society that is giving adults increasing access to leisure time?

Each of the 11 chapters in the book is devoted to one of these contemporary concerns about play and leisure time. A perspective on each of these topics is provided in the general introduction. The selections have been chosen because of their insight, practical advice, and readability. Together, they offer a comprehensive view of the benefits of play and of how these benefits can be enhanced. At the end of each selection, there are questions designed to invite a comparison between the author's view and the reader's personal experience.

This book is intended for a diverse audience, including three groups in particular: (1) parents and teachers of preschool and elementary school children; (2) students of early-childhood education, child development, parent education, elementary physical education, and creative dramatics; and (3) research and development staff of toy manufacturers. The initial motivation to prepare this volume came from families participating in the Parent-Child Laboratory I direct at Arizona State University. It was their wish that the guidance they received from these readings might be extended to other mothers, fathers, and teachers. Encouragement has also been given by executives of the toy industry who have attended my play-research seminars.

All of us who learn from *Growing Through Play* owe thanks to the participating authors for allowing their work to be reprinted. In addition, I want to thank the following people for their helpful suggestions: Ruth Bogdanoff of Purdue University, Donald Gordon of Ohio University, Kevin Oltjenbruns of Colorado State University, Jerome Singer and Dorothy Singer of Yale University, Brian Sutton-Smith of the University of Pennsylvania, and Doug Thomson, President of the Toy Manufacturers of America. John Bergez and Todd Lueders of Brooks/Cole provided valuable ideas for improving the manuscript. Most of all, I am grateful to my wife, Shirley, and to our sons, Steven and Paris, for the play experiences we have shared throughout the world.

Robert D. Strom

Contents

Introduction 1

Chapter 3   Peers at Play   59

Chapter 4   Adults as Play Partners   77

Chapter 5   Teaching through Play   101

Chapter 6   Play and Sex Roles   131

Chapter 7   Sports and Spectators   147

Chapter 8   Places to Play   167

Chapter 9   Selection of Playthings   193

Chapter 10   The Exceptional Players   205

Chapter 11   Education for Leisure   223

Introduction

Parents and teachers want to respect the motivation of children. But is play a worthwhile way for boys and girls to spend much of their time? What do they stand to gain from play?

It has been my observation that people seldom give a direct answer to these questions. Instead, some will review the benefits of early academic training and contend that the results justify a de-emphasis on play. Others will express the opposite view, pointing out that in this century human beings for the first time have a life expectancy that permits full development, yet there are increasing pressures to shorten childhood by insisting that boys and girls grow up faster than ever before. Initially I was surprised by these sorts of roundabout responses, by the regularity with which men and women alike seemed to misinterpret my questions. Later, it became apparent that many of them simply could not provide substantive replies. The fact is that most adults don't know how play affects child development. As a consequence, they sometimes must make unwise decisions about what behaviors to encourage in children and which of their activities deserve priority. In hopes of improving this situation, *The Influence of Play* (Chapter 1) is offered as the first topic for consideration in this text.

During the past decade, significant discoveries have been made about the merits of *Playing Alone* (Chapter 2). As you might suppose, parents and teachers are less informed and less enthusiastic about solitary play than they are about play with peers. In general, adults believe that children should learn quickly and at an early age to play with companions and to share their belongings. This expectation ignores the importance of dominion play and its priority over social play in the natural sequence of development. As an increasing number of boys and girls are placed in daycare and preschool settings, it is essential that their need for dominion or territorial play be acknowledged and provided for. Certainly the need for solitude does not end with early childhood. However, solitary play becomes far more difficult to schedule during the elementary grades as school friends and organized groups demand more of a child's time. The problem of providing sufficient space for solitary play compounds the difficulty. In addition, boys and girls whose preschool experience has not included privacy need to learn how to be alone and how to allow classmates the same opportunity. Despite these difficulties, all the research indicators urge that more of us reconsider our views of solitary play and the value we assign to privacy during childhood.

Children today spend more time with peers than children of any previous generation. Although this condition fosters socialization and enhances children's sense of belonging, it also presents the possibility that immature influences may overshadow adult guidance. Therefore, while approving of *Peers at Play* (Chapter 3), most parents also want to know what's going on. This concern is reflected by the support for Little League Baseball, Pop Warner Football, and other youth sports that are organized and supervised by adults. But what are the consequences when grownups replace children as the primary decision-makers in play? Research is just beginning to provide some answers. Peer play has also undergone some changes within the school setting. There is growing acceptance of the gaming and simulation approach to classroom learning, especially for upper-grade students. Teachers and parents alike ought to become acquainted with the advantages and drawbacks of this instructional innovation. Similarly, each of us should be able to describe the unique benefits children can derive from peer play in and out of school.

The emerging concern with parent education has been accompanied by an increase in studies of family play. Some researchers have tried to assess the potential of the use of toys at home as a medium for teaching. Others have attempted to determine which childrearing goals can best be achieved through play. A valuable by-product of these studies regarding *Adults as Play Partners* (Chapter 4) is our new knowledge about the process of play, especially those factors that inhibit and support satisfying interaction. Some remarkable changes are taking place in attitudes toward adult-child play. Whereas parents once felt an obligation only to read to preschool children, they now consider participation in fantasy play to be another aspect of their responsibility. Parents' growing realization that their children need to play with them as well as with peers and that the benefits of parent-child play are different from those offered by agemates has created a new demand for guidance. Mothers and fathers want to know how they can use play to help children develop language competence, values, creativity, memory and problem-solving skills, and other assets. In short, they have become interested in *Teaching through Play* (Chapter 5). Although this recent transition from indifference to enthusiasm toward parent-child play is a favorable sign, the motivation for such play should go beyond instruction to include mutual enjoyment and gains in the family relationship.

Little children are informed of their sex roles through play. The kinds of toys they are given and the games they are encouraged to play define the behavior that is considered sex-appropriate for them. By the time boys and girls reach elementary school, some are already inclined to deny members of the opposite sex access to certain play activities. In the past, society condoned this kind of discrimination and made it a practice to label children who did not conform to tradition as tomboys or sissies. But perspectives about *Play and Sex Roles* (Chapter 6) are changing. We are in the midst of a revolution in our overall concept of masculinity and femininity. This revolution is supported by federal legislation prohibiting sex discrimination in athletic programs. It is relevant to examine the goals and gains of Title IX. Further, we should consider the long-range implications for sports budgets at all levels of schooling, the criteria for athletic awards, the composition of gym classes, the content of physical education, and the qualifications for membership in after-school activities such as the Little League. There is reason to believe that, besides sports-related materials, toys should also be considered a necessary school purchase in the movement for equal opportunity. To properly begin the group orientation of children to sex roles, preschool and primary-grade teachers must rely on toys more than on organized games. As both sexes are encouraged at school to feel comfortable with nontraditional playthings, they can more readily permit themselves and others a chance to explore new realms of experience.

In what ways do *Sports and Spectators* (Chapter 7) combine to influence child development? The phenomenal growth of Little League Baseball, Midget Football, soccer, and other youth sports has enabled millions of elementary school children to have adults observe them play. This experience also provides grownups a chance to demonstrate for youngsters the kind of spectators they should become. The way these fans—mothers and fathers mostly—react to the opposing team, decisions

by the referees, errors, lineup changes by the coach, and the final outcome of the game all contribute to their influence as observers. Their influence will be far more beneficial if more of them examine whether
their behavior is consistent with good sportsmanship. Another way spectators can help improve organized athletics is by adopting a more
childlike attitude toward games. For many parents, winning is the
ultimate goal in a sports contest, because it has the power to influence
motivation and self-impression in other areas of life. Boys and girls,
however, are more concerned with the process of play and the enjoyment of just being involved. Accepting the children's view means less
emphasis on winning and more emphasis on letting everyone participate.
It also means revising our expectations of coaches. Instead of being
measured strictly on the basis of a won-lost record, a coach would
qualify as successful if every player on the team received help in
developing game-related skills and the desired qualities of sportsmanship.

Finding safe and satisfying *Places to Play* (Chapter 8) can be
difficult, especially for youngsters living in crowded urban areas.
Building more playgrounds seems a reasonable solution until one
recognizes that many of the existing facilities are poorly attended.
Although better toys have been developed because of consumer
pressure, most playgrounds continue to look very much as they did 50
years ago. This time lag for improvement can be attributed to certain erroneous assumptions most adults make about play space. For one thing,
adults tend to assume that youngsters will sustain play whether the
playgrounds are altered or not. This notion contradicts our belief that in
other learning centers, such as the school, it is important to manipulate
and change the environment. The truth is that an unchanging
playground soon becomes redundant and boring, no longer functional. A
second mistake is to suppose that a playground can be designed and
maintained for the initial capital cost. According to this impression, a
good playground is one that requires virtually no maintenance.
However, play is a process of consuming information; when materials
and human resources are consumed, the playground must be changed if
it is to remain stimulating. Perhaps this feature of being responsive to the
growth needs of children is what makes European Adventure
Playgrounds so popular. A number of cities in the United States have
adopted the concept of Adventure Playgrounds. By reviewing the purposes of these facilities, the ways in which they are used, and the evaluations of participating families, we can learn more about the suitability of
similar playgrounds for our communities.

Besides adequate room for play, children need appropriate playthings.
Most parents can recall the frustration, tears, excessive dependence on

adults, and other consequences of poorly chosen toys. Hoping to avoid similar mistakes in the future, mothers and fathers are increasingly curious about the criteria they should apply in the *Selection of Playthings* (Chapter 9). They want to learn what kinds of toys and games will provide fun for children of various ages and also contribute to their learning. The judgment and recommendations of experts will be explored in this chapter.

There are related decisions to be made regarding *The Exceptional Players* (Chapter 10). For a long time it was common to emphasize the limitations of handicapped children, to isolate them from their nonhandicapped peers at school, and to prevent them from being involved in any risk-taking situations. Today, however, mainstreaming is the goal, and our expectations of the handicapped are increasingly guided by what they seem capable of achieving. The wisdom of this change in attitude can be readily observed. More and more handicapped people are getting into competitive sports such as baseball, basketball, skiing, and track. The Adventure Playgrounds are being designed to accommodate the unique needs of persons who are partially sighted, deaf, mentally retarded, or coping with some other disability. At school the integrated play of handicapped and nonhandicapped students is yielding benefits for both groups. And in the classroom, play-intervention strategies by teachers of the learning disabled have begun to pay off. Together these exciting innovations are moving our society closer to its democratic goals.

The primary purpose of schooling has always been to prepare children for the world of work. This goal is hardly sufficient now that the leisure proportion of our lives is beginning to exceed the proportion spent on work, thanks to a longer life span, earlier retirement, shorter workdays, and longer weekends. To be sure, youngsters will continue to be prepared for employment, but they also need help in learning how to use discretionary time. Presently there is no consensus about how to provide children with *Education for Leisure* (Chapter 11). Obviously, many grownups are themselves incapable of coping with free time. Nevertheless, it is becoming apparent that, in a technological society, work is no longer the place for everyone to attain a sense of satisfaction and pride. Millions of people whose jobs are routine and boring necessarily look forward to the weekends, when they can find fulfillment through leisure. As job alienation increases, the schools will need to acquaint students with a broad range of leisure possibilities and encourage their involvement. A less healthy alternative has begun to emerge, the view that people should limit their participation to those leisure pursuits in which they excel. It follows that, unless students are identified as having extraordinary talent in athletics, art, or music, they should withdraw from these activities, which could provide lifelong satisfaction. In this way many potentially active persons are being led to become spectators of the expert few and to enjoy only a vicarious sense of identity. By urging a less restrictive standard for participation in certain leisure activities, we can help more children develop a sense of self-esteem, identity, and well-being.

Chapter 1

The Influence of Play

1

The Rich Rewards of Make-Believe

Mary Ann Spencer Pulaski

Most adults expect children to slip away from reality into occasional dreams, to play make-believe games and to fantasize. A few even share their private worlds with an imaginary friend. We learn to tolerate or ignore such behavior, but we generally become annoyed and concerned when our children repeatedly withdraw into fantasy. After all, Freud made it clear that daydreams and make-believe play are signs of unfulfilled needs and desires, and Maria Montessori frowned upon fantasy as a "pathological tendency of early childhood." As I recall my own childhood experiences, however, I begin to question this dim view of young dreamers, and laboratory studies confirm some of my suspicions.

When I was a little girl, there was no television, no radio, not even many children to play with. My father was a Methodist missionary, and I grew up in a remote region of Japan. We lived in a rather poor district, and after I caught lice from the charcoal-seller's daughter, my mother kept my sister and me away from most of the neighborhood children. But we were not lonely. Our fertile imaginations became our own magical source of entertainment. On rainy days we went up in the attic and dressed up in old clothes. We delighted ourselves, and sometimes our parents, with endless plays. Most of the time we played the parts of characters from stories our parents had read or told us. When I was Peter Pan, my sister was Wendy, and our household pets, or even bushes in the garden, became the Lost Boys, the pirates and the Indians. We had a big woodpile in the backyard that served as a castle, a pirate ship or whatever. We hoisted a skull and crossbones on it, and it became the set for many a bloody battle. At times our games intruded upon family customs. I remember my mother's horror during the singing of grace at the table one evening when my sister and I intoned "and feast in pirate ship with Thee," in place of "and feast in paradise with Thee."

Defying the Gods

I also remember my own private fantasies. I used to lie on the grass, soaking wet in the midst of the Japanese monsoon rains, and pretend that Jupiter was hurling his lightning bolts at me as he roared his

Reprinted from *Psychology Today*, January 1974, pp. 68, 70–72, 74. Copyright © 1974 Ziff-Davis Publishing Company.

frustration in thunder over my head. It never occurred to me that the gods might not be interested in a skinny eight-year-old in a wet bathing suit, defiantly shaking her fist at the torrential sky.

As I grew older my fantasies became more private and less overt. I would spend hours daydreaming about romantic adventures or roles that seemed more glamorous than my own. By then I was the eldest of four girls. I recall traveling with my family on a Japanese train. I was embarrassed by the whole messy business of my baby sister's bottles and diapers, so I packed my own suitcase and chose a seat as far from my family as I could. I pretended that I was a young lady traveling alone. My pretense was probably obvious to the other passengers, since my light coloring clearly labeled me as a member of the only blonde, blue-eyed family on the train. In my fantasies, however, I was remotely and romantically alone.

During adolescence, I daydreamed about boys, and later about courtship and marriage. I planned my wedding and rehearsed every detail long before I met my future husband. How we got together and eventually were married was a far cry from my teen-age dreams. Soon the hard economic facts of life and World War II filled my thoughts, but I never lost the ability to fantasize, and it has stood me in good stead at crucial periods of my life.

During the War, I shoveled coal and snow, purchased food with a meager supply of food coupons, and brought up two children alone while my husband served in the Army Air Corps. I found comfort in retreating into dreams of his homecoming and life's return to normal.

I was over 40 when I went back to graduate school. I still had a family to care for and a first-grade class to teach. It was a long, hard struggle to climb the academic ladder to a doctorate in psychology, and sometimes the obstacles seemed overwhelming. But I learned to put them out of my mind at bedtime, lulling myself to sleep with dreams of the day when I would reach my ambitions. I fantasized that my daughter would graduate from college, my son from Yale Law School and I from my Ph.D. program all on the same day. They beat me by one year, but the fantasy served its purpose; the daydream led to reality.

Value of Fantasy

Daydreams and make-believe have served a very real purpose in my life. As a psychologist I realize they helped me develop cognitive and creative skills and enabled me to endure temporary deprivation while seeking long-range goals. Social scientists recently have learned that fantasies about home and family gave American prisoners of war the incentive to endure torture and deprivation in North Vietnam. Such evidence has encouraged behavioral scientists to study the little understood impact of dreams and make-believe on human development.

Probably the first social scientist to recognize the importance of make-believe in intellectual development was the Swiss psychologist Jean Piaget. Almost 50 years ago, as he watched his own three children growing up, he noted how the symbolism they used in make-believe games helped them bridge the gap between concrete experience and abstract thought. Just over 20 years ago Piaget's theories appeared in English, and since then a number of books have been published on the subject. The most recent collection of research is in Jerome L. Singer's *The Child's World of Make-Believe*. Singer is a clinical psychologist at Yale University who says the ability to daydream and make believe is a cognitive skill that helps us to be more creative, more flexible in solving problems, and it improves our capacity to postpone immediate gratification for future aims [see "The Importance of Daydreaming," PT, April 1968].

In one of Singer's experiments on daydreaming he found that children who have vivid imaginations can sit quietly longer than less imaginative youngsters. He divided 40 young children into high fantasizers and low fantasizers on the basis of tests and interviews in which he asked questions such as, "Do you ever have pictures in your head?" or "Do you have an animal or make-believe person you talk to?" He also asked about birth order, whether their parents read or told them stories regularly, how much time they spent watching television, etc.

After Singer had categorized 19 children as high fantasizers and 21 as low fantasizers, he told the children he was looking for "spacemen of the future" who would have to withstand long periods of solitary confinement. To test each child's ability to fulfill this requirement, Singer asked the children to sit or stand still quietly for 15 minutes.

Fantasy and Future Spacemen
Waiting Time (In Seconds)

	High Fantasizers	Low Fantasizers
15-minute Request	486.10	235.52
Indefinite Request	592.68	241.62

In another procedure he asked the children to stay still as long as they could and then signal when they had had enough. In both situations the mean waiting time was only about six minutes, but the high fantasizers were able to wait significantly longer than the low fantasizers. Those who made believe they were flying rockets or blasting off into space lasted longest. They rolled their eyes, imitated countdowns or engine noises under their breath, or turned an imaginary steering wheel while they were waiting.

Several other characteristics related to the ability to fantasize. The high fantasizers tended to be older children in their families with close relationships to both parents, especially their fathers. Surprisingly, there was no significant difference between the two groups in how much their parents read to them. When Singer asked the children to make up stories, the more imaginative group told more creative stories. Their tales were more original, contained a wider variety of characters and had more changes in time and location than did the stories of the low fantasizers. His interviews indicated that high and low fantasizers had significantly different life-styles. According to Singer a child's tendency to fantasize "seems to be a dimension of experience and exploration whose richness and frequency of employment grows from a set of optimal conditions including parental interest and acceptance of imagination, availability of adults for identification, and opportunity or occasion for practice of fantasy by being alone."

Fantasy for Hyperactive Children?

It occurred to me that this study might have implications for treating hyperactive children who have short attention spans and who cannot concentrate. If the ability to make believe helps children sit still and concentrate on their thoughts, perhaps we should encourage children to develop fantasy rather than medicating them with Ritalin.

There is a considerable body of literature which suggests that children who see human movement in inkblots or other projective tests can inhibit or control their own movements. These youngsters also give more imaginative responses to such tests than other children, which indicates they possess richer inner lives. Conversely, children who tell stories on projective tests with few references to body movements tend to be more active or impulsive in their own behavior. If a child sees an inkblot and says, "It looks like two waiters fighting over a pot of soup," he has the ability to see action in his mind rather than the need to act it out overtly.

A study by Anneliese Riess gives support to this interpretation. She found that wriggly children who could not sit still during an enforced waiting period gave no human-movement responses to projective tests. Those who did were much more likely to sit still or play quietly during the same period of time. When Riess asked the children to select toys to play with, the energetic group chose the more active toys while the more imaginative children picked the quieter playthings.

The studies by Singer, Riess and others led me to wonder what makes a child imaginative and creative when he plays with toys. I thought certain children might have a predisposition to fantasy, or possibly it had something to do with the toys a child's parents gave him to play with. When I was growing up we constructed many of our own toys out of odds and ends. We created entire families of dolls out of corncobs, and we made flower children with hollyhocks, giant azaleas, and pansies. Years later, when my daughter and her friends began to play with Barbie dolls, I was as intrigued as they with the tiny shoes and pocketbooks. But when Barbie began to appear with sexy underwear and glamorous evening dresses, I questioned her appropriateness for these elementary-age children. Later, as I listened to the little girls act out their stilted, stereotyped doll play, it occurred to me that the very completeness of the dolls and their wardrobes left nothing to their imaginations. My beloved rag doll, sent to me in a Christmas box by an Upstate New York church, assumed every conceivable role in my make-believe play; she was a baby, a witch, a bride, and sometimes a fairy princess. I began to suspect that a doll dressed in a white satin gown and wearing a veil would elicit little more than a standard, probably materialistic, and somewhat dull bridal romance.

Barbie Dolls or Clay

With all this in mind, I designed a study based on the hypothesis that simple unstructured play materials, such as paints, clay, or dress-up clothes, would evoke more imaginative play than highly structured materials such as ready-made costumes, Barbie or GI-Joe dolls.

I divided kindergarten, first- and second-grade children into groups of equal intelligence. Using tests and interviews similar to Singer's, I judged which children were high fantasizers and which were low. Then each child played with each kind of toy for two sessions. I also asked them to "make up a story or put on a show," which I tape-recorded. Independent judges rated their stories and plays for the amount and degree of imagination and originality they possessed.

When I analyzed the results, I was surprised to find that the structure built into the toys had little effect on the creativity of the play. By the age of five, the high fantasizers were already playing in an imaginative way with both structured and unstructured toys, while the low-fantasy youngsters simply fooled around and manipulated both types of playthings. The high-fantasy children scored higher in their stories on the number of fantasy themes, their organization and variety, their distance from real-life situations, and the concentration of subjects. They also were more flexible in their ability to switch to another activity when they were interrupted.

These results suggest that children's predisposition to fantasize may be pretty well formed by the age of five. It also indicates that children low in fantasy may be less creative and less flexible in their thinking, and poorer at concentration. They apparently tell more concrete and ordinary stories than youngsters with active imaginations. My study also supported Riess's finding that the more physically active children tended to be low fantasizers.

Fantasy and Aggression

The implication that a five-year-old child's fantasy level is already set has led to studies of nursery-school children. Jerome Singer and Dorothy Singer are conducting extensive research on fantasy among two- to five-year-olds. They classify the children in terms of their imaginative play predisposition (IPP). The IPP measures imaginativeness (from stimulus bound to high originality), emotion (from no interest to extreme delight), and concentration (from highly distractible to intensely absorbed). The Singers also observe and measure the children's moods during both free and structured play, and rate their levels of aggression for each minute of play time.

Though all the results are not in, the Singers do say that "three- and four-year-olds are still in a period of change and growth, and subject to the impact of specific situations on the degree to which they can play various types of imaginative games." More importantly, they find that boys who are low in imaginative-play predisposition are distinctly more aggressive than high-IPP boys. We begin to see a pattern emerging. Low fantasizers tend to be more aggressive and physically active than their highly imaginative peers.

While it is dangerous to generalize on the basis of such limited experimentation, a predisposition to fantasy may be a part of our general life-style, and it may represent a dimension of human competence available for enriching life. It seems to make life more enjoyable, and to help calm aggressive frustration.

One of my colleagues, Ephraim Biblow, conducted an experiment to show how an individual who is skilled in fantasy can reduce feelings of aggression. He selected 30 high and 30 low fantasizers out of a group of 130 white fifth-graders of normal intelligence and gave them a very frustrating job. While the child was working on the task, older children teased him and interfered with his work. After several minutes of this maddening treatment, the experimenter rated each child on his level of aggression. Next Biblow divided the children into three experimental groups and showed them an aggressive film depicting verbal and physical arguments among children, an episode based upon the fantasy, *The Adventures of Chitty Chitty Bang Bang*, or slides that presented mathematical problems. Then the youngsters played with various toys. Biblow rated them on their choice of toys and the moods they displayed towards the playthings and other children.

The high-fantasy children showed a significant decrease in their level of aggression no matter which film they had viewed. The low-fantasy children showed no decrease in aggression after the films, and those who saw the aggressive film had even higher aggression scores than before. The children who viewed the problem-solving slides showed no change in mood.

Fantasy and Aggression

Group	Aggression Scores	
	Before Film	After Film
High fantasy— aggressive film	1.80	.80
High fantasy— fantasy film	1.77	.85
High fantasy— problem-solving slides	1.82	1.63
Low fantasy— aggresive film	2.71	3.11
Low fantasy— fantasy film	2.74	2.71
Low fantasy— problem-solving slides	2.68	2.81

This study implies that individuals with well-developed fantasy skills can use any type of fantasy experience, aggressive or otherwise, to reduce feelings of frustration and aggression. If this is so, perhaps we can change other unhappy moods with an interval of fantasy.

Increasing Creative Play

Several recent studies provide us with information on how to increase fantasy and make-believe play. Joan Freyberg selected 80 kindergarten children from New York City whose economically hard-pressed parents had little education. She divided the children into high-fantasy, low-fantasy and control groups, systematically observed their behavior during free play, and then gave the high and low fantasizers eight training sessions in creative play. She used pipe-cleaner people, Playdoh, blocks and Tinkertoys to act out small plots and engage in make-believe adventures. At first she had to do most of the storytelling herself, but as the children caught on, the stories became spontaneous, original, and sometimes took surprising turns.

Creative Play Training

	High-Fantasy Children (N=20)		Low-Fantasy Children (N=20)	
	Before Training	After Training	Before Training	After Training
Imaginativeness	2.53	4.02	1.06	2.04
Emotion	2.58	3.93	1.24	2.26
Concentration	2.28	4.12	1.17	2.18

At the end of eight sessions both high and low fantasizers had improved significantly in the creativity of their play, as measured by the IPP. Their expression of positive emotion and degree of concentration also increased. The control group, which had eight sessions of play during which they manipulated jigsaw puzzles and Tinkertoys, showed no change. Two months later, the experimental children were still playing with greater imagination and improved verbal communication than before the training sessions. They were also more spontaneous and had increased attention spans. Freyberg's experiment dramatically demonstrates how direct teaching can increase children's ability to fantasize.

Films and Fancy

In another study, Sybil Gottlieb showed abstract movies to elementary and junior-high-school students. She interpreted the films realistically for some groups and imaginatively for others. Then she ran another film for the youngsters and asked them to write their own interpretations of what they had viewed. The junior-high-school subjects classified as high fantasizers wrote original and imaginative stories no matter what story they had heard, while the low-fantasy group consistently wrote concrete, realistic and conventional stories. The elementary-school children, on the other hand, showed a significant increase in the amount of fantasy they used if they had heard a fanciful interpretation of the first movie. Again this supports the notion that the ability to fantasize is a personality characteristic that develops with age and becomes part of one's cognitive life-style.

Adult Models Are Important

These two studies show the effectiveness of an adult model in helping children develop make-believe stories and imaginative thoughts. Sara Smilansky in Israel and D. El'Konin in Russia have conducted research which implies that adult models are not only desirable but necessary for children to carry out make-believe play. Both researchers think that the verbal communication and interaction in fantasy help children develop language skills.

Recently Sophie Lovinger of Central Michigan University conducted a study to find out if training four- and five-year-olds to play imaginatively would improve their verbal expression. First she divided a group of 37 disadvantaged children into an experimental and a control group. She assessed each child's level of make-believe play and recorded his speech. Next she measured their levels of language development with the Verbal Expression Scale of the Illinois Test of Psycholinguistic Abilities. Finally, a woman trained in speech and theater techniques moved right into the classroom during free-play time to help the youngsters in the experimental group act out familiar activities such as cooking, shopping, or taking care of a baby. When the children were already engaged in make-believe play, she joined them, adding novel details and introducing vivid new words to their games. She encouraged one group who were pretending to buy ice-cream cones by saying, "Lick the side where it's dripping," and she suggested that another group take a fishing trip in the school's new rocking boat.

After 25 weeks of this admittedly haphazard intervention, Lovinger retested the children. Her results were encouraging and significant. On the pretest, there was no difference in language skills between control and experimental groups. On the posttest, the experimental groups used significantly more words and sentences than the controls, and they also achieved higher scores on the Verbal Expression Scale. At the beginning of the study, the girls in both the experimental and control groups used more complex forms of play than the boys. At the end of the experiment, sex differences had disappeared, and the experimental group as a whole used significantly more creative play than the controls. Lovinger, like Freyberg, found that children enjoy having adults play with them. Her results also indicate that fantasizing increases a child's language ability and that this improvement will transfer to other cognitive tasks.

Imagination Needs Privacy

Clearly make-believe play is an intrinsic part of normal growth. It is associated with verbal fluency, waiting ability, increased concentration, positive attitudes in life, flexibility, originality and imagination. Psychologists now are learning how to encourage and foster fantasy in children. We have found that children need privacy and time to themselves to think over and replay their experiences. A child cannot fantasize with a television set blaring in his ear or an interfering mother checking up on him every 10 minutes. A child should have a somewhat unstructured environment, free from meticulous order, to help him become more flexible in using materials at hand. He needs a variety of interesting playthings that he can use in a number of different ways.

By sending out subtle signals of approval or disapproval, parents and teachers consciously and unconsciously encourage or discourage children's imaginative play. Adults should become more aware of their impact as models and shapers of young people's behavior.

Theater in the Schools

An exciting program aimed at encouraging creative play is now taking place in some New York public schools. A group of young actors, supported by the Performing Arts Foundation of Long Island, goes into a school to show teachers and students imaginative techniques that add new dimensions to the basic curriculum. The actors, for instance, might start a lesson in communication by teaching children to pantomime, use sign language, or play charades.

One day, I watched two actors ask fifth-graders to improvise with a stick. They used it as a cane, a fishing pole, a toothbrush, a pogo stick, a sword or a guitar. The actors call this a theater game. I call it mind-stretching. Later on, in the gym, the actors helped 300 children put on an imaginary carnival. The players divided the boys and girls into groups and gave them roles as horses, riders on a merry-go-round, members of a side show, etc. Every child had a chance to do something. As the school psychologist, I was fascinated by the way children ended up in suitable roles. When the actors needed someone to challenge the "strong man," the most hostile, aggressive little boy in the school stepped forward. He flexed his muscles, and in pantomime he "threw" the strong man. A great cheer went up from the admiring audience. Ricky was a hero and his glow lasted all day long.

The New Mythology of Television

The imaginary carnival illustrates the final ingredient necessary to develop and encourage make-believe. Children must have content in order to fantasize. They cannot produce a meaningful imitation of a carnival unless they know what a carnival is. Much of this material comes from stories adults read to children, and now television provides additional content for today's young fantasizers. I personally think television time should be limited, but in homes where parents do not read to their children, it may be filling a much-needed gap. Jerome Singer feels strongly that television has had a great impact on the cognitive and fantasy development of children whose parents do not pass on legends, myths, fairy tales, and poems to their offspring. "In this sense," says Singer, "television has widened the horizons of the poor and provided them with a great deal of material that can be used in the course of make-believe."

Only time and more research will tell us whether Singer is correct, but it appears that children play out in fantasy what they see on TV. If parents and teachers enter into and encourage make-believe play instead of shaming or ridiculing it, children will be more likely to develop this skill. It seems strange that we push, drag, and harass our children to adapt to a world that many of us find unsatisfying. We should allow children to enjoy the magical world of childhood. Let us give youngsters the time, privacy and respect necessary for them to play out their fantasies, dream their daydreams and bring imagination, understanding and romance into this tired old world.

Sharing Your Impressions

1. Recall some of the common daydreams you had during childhood and adolescence.
2. In what ways have your fantasies changed since childhood?
3. Identify some of the benefits fantasy provides for children and adults.
4. Speculate about how our lives would be different if we never had daydreams or fantasies.
5. Describe one of the tall tales you made up as a child and the consequences that followed.

6. Recommend some ways of reacting to children that would allow adults to accept and value fantasy while still emphasizing the importance of truth.
7. In your opinion, how is television influencing the fantasy life of children and adults?

2

Child's Play

Jerome Bruner

Experimental psychology tends to be rather a sober discipline, tough-minded not only in its procedures, but in its choice of topics as well. They must be scientifically manageable. No surprise, then, that when it began extending its investigations into the realm of early human development it steered clear of so antic a phenomenon as play. For even as recently as a decade ago, Harold Schlosberg of Brown University, a highly respected critic, had published a carefully reasoned paper concluding sternly that, since play could not even be properly defined, it could scarcely be a manageable topic for experimental research. His paper was not without merit, for the phenomena of play cannot be impeccably framed into a single operational definition. How indeed can one encompass so motley a set of entries as childish punning, cowboys-and-Indians, and the construction of a tower of bricks into a single or even a sober dictionary entry?

Fortunately, the progress of research is subject to accidents of opportunity. Once data begin seriously to undermine presuppositions, the course can change very quickly. A decade ago, while Schlosberg's words still reverberated, work on primate ethology began to force a change in direction, raising new and basic questions about the nature and role of play in the evolution of the primate series. On closer inspection, play is not as diverse a phenomenon as had been thought, particularly when looked at in its natural setting. Nor is it all that antic in its structure, if analyzed properly. But perhaps most important, its role during immaturity appears to be more and more central as one moves up the living primate series from Old World monkeys through Great Apes, to Man—suggesting that in the evolution of primates, marked by an increase in the number of years of immaturity, the selection of a capacity for play during those years may have been crucial. So if play seemed to the methodologically vexed to be an unmanageable laboratory topic, primatologists were pondering its possible centrality in evolution!

A first field finding served to reduce the apparently dizzying variety of forms that play could take. On closer inspection, it turns out that play is universally accompanied in subhuman primates by a recognizable form of metasignalling, a "play face," first carefully studied by the Dutch primatologist van Hooff (Figure 1). It signifies within the species the message, to use Gregory Bateson's phrase, "this is play." It is a powerful signal—redundant in its features, which include a particular kind of open-mouthed gesture, a slack but exaggerated gait, and a marked "galumphing" in movement—and its function is plainly

FIGURE 1.   Sketch showing a chimpanzee play face.

not to be understood simply as "practice of instinctive activities crucial for survival." When, for example, Stephen Miller and I set about analyzing filmed field records of juvenile play behavior made by Irven DeVore while studying Savanna baboons in the Amboseli Game Reserve in East Africa, we very quickly discovered that if one young animal did not see the "metasignal" of another who was seeking to play-fight with him, a real fight broke out with no lack of skill. But once the signal was perceived by both parties the fight was transformed into the universally recognizable clownish ballet of monkeys feigning a fight. They obviously knew how to do it both ways. What was it for, then, play fighting? And why should the accompanying form of metasignalling have been selected in evolution?

We begin to get a hint of the functional significance of play in higher primates from the pioneering observations of the group led by Jane Van Lawick-Goodall studying free-ranging chimpanzees at the Gombe Stream Reserve in Tanzania. Recall first the considerably longer childhood in chimpanzees than in Old World monkeys—the young chimp in close contact with the mother for four or five years during which the mother has no other offspring, whilst in monkeys, the oestrus cycle assures that within a year new young are born, with the rapidly maturing animals of last year's crop relegated to a peer group of juveniles in which play declines rapidly.

Sitting with Mother

David Hamburg of Stanford, a psychiatrist-primatologist working at Gombe Stream, has noted the extent to which young chimpanzees in the first five years spend time observing adult behavior, incorporating observed patterns of adult behavior into their play. Van Lawick-Goodall has a telling observation to report that relates this early observation-cum-play to adult skilled behavior—an observation that deepens our understanding of the function of early play. Adult chimps develop (when the ecology permits) a very skilled technique of termiting, in which they put mouth-wetted, stripped sticks into the opening of a termite hill, wait a bit for the termites to adhere to the stick, then carefully remove their fishing "instrument" with termites adhering to it which they then eat with relish. One of the young animals, Merlin, lost his mother in his third year. He had not learned to termite by four-and-a-half nearly as well as the others, though raised by older siblings. For the young animals appear to learn the "art of termiting" by sitting by the mother, buffered from pressures, trying out in play and learning the individual constituent acts that make up termiting, and without the usual reinforcement of food from catching: learning to play with sticks, to strip leaves from twigs, and to pick the right length of twig for getting into different holes. These are the constituents that must be combined in the final act, and they are tried out in all manner of antic episodes.

Merlin, compared to his age mates, was inept and unequipped. He had not had the opportunity for such observation and play nor, probably, did he get the buffering from distraction and pressure normally provided by the presence of a mother. This would suggest, then, that play has the effect of providing practice not so much of survival-relevant instinctive behavior but, rather, of making possible the playful practice of subroutines of behavior later to be combined in more useful problem solving. What appears to be at stake in play is the opportunity for assembling and reassembling behavior sequences for skilled action. That, at least, is one function of play.

It suggests a more general feature of play. It is able to reduce or neutralise the pressure of goal-directed action, the "push" to successful completion of an act. There is a well known rule in the psychology of learning, the Yerkes-Dodson law, that states that the more complex a skill to be learned, the lower the *optimum* motivational level required for fastest learning. Play, then, may provide the means for reducing excessive drive. The distinguished Russian investigator Lev Vygotsky in a long-lost manuscript published a few years ago reports an investigation in which young children could easily be induced not to eat their favorite candy when laid before them when the candy was made part of a game of "Poison." And years before, Wolfgang Köhler had reported that when his chimps were learning to stack boxes to reach fruit suspended from the high tops of their cages, they often lost interest in eating the fruit when they were closing in on the solution. Indeed, Peter Reynolds in a widely acclaimed paper on play in primates given to the American Association for the Advancement of Science in Philadelphia in 1972 remarks that the essence of play is to dissociate goal-directed behavior from its principal drive system and customary reinforcements. It is no surprise, then, to find results indicating that prior play with materials improves children's problem solving with those materials later.

Kathy Sylva of Harvard and I worked with children aged three to five who had the task of fishing a prize from a latched box out of reach. To do so, they had to extend two sticks by clamping them together. The children were given various "training" procedures beforehand, including explaining the principle of clamping sticks together, or practice in fastening clamps on single sticks, or an opportunity to watch the experimenter carry out the task. One group was simply allowed to play with the materials. They did as well in solving the problem as the ones who had been given a demonstration of the principle of clamping sticks together and better than any of the other groups. In fact, what was striking about the play group was their tenacity in sticking with the task so that even when they were poor in their initial approach, they ended by solving the problem. What was particularly striking was their capacity to resist frustration and "giving up." They were playing.

The Young Lead the Way

There are comparable results on primates below man where the pressure is taken off animals by other means—as by semi-domestication achieved by putting out food in a natural habitat, a technique pioneered by Japanese primatologists. It appears to have the effect of increasing innovation in the animals studied. Japanese macaques at Takasakiyama have taken to washing yams, to separating maize from the sand on which it is spread by dropping a handful of the mix into seawater and letting the sand sink. And once in the water, playing in this new medium to the edge of which they have been transplanted, the young learn to swim, first in play, and then begin swimming off, migrating to near islands. In all of these activities, it is the playful young who are centrally involved in the new enterprises, even if they may not always be the innovators of the new "technologies." But it is the young who are game for a change, and it is this gameness that predisposes the troop to change its ways—with the fully adult males often the most resistant, or at least the most out of touch, for the novelties are being tried out in the groups playing around the mother from which the big males are absent. Jean Claude Fady, the French primatologist, has shown that even ordinarily combative adult males will cooperate with each other in moving heavy rocks under which food is hidden—if the pressure is taken off by the technique of semi-domestication.

Ample early opportunity for play may have a more lasting effect still, as Corinne Hutt has shown. She designed a super-toy for children of three to five years old, consisting of a table with a lever, buzzer, bells, and counters, different movements of the lever systematically sounding buzzers and turning counters, etc. Children first explore its possibilities, then having contented themselves, often proceed to play. She was able to rate how inventive the children were in their play, dividing them into non-explorers, explorers, and inventive explorers, the last group carrying on all the way from initial exploration to full-blown play. Four years later, when the children were aged seven to ten, she tested them again on a creativity test designed by Mike Wallach and Nathan Kogan in the United States, as well as on some personality tests.

The more inventive and exploratory the children had been initially in playing with the super-toy, the higher their originality scores were four years later. The non-exploring boys in general had come to view themselves as unadventurous and inactive and their parents and teachers considered them as lacking curiosity. The non-exploratory and unplayful girls were later rather unforthcoming in social interaction as well and more tense than their originally more playful mates. Early unplayfulness may go with a lack of later originality.

Obviously, more studies of this kind are needed (and are in progress). But the psychiatrist Erik Erikson, reporting in his Godkin Lectures at Harvard in 1973 on a thirty-year follow-up of children earlier studied, has commented that the ones with the most interesting and fulfilling lives were the ones who had managed to keep a sense of playfulness at the center of things.

Play Has Rules

Consider play now from a structural point of view as a form of activity. Rather than being "random" it is usually found to be characterized by a recognizable rule structure.

New studies by the young American psycholinguist Catherine Garvey show how three- to five-year-old children, playing in pairs, manage implicitly even in their simplest games to create and recognize rules and expectancies, managing the while to distinguish sharply between the structure of make-believe or possibility and the real thing. Amusing though Catherine Garvey's protocols may be, they reveal a concise, almost grammatical quality in the interchanges and an extraordinary sensitivity on the part of the children to violations of implicit expectancies and codes.

It is hardly surprising then that different cultures encourage different forms of play as "fitting." Ours tend, in the main, to admire play and games of "zero sum," one wins what the other loses. The anthropologist Kenelm Burridge contrasts our favorite form with a typical ritual food-exchange game of "taketak" among the Tangu in New Guinea, a tribe that practices strict and equal sharing. The object of their game is to achieve equal shares among the players—not to win, not to lose, but to tie. It is reminiscent of a game reported years ago by James Sully. He tells of two sisters, five and seven, who played a game they called "Sisters," a game with one rule: equal shares for each player, no matter what, in their case quite unlike life! We are only at the beginning of studying the functions of play in fitting children to their culture, but there are some classic studies.

If the rule structure of human play and games sensitizes the child to the rules of culture, both generally and in preparation for a particular way of life, then surely play must have some special role in nurturing symbolic activity generally. For culture is symbolism in action. Does play then have some deep connection with the origins of language? One can never know. Yet, we have already noted the extraordinary combinatorial push behind play, its working out of variations. Play is certainly implicated in early language acquisition. Its structured interactions and "rules" precede and are a part of the child's first mastery of language. Our own studies at Oxford on language acquisition suggest that in exchange games, in "peek-bo," and in other structured interactions, young children learn to signal and to recognize signals and expectancies. They delight in primitive rule structures that come to govern their encounters. In these encounters they master the idea of "privileges of occurrence" so central to grammar, as well as other constituents of language that must later be put together.

Indeed, there is a celebrated and highly technical volume by Ruth Weir on language play in a two-and-one-half year old child, *Language in the Crib,* in which she reports on the language of her son Anthony after he had been put to bed with lights out. He pushes combinatorial activity to the limit, phonologically, syntactically, and semantically, often to the point at which he remonstrates himself with an adult "Oh no, no."

Much more is being learned about play than we would have expected a decade ago. We have come a long way since Piaget's brilliant observations on the role of play in assimilating the child's experience to his personal schema of the world, as preparation for later accommodation to it. A new period of research on play is underway. Nick Blurton-Jones has shown that Niko Tinbergen's ethological methods can be applied to children at play as readily as to chimps in the forest. The new work begins to suggest why play is the principal business of childhood, the vehicle of improvisation and combination, the first carrier of rule systems through which a world of cultural restraint is substituted for the operation of impulse.

That such research as that reported raises deep questions about the role of play in our own society is, of course, self-evident. Although we do not yet know how important play is for growing up, we do know that it is serious business. How serious it is can perhaps be condensed by citing the conclusion of a study done on children's laughter by Alan Sroufe and his colleagues at Minnesota. They find that those things most likely to make a child laugh when done by his mother at a year are most likely to make him cry when done by a stranger.

Sharing Your Impressions

1. Describe some of your own observations and conclusions regarding animals at play.

2. Compare the level of task persistence children show during play with their level of persistence in other tasks.
3. Describe some of the things your child has learned to do by playing.
4. What are some skills you learned during child play that you still use?
5. In what ways does play contribute to a child's problem-solving ability?
6. Why do you suppose so many children lose their sense of playfulness as they grow up?

3

Children at Play

Brian Sutton-Smith

Our civilization has not paid much rational attention to play. Rather, we have considered it to be irrational, trivial, ephemeral—not really critical. The seventeenth-century creation of an "innocent" childhood has led us, until recently, to consider play unimportant in adult existence. Although in the past fifty years some intuitive investigators have sought to rescue something from this pejorative definition by saying that play is a child's work, little has been accomplished in the systematic understanding of play.

The Genevan psychologist Jean Piaget demonstrated that much of what we had called play is really the activity of intelligence. From the very first days of life, the child is learning discriminations and forms of effective behavior. A generation of American psychologists showed that much of the time a child is intently "exploring" his world and that we should not call that play either.

What then is play? To answer this question we need to say something about the special feelings, the special volitions, and the special structure of play. Entering into play seems to involve a relaxation of feeling. A baby who has had his bottle and is "playfully" sucking and tonguing in his mouth has a quiescent, euphoric, ruminative quality. Paradoxically, once play gets under way, new forms of feeling and tension often rise. For example, a championship chess player was recently quoted as saying, "For the most part chess is everything. It's a tight world of 64 squares. It's an unreal fascination. You're always thinking. You're always in the present time. You know you're alive. You're always being challenged and threatened."

Reprinted with permission from *Natural History Magazine*, December 1971.

Perhaps play has a temporal sequence: first, a relaxation of customary feelings; then the induction of new, play-appropriate tensions, followed by relaxation at the end. The "pleasure" of play has a distinctive alternation between relaxed and heightened affect.

Play and game involvement are customarily voluntary. The player begins because he wants to, and once in the play he makes his own choices and behaves in the novel ways he wishes. The player has more freedom and can sustain his chosen activity without interference for considerable periods. Being active rather than passive before fate may account for the immediately euphoric quality of play, while the exigencies of the new game may account for the novel tensions that then arise.

These considerations lead us to define play briefly as a transformation of feelings, volitions, and thoughts for the sake of the excitements of the novel affective, cognitive, and behavioral variations that then occur. In play the ends are indeed subordinated; the means justify the ends. Within this context, play of children can be usefully divided into four categories: imitative, exploratory, testing, and model building.

Imitative Play

In the first year of life, the earliest forms of imitative play usually involve the child imitating the parent imitating the child. The baby can only do well what he has already done. The mother who imitates the six-month-old baby's sucking sound may then induce the baby to reproduce that same sound. The difference between the original sucking and the new sucking noise causes them both to laugh during this game. By the end of the first year a number of mother-child games (for example, handclapping) have this circular imitative basis.

By the second year the infant can imitate other people by himself. This deferred imitation is illustrated when the 18-month-old child "pretends" to rub the face cloth all over his face as if washing, although he is nowhere near the washbasin. If he does this washing at the basin, we might say that it is intelligent imitation, a mode of knowing. If he does it nowhere near its proper setting, we can say it is imitative play. In this second year of life most of the imitative play will be partial acts borrowed from sleeping, eating, and washing.

In the third year, children show a greater awareness of their own pretense and tend to copy other people as a whole. They become mothers and fathers. The imitation of whole people can be difficult in some modern societies where the father's work is outside the child's sphere. For example, in a suburban nursery school, children did not like to be assigned the role of "father" in their dramatic play. Most of them refused. One boy who reluctantly took the part rapidly rode his tricycle (car) away from the "house," turned around at the end of the room, tore back, clasped "mother" in his arms and gave her a loud kiss, stretched, and said, "Well, I guess I'll take a nap."

In most of this early imitative play the child imitates the important and powerful people in his life. In homes or in cultures where the parents are highly authoritarian and inflexible, play throughout early childhood is usually rigidly imitative. Alternatively, in cultures where adults have much greater flexibility in their roles as adults and in their adult-child relationships, at about the fourth year the characters in children's play become increasingly imaginary and less faithful copies of rigid parental prototypes. Cross-cultural information suggests that the rigid imitation of parental power has been the rule throughout most of human history, and that the rather imaginative play we have come to observe in modern nursery schools is a late product in cultural development.

Similarly, toys may reflect the children's needs for exact replication of overpowerful superiors or for more flexible venture into novel worlds. The social play of the fourth year also reflects these differences. In the more rigid tradition the play involves a dominant child forcing the less powerful children into inferior roles. The dominant child arbitrarily fixes the parts the other children shall play and refuses to reverse the roles. This order of events is then maintained by threats and bribes. In modern nursery schools there is more readiness to take turns and to alternate the desirable roles.

Between four and six, imitative social play tends to be governed by one player acting as a central person and the others acting in satellite roles, or by players taking turns and alternating the roles, or by all the players doing much the same thing at the same time.

In earlier times in America this age group performed a number of circular group-singing and rhythmic pastimes that emphasized choral imitative behavior. These circle pastimes are still found in some nursery schools and in certain rural or immigrant environments. Many were simply group pantomimes such as "ring-around-the-rosy," "baloo, baloo, balight," "looby loo," "mulberry bush," but most were choral celebrations of marriage or funeral customs such as "Poor Alice is a-weeping," "Sally Waters," "Knights of Spain," "Green Grow the Rushes, Oh," "Green Gravels," and others.

Today we see less of these traditional pastimes, and more informal, imitative group games known by such names as "houses," "cars," "trucks," and "schools." These latter games have seldom been studied systematically, perhaps because they are found in homes and neighborhoods more often than in the more accessible school playgrounds. Whatever the reason, the meaning behind these games probably could give us a better indication of how our civilization is going than anything else that children have to tell us.

Exploratory Play

It is difficult to separate exploratory play from exploration. When a child discovers a novel object and examines it, he is not playing. But what if the novel object is a toy that the child is examining in his usual play milieu? Is that play? Because the answer lies in the child's attitude at the time, it is difficult to provide an answer, particularly for the first two years of life when play consciousness is not clearly differentiated.

Still, even in the first six months the child occasionally seems relaxed and pleased when he plays with his tongue and lips or his hands and fingers. This might well be exploratory play. And in the second six months, play with the parents' face and hair is often accompanied by smiling and laughter. In the second year, exploratory activities that may well give rise to exploratory play include tasting, scribbling, emptying, filling, inserting, putting in and out, pulling, stacking, rolling, and climbing into and under small spaces.

By the third year this exploration grows increasingly complex. Various patterns of organization become manifest. The child arranges, heaps, combines, transfers, sorts, and spreads. The child is also aware that he is playing and that his objects are toys. He piles the blocks in new and amusing ways. Novel manipulations and effects excite him. Much so-called destructive block play has this character. Towers of blocks make marvelous effects as they crash to the ground or get higher and higher before falling. Blocks do odd things when a child pushes one against another, then another against the first one, and then another and another. Clay can be pushed and squeezed and torn into pieces that yield funny shapes and feel different to his fingers. Sand pours from buckets and over his legs in pleasant ways. There are again novel feelings, novel effects, and novel relationships in a familiar setting.

At the same age level, from three to four years, we should not neglect the extensive verbal exploratory play that children exhibit. They put words and sounds together in novel combinations, most frequently while sitting in bed early in the morning or before sleep at night.

In childhood today, exploratory play is facilitated by innumerable toy models—cars, ships, and skeletons. These models partly confine play, but children often build fantasies during their examination and construction of the toys. Verbal exploratory play is also conventionalized in childhood through prescribed humor and nonsense. Riddles expose the child to novel contingencies in semantic relationships: "Why did the dog get out of the sun? He didn't want to be a hot dog." Nonsense yields absurd possibilities: "I took a chair and sat down on the floor."

Testing Play

In many types of play and playful contests, the child is testing himself. During his second year, he does a great deal of large motor testing. He crawls under and into things, pulls wagons, lifts objects, pushes, hammers, splashes, rides, balances, climbs, digs, opens, closes, runs, throws. Much of this is not play, but direct testing and adaptation in a given situation. At times however, an exuberance to the pulling, the pushing, the creeping into cupboards makes it play. Testing play is a form of self-validation.

As the child becomes older, the tests he enjoys increase in variety and character. The baby climbing the stairs gives way to the child jumping down them three at a time or sliding down the bannister. The most obvious way in which testing takes place in play is in the social form of games. In these games the child obtains his self-validation by using others as his standard of competence. He seeks out competitors with talents matching his own. Against them he can measure his progress.

Most testing games are contests that deal with some of the major forms of emotional life. There are games of approach and avoidance, incorporating the behaviors of withdrawal and escape (hide-and-seek), in which the emotion of fear and the adaptive function of protection are tested out. There are games of attack, in which anger and the adaptive function of destruction are tested (dodge ball). There are games of choice, in which joy or sadness, mating or deprivation are tested (flashlight kissing); games of observation in which expectancy, sensory functions, and exploration are exercised (memory); games of impulse control, in which surprise, stopping, and orientation are critical (priest of the parish).

Each of these types of contests can be arranged in a developmental sequence that children go through between the ages of five to twelve years. This development can be illustrated through four levels of approach and avoidance games. At each level in the game there are particular spatial and temporal relationships, different approach and avoidance actions, and special relationships between the players.

Level I (Hide-and-Seek, Tag)

First played extensively between five and six years, these games continue for many years, particularly in the play of girls. There is one central person (the *It*) who has most of the power (he can select whom to chase, when to run) and a number of other fugitive persons who try to hide or escape by holding on to a safe base or saying some safe term. The players' actions are reversible. The space is differentiated into "hiding places," or "safe" spaces, and dangerous territory. These two qualities of space (security versus danger) may be analogous to the division of religious and mythic spaces into the sacred and the profane. The temporal arrangement is episodic. Each incident is of equal weight, and one follows the other interminably. When the *It* tags another player, he is replaced by that player and the game continues.

Level II (Release and Ring-a-Lievo)

In these games, which become popular at seven to eight years, a central *It* figure again attempts to capture the other players. But now these other players can harass him and rescue each other. While the *It* is accumulating the captured at his base, all the captured players can be freed if one of the free players rushes through that base and cries "release." As well as "hideaways," there is now a "captive base." Space has been differentiated into these two special types of territory. Time has also changed. It is now cumulative. Each episode adds to the previous one until the *It* catches all players and is then relieved of his role.

Level III (Red Rover)

In this game, which is popular among nine- and ten-year-olds, the *It* player calls the others across from one base to the next. As they race from base to base he attempts to catch them. If he succeeds, the captured player joins him in the middle and helps him catch the other players. The play takes place now within defined boundaries, with two safe bases at each end. At some middle point, the play resembles a team game with half the players on each side. The play reaches an exciting climax when everyone except the last player has been caught. He is the fastest, the most cunning of all, and all the other players join to capture him. The game has a crescendo effect, and the exciting capture of that last player is a climax time.

Level IV (Prisoners' Base)

In a complex game usually played first at 11 or 12 years of age, two relatively undifferentiated teams pursue each other over a large, but undefined, territory. The pursued players attempt to return to base before they can be hunted down. There are home bases and prisoners' bases and one team attempts to eliminate the other. When this is done, the game is over.

In these four levels of play, the child first tests his powers against "magical" *It* figures, and finally, at an older age, against other players of relatively the same skill. The actions in this sequence evolve from chasing and escaping to capturing and rescuing, with the final game of prisoners' base containing both sets of elements. Each level has a new form of spatial and temporal arrangement, which corresponds to parallel forms of cognitive organization in children of these age levels. But the spatial and temporal qualities take on a vividness in games that they may not have in other situations. Notions like episodic, cumulative, and climax time are also illustrated in the picaresque stories, folktales, and dramas for children. Some cross-cultural data show that games of chase, escape, capture, and rescue exist in cultures where children are made anxious about independence. The children's running back and forth between bases may represent attempts to come to terms with their apprehensions about becoming independent as against remaining dependent. In these games they test their ability to hide, to escape, to capture, to rescue without becoming overwhelmed by fear.

Similar levels can be illustrated for the other types of games. The relationships between the levels in games seem to be additive. Rather than disappearing, the younger elements are added to the next level of games. A sport of adults, such as football, may include many elements of child play.

When game progress is viewed in this developmental fashion, it seems clear that as children proceed through the series, they gain an understanding of social relations, social actions, space, and time.

Model-Building Play

Although difficult to observe in the very young, model-building play becomes explicit by about four years when the organization of houses, tea parties, blocks, cities, trucks reaches a peak. It becomes a different type of play when the child puts elements of his experience together in unique ways, especially when these involve flights of his imagination. During childhood, play with model worlds of trains, dolls, and cars may be facilitated by commercial toys. This is the play that the psychoanalyst Erik Erikson has suggested is the analog of the adults' "planning" activity. There is a widespread, but unsubstantiated, belief among many adults that because children today have so many toys and models they spend less of their time in these solitary constructive pursuits. Actually the problem may lie less with the toys than with the parents' inability to provide examples of creative adult activities.

In today's society (as indicated by movies and television), fantasies about novel human interrelationships are a key form of model building. The industrious, product-oriented play that we of an older generation encourage in our children is more related to nineteenth-century industrialism than to tomorrow's customers. I have been impressed at the speed with which today's children construct gregarious fantasies with humor and versatility in their informal play. Here is another fitting area for research into the future of our own society.

A great deal of systematic observational work, probably with video tapes, will be necessary before we can decide what we mean when we say a child is at play. I am certain, however, that most readers will be unsatisfied with this state of affairs. They will want to know what play does. Why is it so important to define it? Unfortunately, answers to this sort of question must be even more imprecise than the missing observations.

From the analysis of play in animals we know that play increases as we ascend the phylogenic order. The more complex the animal, the more it plays. From cross-cultural studies we know also that as culture becomes more complex, more types of games are added, and that different types of games are systematically related to other cultural variables. For example, games of strategy appear in cultures when diplomacy, class stratification, and warfare are institutionalized. Games of chance appear when survival conditions are uncertain. Studies of devoted game players in our own culture show that they have distinctive attributes that go along with their game playing. The players seem to be molded by their games, they don't just "play" them.

Such general discoveries indicate that play and games are functional in culture. Just what this functionality is, however, is another question. I suspect that the primary function of play is the enjoyment of a commitment to one's own experience. In play, the player makes the choices. In modern society, where individuals are increasingly aware of their alienation, such a commitment may have considerable survival value.

Once the player begins the game, the uniqueness, nonsense, triviality, distortion, or serendipity that follows may well bring secondary gains. The experience of play heightens the player's flexibility and imaginative capacity in addition to improving his physical and strategic competence. But these secondary gains are clearly indirect.

Games are in part imitative of the larger culture and therefore embody its processes and attitudes. But because play is voluntary, it admits madness as well as sanity. So that what ensues may be only partly a rehearsal for any specific cultural outcome. The primary purpose of play has a deeper importance for every individual. Playing children are motivated primarily to enjoy living. This is the major rehearsal value of play and games, for without the ability to enjoy life, the long years of adulthood can be dull and wearisome.

Sharing Your Impressions

1. What is your definition of play?
2. Why do you suppose American four-year-olds imitate their parents less than they imitate imaginary characters during play?
3. Recall some of the testing games that you played as a child.
4. Compare your child's opportunity to engage in testing-type play with your own opportunity to do so during childhood.
5. What types of play do you feel most and least comfortable with as an adult?
6. Make some suggestions for helping parents and teachers participate in model-building play with children.
7. Why do you suppose that, after elementary school, game playing decreases with age?

Chapter 2

Playing Alone

4

Dominion in Children's Play: Its Meaning and Management

Mary Nicolaysen

When children play, sometimes a child will arbitrarily take possession of an area or place which he occupies and treats as his private property. He may fence off a space with blocks, furniture, or other available materials; he may build his own "house" or "hideout" or whatever he names it; or he may appropriate a ready-made nook or enclosure, at times even taking over an entire play center in nursery school. He may choose to play by himself; again, he may be willing to share it with a playmate—perhaps more than one—while all others he firmly keeps out. This behavior might be considered an example of territoriality—"the technical term ethologists use to describe the taking possession, use, and defense of a territory on the part of a living organism" (Edward T. Hall, *The Silent Language*. Doubleday & Co., 1959).

The Authority to Possess

Similar behavior of children in their play I call *dominion play*. Dominion means the authority to possess, use, and control territory. A child, along with his possession of space, may exercise jurisdiction over certain objects, which he may actually own or may be using only temporarily. This paper, however, will focus on children's efforts to possess space itself and the bearing of this behavior on their emotional and social growth.

Children take possession of space in both approved and disapproved ways. It is acceptable, for example, when a child draws a line in the sand to avoid conflicts with his neighbor, when he insists on keeping his cubby or coat hook for his own exclusive use, or when he produces marvels of creative construction with blocks or other materials. As long as his structures or boundaries do not interfere with the activities of

Reprinted by permission from *Young Children*, Vol. 22, No. 1 (October 1966), pp. 20–28. Copyright © 1966, National Association for the Education of Young Children, 1834 Connecticut Avenue, N.W., Washington, D.C. 20009.

others, all goes well, but when his exercise of dominion distresses others, problems arise. For once a child has taken possession of a certain place or portion of space, he vehemently rejects unwanted companions and, if necessary, uses physical force to defend his domain. The emotional intensity of this child's response indicates how important his activity is to him.

Adults, however, are inclined to take a dim view of exclusiveness in play. They are displeased by a child's rude retorts to would-be sharers and by their outraged protests; and, usually, a teacher's first impulse is to step in and restore harmony as quickly as possible. To this end she may urge the child in possession to be friendly and permit others to play with him; she may even remove his barriers. When such measures are taken the frustrated child will respond with anything from silent compliance to a full-blown tantrum, depending upon his ability to protest and the strength of his need for dominion play.

Dominion Play Contagious

However, whether the child obeys or not, and whether or not his play infringes on the rights of others, the situation has not been adequately handled until the children's feelings and needs, or dynamics, have been explored and dealt with. Such guidance demands both skill and sympathetic understanding; it is easier simply to discourage dominion play. The play may be discouraged for another reason also; it is highly contagious. If Susie sets up housekeeping under a table, Karen wants to do the same thing, and Julie, too, is likely to insist on making a similar "house." In homes, materials and "building sites" are plentiful; in preschools, however, there may be problems of space and equipment as well as interpersonal difficulties.

Children's ways of playing merit our trust and cooperation rather than our suspicion and frustrative intervention. If we want to foster the development of personality rather than merely control children's behavior, we must be concerned with motives and meanings; and the motivations behind a child's behavior may be unclear even to a knowledgeable adult who is also familiar with this child's particular play patterns. While we do not permit inappropriate behavior to continue, neither do we block a child's purpose if partial realization of his aims can be effected without violating mutual rights.

Setting limits to insure mutual rights is not so simple in practice as in theory. It involves knowing what limits are appropriate as well as when and how to set them. A child should not be prevented from doing what he very much wants to do, unless there is an extremely good reason why permission should be refused. Even without further inquiry, dominion play deserves our thoughtful consideration because of its frequency, its attractiveness, and the emotional involvement with which children pursue it. Rather than discourage dominion play, we may well ask why children want to engage in it. Let us consider some of their motives.

Why Dominion Play?

(1) It is satisfying to possess something of one's own. Aristotle said, "How immeasurably greater is the pleasure when a man feels a thing to be his own; for surely love of self is a feeling implanted by nature and not given in vain." (*Politics*, by permission of the Clarendon Press, Oxford.) Whatever combination of nature and nurture is involved, to own space gives pleasure and a certain sense of security. A child's real experiences with territoriality begin early. His use of space is limited both by other controls and by his own immaturities: there are places where he may go and be, and others he must avoid. He may have jurisdiction over his few personal possessions but rarely does he own space. Such ownership is in fact only nominal, and he is almost always subject to intrusion. But in his play, as in his fantasies and dreams, a child is free from the restrictions of reality and can, if he wishes, own the whole world!

(2) Humans as well as other animals take possession of territory, use, and defend it. Anthropologist Edward T. Hall writes: "To have a territory is to have one of the essential components of life: to lack one is one of the most precarious of all conditions" (*The Silent Language*). In our society acquisitiveness is accepted as part of human character, and personal property rights are protected by law. Customs and sentiments regarding the uses of space, especially the spaces between persons, are acquired by a child with other aspects of his culture. He characteristically imitates adults and seeks to participate in the larger world of reality. Dominion play is one of his many attempts to "try on life," in Elizabeth Campbell's apt phrase.

(3) In play a child can safely express his reactions to the many directions, commands, and prohibitions that he commonly receives from others. In play he can control instead of being controlled; he can be autonomous and powerful instead of compliant and weak. This reversal of roles might be considered a form of "identification with the aggressor," a mechanism for getting emotional release from outside pressures. Also, in arrogating a place of his own he provides himself with a secure base of operations and enhances his personal power, much the way a dog gains more courage when in his own back yard! Freedom to act out feelings

and fantasies provides emotional outlet; appropriate limits keep the child close enough to reality for his security and self-respect.

(4) A child's maneuvers to isolate and enclose himself in a chosen place may express his needs for security and protection, normal human needs especially strong in children. Their satisfaction fosters self-confidence and well-being. Feelings of security enable a child to trust those who give him security and who also respect his own efforts to gain it. In preschools, where disturbing contacts with others are almost unavoidable, the need for protection may be intensified. Acting out wishes for coziness and safe enclosure are time-honored themes in children's play. James Hymes, in *The Child under Six,* points out how such play expresses needs for dependent satisfactions and describes how the child in this play re-experiences the joys of "littleness" and helplessness so fully known, we add, in his mother's arms.

(5) Occasional preference for solitary play may have quite desirable indications. For example: (a) the child is expressing a healthy need for autonomy; (b) he is learning to cultivate and enjoy his own interests; (c) he is able to form and carry out creative purposes of his own; (d) he is learning to think independently. Children should have opportunities for these activities and at times guidance in pursuing them appropriately in a social setting.

(6) The child's concept of space is related to his developing concept of self. His needs for isolation and dominion are linked with his growing consciousness of himself as a being differentiated from his environment. To quote Werner Wolff in his book *The Personality of the Preschool Child* (Grune & Stratton, 1947):

> Every child goes through a stage of isolation and monologous behavior, but the degree of this isolation varies with different children. . . . The stage of isolation prepares the development of the child's individuality and the emergence of his self. Since the child deals with objects of his environment as with parts of his personality, he isolates not only himself but also certain objects from the environment. With the isolation of objects there starts the concept of property. . . . Property becomes a symbol of power invested in the personality and is used for the goal of differentiating the individual from the environment. . . . This need of gradually limiting the personality from its fusion with the world appears . . . in children's expressive behavior as when, for instance, they surround their drawings by a circle, or build a fence around their playground, or desire a screen or other enclosure when sleeping. . . . A child isolating himself from a group might be compared with an adult taking a walk alone to find himself. [pp. 56, 57.]

Such motives for dominion play suggest that those who live and work with young children would do well to recognize its values and provide for it with suitable equipment and enlightened guidance. Equipment is surprisingly easy to procure, for ingenuity can often substitute

for spending, and the possibilities are many. Prefabricated playhouses
are not so satisfying to children as materials they can easily put together
themselves.

It is also essential that enough equipment be available to
them. A folding card table with a cloth draped over it makes a fine
"house" under which a youngster can sit upright. Very satisfactory
covers are two-yard squares of wool-and-rayon felt in rich colors,
lightweight and soil-resistant. Tables can be folded away when not in
use. Wooden fences and dividing screens are available at pre-school supply houses or may be home-made. Partitions of various heights may be
made of adjoining sides of cardboard cartons, costing nothing. These too
can be folded away for storage. Such dividers or fences leave the blocks
for building and serve many uses in play.

Alertness, Guidance Required

Children's enjoyment of dominion play in a setting of mutual
rights and respect calls for alertness and wise guidance on the part of the
teacher. Let us observe an incident that occurred in a group of four-year-
olds early in the school year. Carol, close to tears, complains to her
teacher, "Dale won't let me come in his house."

Teacher: "I guess that makes you feel pretty unhappy. What
did he say?"

Carol: "He said, 'Go away!' I can't come in."

Teacher: "Let's go and talk with him." Carol takes her hand,
and they walk over to where Dale has made what children often call a
"house"—an area two or three feet wide walled around with blocks. He
sits inside arranging some rubber animals. For the children's
understanding of the situation, as well as her own, the teacher encourages them to talk about it. "This is a good strong wall you've made,
Dale. Did you tell Carol what you're doing in here?"

Dale: "I'm making a zoo."

Carol: "I want to get in there and make your zoo, too."

Dale: "You can't. This is my house. I don't want anybody in
here."

Since Dale is busy with his own absorbing play and is not in-
fringing on anyone, the teacher supports him. "Carol, Dale's busy now;
he wants to play all by himself. You could find somebody else to play
with, dear."

To force Dale to play with Carol against his will would be
unlikely to make him actually feel friendly toward either Carol or the
teacher herself; and she wants the children to develop genuinely friendly
feelings rather than merely "go through the motions." She also wants to

help Carol accept calmly another child's desire to play alone. The teacher's own easy, natural acceptance of the situation, without regarding Dale as unkind and with sympathy and encouragement for Carol, guides the children toward self-acceptance and mutual respect.

Dale happily echoes her words, "I'm busy now. You can find somebody else to play with." He continues his animal play, and the teacher, hoping to see Carol also find interesting play, suggests, "If you want to play zoo, you could make a zoo of your own." Carol replies, "Okay," but seems not to know how to begin.

Teacher: "Did you see these fences we have? You could use them to build your own zoo." As Carol takes the fences and sets them up Dale cheerfully offers, "You can have this lion, and there's lots of animals on the shelf." Soon the two children are playing contentedly each in his own place but with occasional conversation and trading of toys back and forth. A certain emotional balance, along with mutual acceptance, has been achieved.

There are times, however, when a child's dominion play interferes with the rights of others; then limits must be set, not to deny the child an area of his own but to help him satisfy his need appropriately. If other children, who are sure to complain, fail to gain his cooperation, the teacher will have to help restore mutual rights.

One teacher handled such a situation as follows. Jim came to nursery school full of excitement about his visit to the railroad yards to see the trains. Later in the morning he built an elaborate "roundhouse" of blocks which he would not let anyone touch. Unfortunately he placed it so close to the block shelves that it interfered with access to them. The teacher, who had briefly observed the futile efforts to get Jim to move his structure, finally decided to intervene.

Teacher: "Jim, do you know why they want you to move your roundhouse? They can't get to these shelves."

Jim: "They can't walk here. They'll knock it down."

Teacher: "But they want to play with the blocks, too. Where could you move your roundhouse so the other children can get blocks without bothering you?"

Jim: "I don't want to move it."

Teacher: "I know you don't and I'm sorry, but you'll need to find a better place for it. Here, it's in their way."

Jim: "I can't move it 'cause it's all built."

Teacher: "Can you find a new place yourself, or shall I find one for you?" Jim replies, "No!" so she offers him another choice: "Look Jim. Would you rather put your roundhouse here by the wall (pointing) or over here? You choose."

Jim: "It's not going to get moved, I said."

Teacher: "I'll be glad to help you move it, or will you do it yourself?" No answer. Since she could not get the child's cooperation, the teacher herself quietly moved aside enough of his structure to clear the way to the shelves. Not every child will hold out to the very last of such a series of alternatives, but even when he does, face-saving choices are easier to accept than specific commands.

In dominion play a child's efforts to exclude others from his territory may sometimes cause resentment and hurt feelings. It is hard to take such remarks as "You can't come in. You're not my friend," or "I don't want you in here. Go away," or just plain "Get out!" The rejected child has a right as well as a need to respond, whether or not he is able to. Usually children require some help in learning to manage the personal relationships that grow out of dominion play, at least in their early experiences. Guidance can reduce unhappy tensions.

Reverse Approach Used

Judy has rudely forbidden Beth to come into her "house," and now Beth is crying helplessly. She is a rather diffident little girl, and being rejected is especially painful to her. The teacher, seeing the girls in need, takes Beth a fresh tissue for her tears and offers a comforting embrace. She deliberately directs her attention to the troubled child, purposely reversing the usual approach in which the child suspected of causing a problem is dealt with first. Her intention is to reassure and disarm the offender enough to secure the child's interest and cooperation in solving the situation, as well as to lend emotional "first aid" to the injured.

Teacher: "Beth, I think you'd better tell Judy how you feel." But Beth only shakes her head and clings tightly to the teacher, who then turns her attention to Judy. "Beth needs to tell you something." She encourages Beth by promising, "I'll stay right here beside you while you tell her how you feel." Finally, Beth is able to say, "Those words made me cry." Judy does not reply.

Teacher: "Judy, look at Beth's face. How do you think she's feeling?"

Judy: "She's crying. She wants to play in here but she can't."

Teacher: "You don't have to let her in your house, but if she built a house of her own then you could be neighbors. How about it?"

Judy: "Okay, she can make her own house."

Teacher: "You could tell her about that." She would like the two girls to achieve a friendly relationship as soon as possible; she also wants Judy to have actual practice in handling this common situation.

Judy: "You can build a house, too. Right next to mine if you want. We'll be neighbors and we'll each have our own house."

After some discussion about materials Beth goes about making a house "just like Judy's." When she moves in Judy calls, "I'm making a cake and I want you to come to my house for lunch. Okay, Beth?"

Time and again when a child's right of ownership is respected he becomes less defensive, relaxes, and often welcomes the very child he recently refused to play with. Secure possession promotes expansive feelings and enables a child to learn from his own experience to understand and respect the property rights of others. It is amazing to see how that small recognition of ownership and privacy, a knock at another child's "door," so often has the dramatic effect of producing instant hospitality!

As a child grows older his developing social consciousness influences his ways of seeking both isolation and dominion. More often now he wants to share his domain with one or more companions of his own choosing, while he excludes all others. Adults often disapprove of such selectivity; they want the child to like everyone. They tend to regard preferences as limiting and unfriendly and urge the child to behave more maturely. Indeed, they often seem to expect children to exhibit an all-embracing acceptance of others that is seldom, if ever, achieved by adults themselves.

Except in unusual circumstances a child should be allowed to choose his own friends. Such freedom will not prevent problems, but if children are wisely guided in solving them, they will learn and grow. Moreover, when permitted to choose their own playmates, children reveal themselves more clearly to the trained observer, who can then guide them more effectively.

In dominion play a child's selection or rejection of other children may have motives and meanings that are far from obvious. Not only his developing personality structure but also the particular preschool setting in which a child finds himself may be influencing factors in his behavior. Let us consider some possibilities.

(1) A child's early experiences as a member of a group may overwhelm him with anxious feelings. Having to deal with strange persons in a strange place commonly makes young children insecure. A child may seek relief in isolation or in efforts to control his surroundings, including dominion play.

(2) A child may feel most secure with one special companion, who may be a familiar friend or an attractive new acquaintance. Each child can depend on the other for nonthreatening behavior; and mutual support permits them to develop social skills in safety. Often such a couple may be stimulated by subtly arranged contacts with one or two other

children but often enough the self-confidence that the two develop in each other's company enables them quite spontaneously to include others.

(3) Friends need to be alone together: a developing friendship needs a certain measure of privacy to be fully experienced. Furthermore, the nature of a relationship can be better understood by a teacher if the children are allowed to pursue it. Is this an enriching relationship? Would the children profit from additional contacts outside school hours? Or is it one, for example, of dominance-submission in which the passive partner needs help in becoming more self-confident and assertive?

(4) A child may be anxious about possible encounters with certain children whom he is afraid of. He wants to play with other kids but doesn't know how to deal with them. His isolating and rejecting maneuvers offer clues to his emotional needs. Teachers may well ask themselves whether this child is receiving adequate guidance in learning to express and assert himself. Are they teaching him how to set limits on unwelcome behavior in others? Are the aggressive ones being wisely guided?

(5) The imaginative, creative child often seeks cooperative companions to help him carry out his ideas for play. Some children are more cooperative, some quicker to understand, some better natured than others; some have interesting ideas of their own to contribute. A child simply chooses playmates that are congenial to him.

(6) Perhaps the most obvious reason for excluding others is that, when only a few children occupy a play center, there is a wider choice of toys and more room to play and consequently less frustration about sharing and taking turns. However, children should have enough equipment and playthings so that they do not have to endure persistent frustrations. Teachers might take a fresh look at their provisions for children's play, in the interest of smooth relationships and personal satisfaction.

Let us watch Danny and Laurie playing in the little kitchen of their nursery school. They stand at a table full of containers and utensils for water play; each child has a big plastic pan and is busy filling and pouring. Now Tom gets a pan from the shelf and says, "I'm going to get some water and play with you."

Danny: "You can't play in here. We're making ice cream."

Laurie adds, "This is our kitchen, and there isn't any more room."

Nevertheless, Tom fills his pan at the sink and asks a teacher to carry it for him to the kitchen. There Laurie and Danny renew their protests: "We don't want him in here," and "This is our table and our stuff." But the teacher thinks that the kitchen, which is large enough for several children, should not be monopolized by only two. First, however, she assures them, "You don't have to play with Tom." Then she offers them a plywood screen and suggests, "If you use this for a wall, you can make two apartments and each have your own kitchen. Where should it go?" Laurie takes the initiative: "Tom can have the little table and the cupboard. This is your place, Tom." Danny compromises with, "You have to ask us when you want to cook on the stove." Everyone seems content.

Possession of Space Important

When there is adequate equipment this expedient is usually acceptable to children, perhaps because the right to possess space appears to be more important to a child than the extent of his domain. If dividing a play center does not solve the problem of who shall play where, sometimes a child can conveniently play alone elsewhere.

The basic plan, arrangement, and equipment of a preschool can either cause or minimize problems relating to possession of space. Careful consideration of children's needs and interests can lead to new and creative spatial arrangements. For example, conflicts are fewer when the play kitchen with its inevitable spills and clatter is distinctly separated from other areas for housekeeping play. Good arrangement furthers children's own responsible handling of their relationships and lessens the need for adult interference.

In summary, dominion play may be seen as an aspect of a child's deep need to realize himself, to achieve security and mastery, and to participate in the world. In a setting of mutual respect, secure ownership of "territory" enhances self-awareness and self-respect, and fosters the joys of friendship and spontaneous sharing. In dominion play the usual finding is that the satisfaction of a child's needs is a condition of, rather than a deterrent to, his feeling friendly toward others.

Bibliography

Frank, Lawrence K. *The Fundamental Needs of the Child.* New York: The National Association for Mental Health, Inc., 1952 edition.

Hall, Edward T. *The Hidden Dimension.* Garden City, New York: Doubleday & Company, Inc., 1966.

Hymes, James L. *The Child under Six.* Englewood Cliffs, New Jersey: Prentice-Hall, 1960.

White, Robert W. Motivation reconsidered: The concept of competence. *Psychological Review,* 1959, *66*; 297–333.

Sharing Your Impressions

1. What could you tell a child who is crying because Dennis and Tom wouldn't let him play and told him to 'go away'?
2. How do you feel when you see a child purposely isolating himself or herself if there is an opportunity to socialize with other children?
3. Describe some of the benefits children gain from dominion play.
4. How do you feel when your child claims a territory and refuses to let others play there?
5. Give your opinion about whether children should be expected to resolve their own conflicts relating to dominion play.
6. What degree of influence do you feel parents and teachers should have on a child's choice of playmates?
7. How do boys and girls differ in dominion play?
8. What do you suppose are the effects on children when parents and surrogates do not respect their right to privacy?

5

The Merits of Solitary Play

Robert D. Strom

Most parents want their young children to have playmates. Play with peers is expected to encourage getting along with others and learning to share—social skills that will be required at school. In some families where childrearing is left entirely to the mother, her own natural desire for periodic relief can also be a motivation for encouraging peer play. Whatever the reason, parents tend to agree that during early childhood peer play is essential. Many are less certain about the merits of *solitary* play and consequently less enthusiastic about arranging uninterrupted time for children to be alone. But recent research on creativity may call for a reconsideration of these attitudes.

Creative Adults

Over the past fifteen years numerous attempts have been made to determine what creative people are like and how their extraordinary abilities can become more common. Under the direction of

From *Childhood Education,* January 1976, pp. 149–152. Reprinted by permission of the author and the Association for Childhood Education International, 3615 Wisconsin Avenue, N.W., Washington, D.C. Copyright © 1976 by the Association.

Donald MacKinnon, psychologists at the University of California have studied some 600 mathematicians, architects, engineers, writers and research scientists. All of these people were nominated by experts in their field as being highly creative. As a result of the California research, we are more familiar with the personality characteristics of creative adults.

It seems that, in addition to being highly imaginative, most of them prefer solitary activities; they are able to concentrate for extended periods of time; and they exhibit an unusual level of task persistence. But how did they get this way? What growing-up experiences did they share in common? Some clues are provided by their autobiographical narratives. Generally, because they were either the eldest child in a family or were distantly spaced from brothers and sisters, they spent more time alone and with adults than did their peers, and they learned at an early age to enjoy the company provided by their own imagination (MacKinnon, 1962; 1972).

High and Low Daydreamers

Although the privacy most creative adults experienced during childhood is suggestive of an environment other people may need to become more creative, the value of solitary play has generally been overlooked. Then in the 1970s Jerome Singer and his colleagues at Yale University made some important discoveries. One experiment involved a population of nine-year-olds who were all similar in intelligence, level of education and social background. After intensive interviews, the children were divided into two groups. The so-called "High Daydreamers" were boys and girls who had created imaginary companions, enjoyed playing by themselves, and reported more daydreams. Children qualified as "Low Daydreamers" if they preferred more literal play, expressed disinterest in solitary activities and reported infrequent daydreams. All the youngsters were told that they were being considered as potential astronauts. Since astronauts must spend long periods of time in a space capsule without moving about much or speaking to others, the purpose of the experiment was explained to the "candidate" as that of seeing how long they could sit quietly without talking to the experimenter.

The results were significant. The High Daydreamers were able to remain quiet for protracted periods of solitary activity and to persist without giving up, factors closely related to concentration ability. In addition, the High Daydreamers were less restless, less eager to end the test; and they seemed serenely able to occupy themselves inwardly to make time pass. Later it was learned that they each transformed the situation of forced compliance into a fantasy game which helped them increase waiting ability. By contrast, the Low Daydreamers never seemed able to settle down. They would leap up repeatedly and inquire, "Is the time up yet?" They continually tried to involve the experimenter in conversation. Further testing revealed that the High Daydreamers were also superior in creativity, storytelling and need for achievement.

"There's Nothing to Do"

Teachers and parents can confirm Singer's (1973) findings for themselves. It is a common observation that slum children are usually crowded together and seldom have a chance for solitary play. As a result, many of them come to school restless, unable to sit still or persist at tasks, inclined to act out impulses rather than reflect on them. Because these children tend to lack the ability to concentrate, they often interrupt and distract each other. In one study of inner-city schools, Martin Deutsch (1960) found that teachers had to devote as much as 80 percent of their time trying to establish the discipline they felt was necessary for learning. Many of these teachers complained that their students had never developed the inner resources needed for sustained inquiry. The forecast is not much better in homes of higher income levels where children are heard to complain that "there's nothing to do" when playmates or television are unavailable. It is a sad commentary when the very young already bore themselves (Strom, 1974; 1975).

Fortunately, if solitary play is permitted a larger place in early childhood education of the future, boredom and inattention may become far less common. The transition will not be easy because grownups have traditionally felt that children do not need privacy.[1] Although adults themselves resent child intrusion when they are occupied in trying to concentrate, the tendency to underestimate the seriousness of children at play is nearly universal. One contrary view is expressed by researchers Buchsbaum (1965) and Farnham-Diggory (1971), who find that the frustration effects of interrupted solitary play include reduction of a chld's persistence for mental tasks as well as a lowering of his ability to concentrate. A further finding is that the younger the child, the more he is vulnerable to play disturbances (cf. Freyberg, 1970; Pulaski, 1974).

In this connection, the conflicting privacy needs of some mothers and their children bear mention. More fathers should assume their proper share of childrearing in order to reduce the necessity of

---

[1]Too often children are led to feel that being alone is more a form of punishment than an opportunity. When we say, "Get to your room and stay there by yourself," the solitude is intended as a form of punishment, a type of solitary confinement (Strom, 1969).

mothers having to be with children more than they can tolerate. A probable consequence would be a decline in the need to over-rely on early peer encounter for the sake of maternal relief. For children, the outcome might well be a more reasonable chance for solitary play.

Learning to Be Alone

Unlike learning to be with age-mates, a socialization skill that can be acquired after starting school, learning to be alone will probably begin at home or not at all. Obviously the number of children in a class and the frequency of interruption make solitary play a low-priority activity at school. Moreover, once the school-year begins, such organized groups as Cub Scouts, Brownies, Little League, YMCA are available along with other peer pressures to spend less time alone. Some of these group experiences can offer a child much and should be encouraged. At the same time, however, parents should help children arrange a schedule that continues to allow ample opportunity for solitude each day.[2]

Many adults today appear unsure of their identity or sense loneliness even though they belong to social groups that identify them and provide companionship. Apparently, belonging is not enough. Parents who arrange solitary play avoid depriving their child of needed early self-encounters.

Fantasy and Solitary Play

When children engage in solitary play, they fantasize more than during peer play or parent-child play. Still, even though we recognize solitude as the best condition for fantasy practice, we sometimes look with concern upon the child who prefers to play alone. This apprehension relates to the high esteem our culture attaches to extroversion and sociability. Indeed, generally we tend to ignore the evidence suggesting that two-thirds of creative people are introverts and that 90 percent of them are intuitive. Some parents even express anxious reservation about whether their child's solitary play is actually unhealthy. One father suggests: "Playing alone is fine but our four-year-old seems to be the victim of hallucination. He often makes reference to

[2]Many adults find it difficult to arrange uninterrupted time for even their own important business. One common example involves professional educators who work together daily but find it necessary to schedule out-of-town retreats in order to be undisturbed.

Roy, a nonexistent companion." When such parents listen more closely, they realize that unlike the mentally ill person who is dominated by his hallucinations, during solitary play it is the child who controls his imaginary friend. In fact this total control of the companion may be what bothers some parents the most. Perhaps they suppose that being the boss is not good for children because it invites them to develop uncooperative behavior in relation with real people. The fact is that cooperation implies *sharing* power. Children who sense powerlessness cannot cooperate; they can only acquiesce.

    In any event, if imaginary companions appear at all, they are usually created by children between ages three and six; seldom will they remain beyond the age of ten. Incidentally, these children do not classify as the lonely, the timid or the maladjusted. Instead, they are normal and live in families of all sizes and social circumstance. Estimates ranging from 20 to 50 percent are given as the proportion of us who at some time experienced fictitious companions. That bright persons are more likely to have fantasy friends shows up in child studies and later in studies of creative college students, whose recall of imaginary companions is one of several retrospective variables that they have in common (Jersild, 1968; Singer, 1971).

Conclusion

    Society now tolerates the consequences of failing to provide uninterrupted time for solitary play. Hyperactivity, disruptive behavior, impulsivity, inattentivenes – these are problems with which teachers and parents reluctantly feel they are obliged to cope. But can we live with the long-term effects, the adult consequences? When people have no recourse to imagination, reflection, analytic thinking and self-examination, then their mental health and the well-being of others they can influence are all in jeopardy. A better future for all is more likely if more parents come to see imaginative play as a base for problem-solving through its direct influence on the development of concentration, task persistence, self-control and delay of closure. Then our emphasis on getting to know others will be joined by an enthusiasm for getting to know oneself. Surely children must learn to effectively relate with peers but unless they also learn the productive use of privacy, they will have little to offer when in the company of others. Thus, to achieve either goal requires that we support both. In my view, these are sufficient reasons to recommend that every child's experience include a generous period of time for solitary play.

References

Buchsbaum, B.C. "The Effect of the Frustration of Interrupted Play on Cognitive Level as a Function of Age." Doctoral Dissertation, Yeshiva University. Ann Arbor, MI: University Microfilms, 1965, No. 66–2882.

Deutsch, Martin. *Minority Group and Class Status as Related to Social and Personality Factors in Scholastic Achievement*. Ithaca, NY: Society for Applied Anthropology. Monograph No. 2, 1960, 3–23.

Farnham-Diggory, S. & B. Ramsey. "Play Persistence: Some Effects of Interruption, Social Reinforcement and Defective Toys." *Developmental Psychology 4*, 2(1971): 297–98.

Freyberg, J. T. "Experimental Enhancement of Imaginative Play of Kindergarten Children in a Poverty Area School." Doctoral Dissertation, City University of New York. Ann Arbor, MI: University Microfilms, 1970, No. 70–24, 464.

Jersild, Arthur. *Child Psychology*. Englewood Cliffs, NJ: Prentice-Hall, 1968. Pp. 391–96.

MacKinnon, Donald W. "The Nature and Nurture of Creative Talent." *American Psychologist 17*, 7(July 1962): 484–95.

_____."Maslow's Place in the History of Psychology." *Journal of Creative Behavior 6*, 3(1972): 158–63.

Pulaski, M. "The Rich Rewards of Make Believe." *Psychology Today 7*, 8(Jan. 1974): 68–74.

Singer, Jerome. "Exploring Man's Imaginative World." In *Teachers and the Learning Process*, Robert D. Strom, ed. Englewood Cliffs, NJ: Prentice-Hall, 1971. Pp. 333–50.

_____.*The Child's World of Make Believe*. New York: Academic Press, 1973. 289 pp.

Strom, Robert. "Dangers and Advantages of Solitude." In *Psychology for the Classroom*. Englewood Cliffs, NJ: Prentice-Hall, 1969. Pp 233–36.

_____."The Slumdwellers." In *Education for Affective Achievement*, Robert Strom & E. Paul Torrance, eds. Chicago: Rand McNally, 1974. Pp. 54–64.

_____."Observing Parent-Child Fantasy Play." *Theory into Practice 13*, 4(Oct. 1974).

_____."Parents and Teachers as Play Observers." *Childhood Education 51*, 3(Jan. 1975): 139–41.

_____."Education for a Leisure Society." *The Futurist 9*, 2(Apr. 1975): 93–97.

Sharing Your Impressions

1. Give some reasons why you occasionally feel the need to be alone.
2. What factors would you consider in deciding how much time a child should spend alone?

3. How do you feel when your child or student prefers to play alone instead of with others?
4. What do you suppose are the benefits of solitary play for children?
5. What are some materials that are appropriate for the solitary play of preschoolers? Elementary school children? Teenagers?
6. How can solitary play be arranged within the early-childhood facilities where some boys and girls spend most of their time?
7. How do you react to children's daydreaming?

6

Privacy: A Child's Need to Be Alone in the Classroom

Don Mack

Coexisting in a crowded noisy environment—whether the classroom, the home or the streets—creates a personal dilemma for many children. How to be alone? In a class of 35 or even 25, children are hard put to find a private uninhabited space to think, work, read, confer quietly or wonder.

Many voice displeasure when a teacher or other students hover near their work space. "It bothers me to have someone standing over me," they explain. Others will cry, "I just need a place to go to figure this out for myself. I can't think clearly when I'm crowded." What they seem to be pleading for is a private, quiet refuge where they can curl up with a book, have a private discussion with a friend, air a conflict that needs resolving or simply keep their supplies and possessions.

But where, you might ask? Where in my already overcrowded room is there an extra inch of space? That was my initial question, too. Early in the year we had used up what I thought was the last unoccupied space for a sofa and rug area, closed off by a folding screen. It provided some privacy, but for just a few children at a time. Too many others were frustrated.

Then I mentioned that anyone who could find a vacant space located out of the mainstream of class traffic could occupy it and turn it into a private area. Many students responded immediately. In a matter of days, students had scrounged workable spaces and fashioned a marvelous motley variety of forts, perches, cubbies and offices out of

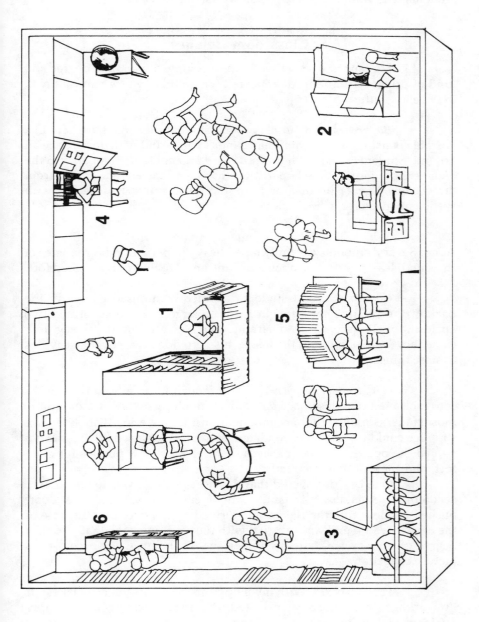

chairs, desks, strips or sheets of paper and other assorted materials. For students who wanted the same spot, we established a rotating schedule.

Classroom Refuges

Student refuges varied both in complexity and the degree and kind of privacy afforded. All appeared where there was a natural break in the class pattern.

Bookcases. In our classroom, student mailboxes are kept in a portable waist-high bookshelf that stands as an island with open space all around. Students attached light cardboard and construction paper to the ends, creating a right-angle partition that separates anyone inside from direct view (see #1 on diagram)—perfect for a semiprivate office with sufficient space for a single desk.

Stands. The TV set in our room is on a high, movable metal stand. Several students carefully taped heavy paper around three sides of the stand, leaving one side open as an entrance, to make an enclosed fort.

Corners. Several students claimed an unused corner in the back of the room. They brought in three large boxes that formed two enclosing walls (see #2 on diagram). The boxes ensured privacy and, since they were open from the inside, also provided two cavelike cavities to store things.

Closets and storage areas. A pair of children moved their desks into a cleaned out closet (see #3). Since full closets were at a premium, most students made other accommodations. Discovering that classroom supplies could be easily consolidated, students rearranged them and occupied the opened-up crawl spaces themselves. A few pillows for comfort, and their nests were ready.

One boy discovered that the storage closet was too narrow to accommodate his desk. Undaunted, he opened one storage closet door, pushed his desk into the right angle formed by the door and the base of the closet (see #4) and was satisfied with the resulting nook that offered a degree of privacy and, equally important, abundant wall space for his picture collection.

Packing boxes. With my help, some students made a makeshift "recording studio." They insulated the inside walls of an empty refrigerator box with scraps of felt and crumpled newspapers, and covered all with burlap. Inside they placed a small table, a stool and a mirror.

Only a muffled noise could be heard by the class, while a "recording artist" was in session. Frequently, however, the studio was used for other purposes. Some students practiced facial expressions or rehearsed lines for plays in front of the mirror. More often it became a place for a child to be alone.

Tables. Territory under tables proved to be an ideal solution for several students. One child covered a round table with an old tablecloth. It flopped to the floor enclosing the space on all sides.

Two girls cleverly taped book covers together to make a long strip that they attached to the outer edge of the rectangular work table they shared. Only their eyes and the tops of their heads could be seen over the top of the screen (see #5). Group privacy is what they wanted and achieved. Another group followed their example by balancing a long strip of corrugated cardboard on the front length of their table.

The "roost". The strangest innovation by far is what the students refer to as the "Eagle's Roost" (see #6). Three students decided that, since all the floor space areas had been commandeered, they would step up on the window counter, which has a waist-high portable bookcase in front of it at the far right end. The bookcase stands close to the edge of the counter, leaving about a foot and a half of closed-in space between the bookcase and the windows behind.

Students stand behind the case leaning on its top, which is high enough for them to rest their arms on, and read or write comfortably. Or they often sit on the windowsills behind them. Students in the "Roost" can also close the darkroom curtains behind them, so that they can't be seen from outside.

In addition to offering relative privacy, the "Eagle's Roost" provides an ideal perch for observing all classroom activities. For students who have difficulty sitting still for long stretches of time, this stand-up outlet is ideal.

Office Contents

Articles kept in student offices varied according to the occupant's tastes, interests and needs. Most frequently children organized their school supplies such as memo pads, staplers, assignment papers, scissors, rulers, pencils, crayons and tape. Many devised clever ways of storing their possessions by tacking, taping or hanging envelopes or cups to the walls, adapting these innovations to the structural possibilities of their particular office.

Individual interests were reflected in office decor. Some children added a personal touch by hanging family or friends' photos or mirrors or displaying apothecary jars or bottles. Others hung models of planes or cars and handmade craft items or decorated the walls with stamp collections, decals, maps or calendars. One boy practically wallpapered his nook with his motorcycle picture collection. Besides offering this student a private place, the refuge was an interest center for the whole class. In a few cases students felt the need to post signs such as "Please knock before entering" or "Keep out." Whether or not signs appeared, students abided by an unwritten law that these areas were not to be disturbed – and they weren't.

From the time the first private place emerged, it did not take students long to verbalize their opinions about the areas. "Before I had my fort I would leave my desk and come back to find something gone or missing. Now I don't have to worry." "Now I can get my work done. I can't study at home because of my brother who is a noisemaker." "My office helps me keep my things neat and organized because of the shelves on the edge of it." "I like to be alone and think. I can imagine many different things, but I can't stand it when someone interrupts me. I've enjoyed my privacy."

Few negative comments were voiced. As a teacher I agreed with the students' thoughtful and honest reactions and felt comfortable permitting the private places to exist. They were functional, and the children respected the rights they offered and responsibilities that went with them.

One mystery, however, perplexed me. Though most of the private places became "home" for the students, several seemed to exist only as storage areas for learning materials and private possessions. Students had meticulously organized and decorated these places, yet seldom used them.

I asked about this. Though responses were vague and inconclusive, I finally realized that the children who used their areas this way came from large families or lived in small apartments. Several had spoken about their difficulties at home attempting to find enough space to spread out their things or a spot where their possessions would be left untouched. For them, the special area in the classroom served as a sanctuary where no adult or meddlesome sibling would disturb their treasures.

The private areas were flexible, changing from month to month with childrens' interests, problems and immediate desires. What didn't change during the year was the students' pervasive need to be alone in the room and the feeling of relief that they could be.

Sharing Your Impressions

1. How can schools make up for the lack of privacy experienced by children in crowded homes?
2. Where do you go when you want to be alone?
3. What are some benefits of allowing children to have their own territory at school? At home?
4. Speculate about the effects that providing for student privacy might have on classroom organization and instruction.
5. How do you feel about permitting students to find and claim their own territory in the classroom?
6. Share your observations of the way students try to create privacy in the classroom.
7. What do you remember doing in school to achieve privacy?

Chapter 3

Peers at Play

7

Games Children Play

Edward Devereux

Whatever happened to children's games?

This question occurred to me during a recent visit to Japan. Watching children in parks and neighborhood playgrounds, what struck me most forcefully was the observation that Japanese children seemed to spend very little time just "hanging around." Whenever two or more children found themselves together, they seemed to move very quickly into some kind of self-organized game, of which they seemed to know an enormous variety.

This caused me to puzzle about what has happened to the culture of children's games in America. Looking back to my own childhood, some fifty years ago, I could recall literally dozens of games we played regularly and with enthusiasm—puss in the corner, red rover, capture the flag, one-o-cat, statues, stealing sticks, blind-man's buff, croquet, leap frog, prisoner's base, duck on the rock, marbles, mumble-de-peg, tag, hide and seek, follow the leader—all these and many, many more.

It occurred to me that in recent years I had rarely seen games like these being played spontaneously by American children. Those games that are played always seem to be adult-instigated and supervised, in schools, camps, or other organized play settings, or in party settings in homes.

A research study of game preferences of American children over a sixty-year period tended to confirm these impressions. This study concluded that virtually all of the traditional games of childhood have either vanished entirely or declined in interest among American children and that those which survive have retreated to progressively younger age ranges. Especially the older boys, from 8 or 9 on, seem to be devoting more and more of their play time to a bare handful of major sports, essentially those which are currently most salient for the adult sports fans.

How can we account for this rapid impoverishment of our children's game repertories and, in particular, for the drastic circumscription of play roles among the older boys? Part of this answer surely

From *Cornell Alumni News*, 77, May 1975, 25–28. Reprinted by permission.

lies in the enormous number of hours our children currently devote to
television watching. But still more important is the way in which the
adult-sponsored sports culture has invaded the world of childhood.
Across the nation, literally millions of young boys have been organized,
by adults, into tens of thousands of teams for league competition, in such
sports as Pop Warner football, Pee Wee hockey, basketball, soccer, and
Little League baseball. Even those children who do not participate in
these league sports are surely aware of the extraordinary payoff value of
success in major sports in America. And they know how pleased their
fathers will be at any athletic achievements of their own. Against these
heroic models, who would dare propose a simple game of puss in the corner or tag? Kid stuff, unworthy of the time and attention of any red-
blooded American boy beyond the age of 7 or 8!

Why should we care about what has been happening to the
recreational and spare time activities of our children? It is easy to say—
and this is surely part of it—that our kids are missing out on a lot of
things that provided a great deal of innocent fun for children in earlier
generations. But I believe there is more to it than just that.

Let me make just four general observations about the "functions" of games for children. First, the traditional games represent
miniature and playful models reflecting a wide variety of almost universal cultural and social activities and concerns. Such elemental themes as
leading and following, chasing and eluding, capturing and rescuing, at-
tacking and defending, concealing and searching—these and many more
are endlessly recombined in games of varying complexity into what has
been called a "syntax of play." Through their participation in a variety of
game types, each representing some microcosmic social structure and
variously combining the elements of skill, chance, strategy and physical
prowess, children gain experience with many different success styles
and coping skills.

Second, spontaneously organized games tend to occur in a
"having fun" context. Since the "reality consequences" do not have to
be faced, games allow children to gain some experience, safely, in handling many potentially dangerous psychological and emotional problems—such as anxiety and aggression. Games constitute for children a
kind of "buffered learning setting," introducing them to a variety of
cultural, cognitive, and emotional processes which cannot yet be learned
in full scale cultural participation.

Third, when children are left to organize and govern their
own play activities, much incidental social learning also occurs. As
Piaget, the famous Swiss psychologist, observed, little children tend to
be "moral realists": the "rules" are something out there in the external

world, defined and enforced by powerful adults. Initially, the child learns to conform to avoid punishment, without feeling any particular moral commitment to the rules. In self-organized games, because the rules are vague or in dispute, and because no adult rule-enforcers are present, children are forced to recognize the need for rules of some sort and to bargain among themselves about what is "fair." They must all participate in establishing the rules and learn how to enforce these on themselves and the others. Experiences of this sort, Piaget argued, are essential in helping children move to a more mature, principled stage of moral development, based on the principles of cooperation and consent.

Finally, whatever it is they learn, there is good reason to believe that children may learn it better in a self-supervised game setting than they do in a traditional classroom or in an adult-supervised sport setting. Why? Consider what some psychologists are saying about the properties of an "optimum learning environment": that it should permit free and safe exploration, that it should be responsive to the child's own initiatives, and provide immediate and relevant feedback, that it should be so organized that, through his explorations, the child can infer a variety of ramifying principles and interconnections, and finally that activities should relate directly to the child's own spontaneous interests and motivations. These principles, so widely violated in traditionally organized classrooms, are all most admirably present in spontaneously pursued children's games.

What happens to all these kinds of incidental learning when adults move in and organize the kids' games for them? To answer this question, let me compare a typical game of backyard baseball with the Little League version of the game.

One version we played in my neighborhood fifty years ago was called one-o-cat. There were no teams. With a minimum of five kids you could start up a game, but once you got started usually a few more kids would wander over to join. There was only one base—usually a tree, or somebody's cap. Home plate was a flat stone. A tree to the right and some shrubs on the left were designated as foul markers. There were two batters, a pitcher, a catcher and first baseman; everyone else was in the field.

The rules of the game, as we vaguely understood or invented them, were simple. Since there was no umpire to call balls or strikes, pitches not swung at didn't count, and the pitcher was disciplined mostly by shouts of "put it over!" A good hit could get you to first base and back for a home run. A lesser hit could leave you stranded at first, to be hit in, maybe, by the other batter. Three strikes or a caught fly put you out; or you could be put out at first or home plate in the usual fashion. Since there was no fixed basepath, when a runner was caught between the catcher and the first baseman, a wild chase all over the yard frequently ensued. When you went out, you retired to right field, and everyone else moved up one notch; the catcher to batter, pitcher to catcher, etc. The object seemed to be to stay at bat as long as you could; but during the afternoon everyone had plenty of opportunities to play in every position, and no one was ever on the bench. No one really bothered to keep score, since there were no teams, and besides the personnel of the game kept changing as some kids had to leave for their chores and as others joined in.

Maybe we didn't learn to be expert ball players, but we did have a lot of fun. Moreover, in an indirect and incidental way, I think we learned a lot of other things which are really more important for children in the 8 to 12 age range to learn. Because there was no rule book or rule enforcer, we had to improvise the whole thing by ourselves—endless hassles about whether a ball was fair or foul, a runner was safe or out, or, more generally, simply about what was fair. On the anvil of experience, we gradually learned to understand the invisible boundary conditions of our relations to each other.

Don't be a poor sport or the other kids won't want you to play with them. Don't push your point so hard that the kid with the only catcher's mitt will quit the game. Pitch a bit more gently to the littler kids, so they can have some fun too; besides, you have to keep them in the game because numbers are important. How to handle poor sports and incompetents, when the easy out of excluding them from the game entirely was somehow impractical. How to get a game going and somehow keep it going so long as the fun lasted. How to pace it. When to quit for a while to get a round of cokes or just sit under a tree. How to recognize when the game was really over—not an easy thing, since there were no innings, no winners or losers.

In terms of the models for incidental learning mentioned above, it was all there. It was fun, the scale was small, and the risks minimal. We felt free and relatively safe. The game was self-pacing, responsive to our initiatives, and the feedback was continuous and relevant. Above all, the game was so loosely structured that it forced us to exercise our utmost ingenuity to discover the rules behind the rules—the general principles which make games fair and fun and interesting, and which had to govern our complex relationships with each other.

How does Little League baseball stack up against this model? Rather badly, in my opinion. Granted that the Little Leaguers undoubtedly do learn more about the rules and strategies of our national sport and gain more experience and coaching in the complex skills of ball

handling. If the object is to train future high school, college, and professional athletes, then Little League is unquestionably the winner.

But if we look at the matter in a broader educational perspective, it seems that these gains are not achieved without serious cost. In
educational terms, the question must always be, not what is the boy doing to the ball, but what is the ball doing for the boy? Almost inevitably,
in highly organized, competitive sports, the focus is on winning and the
eye is on the ball. How many Little League coaches or parents really stop
to think about the total experience each boy is having, including those
who have made costly errors, or who have warmed the bench all afternoon, or who were not selected for league competition?

With respect to our models for incidental learning, consider
what is happening. The scale is no longer miniature and safe, what with
scoreboards, umpires, parents, and spectators all looking at you and
evaluating your every move with a single, myopic criterion. Perform!
Win! The risks of failure are large and wounding. Spontaneity is largely
killed by schedules, rules, and adult supervision—a fixed time and place
for each game, a set number of innings, adult-dictated lineups, and a
commitment to a whole season's schedule, at the expense of all other activities.

The major problem with Little League baseball is that the
whole structure of the game is rigidly fixed once and for all. It's all there
in the rule books and in the organization of the League and of the game
itself. It is all handed to the children, ready-made, on a silver platter,
together with the diamonds, the bats and the uniforms. It is all so carefully supervised by adults, who are the teachers, coaches, rule enforcers,
decision makers, rewarders, and punishers, that there is almost nothing
left for the children to do but "play" the game. Almost all the opportunities for incidental learning which were present in the backyard game
have been sacrificed on the altar of baseball competence.

Still more fundamentally, my concern is with what "Little
Leaguism," in baseball and other sports, is doing to the whole culture of
childhood, to participants and non-participants alike, in the schools,
families, neighborhoods, and communities where it has taken root.
Because of its peculiar fascination, for parents more than for the children
themselves, it ends by monopolizing the field and driving almost to
bankruptcy the traditional and spontaneous culture of play and games
among American children.

In a few short decades, our children have nearly lost this rich
heritage which had been passed along from generation to generation
among the children themselves. Today our children have almost forgotten how to play. It is more than just fun they are missing.

Sharing Your Impressions

1. What do you remember about participating in spontaneously organized games?
2. Make some guesses about why children no longer play some of the once traditional games.
3. How do you feel when a group of older children gather at night on your street to play?
4. Describe a spontaneously organized game you used to play and would recommend for today's children.
5. In what ways has the attitude of adults changed toward neighborhood street games since your childhood?
6. Compare the benefits of children's games that are organized by adults with those of games spontaneously organized by children.
7. Explain why you find particular games exciting and other games boring.

8

Play and Peer Teaching

Robert D. Strom

Whenever I talk with boys and girls about age prejudice, I begin with a couple of questions: "Have you ever wanted to be older than you are? How old would you like to be?" Usually the children answer, "Twelve," "Sixteen," "Eighteen," or "Twenty-one." Most children want to be older because to them being older means getting bigger, growing stronger, and having more privileges, such as staying up late or driving a car. Sometimes children tell me what it is like to be left out because others consider them too young. Maybe a seven-year-old has been told by a group of nine-year-olds, "You can't play with us because you're only seven." Children attach great importance to a few months' difference in age. I can't imagine a thirty-five-year-old saying, "That couple shouldn't be invited to our bridge party because they're only thirty-three." In any event, young children do look to older children for a glimpse of what comes next in life and for ideas about how to behave. These are important reasons for considering ways of improving the influence of older children.

Reprinted from *Elementary School Journal,* November 1978, 79(2), 75–80, by permission of The University of Chicago Press. © 1978 by The University of Chicago Press.

Perhaps we should begin by helping parents answer the question: "Why should my children spend time with children their own age?" Age-mates share the same interests and are willing to recreate play situations again and again without a loss of enthusiasm. For certain kinds of early learning, this tolerance for repetition is essential even though it may seem boring to older and more competent children. Young children need someone their own age to find out how well they're doing. In the company of older boys and girls there is less chance for younger ones to assert themselves or to assume a leadership role. Age-mates encourage one another to protest family decisions and to strive for independence; older peers often demand dependence from younger ones. Ordinarily children pay a price for associating with older peers. Part of the price may be living with the uncomfortable fact that the only strengths that count with older children are those strengths a young child has not yet developed. Small children readily accept one another's imaginations, spontaneity, and fears. Peers are less likely to ridicule one another about competence, less likely to overstimulate and strain their companions than older children. Big children frequently make small ones feel unwanted; age-mates share secrets and private jokes, make one feel special, and help give one a sense of belonging to a group—a feeling that everyone needs.

Sometimes parents who favor interaction among age-mates worry when children of different ages spend much time together. Parents fear that the younger party may be abused, exploited, or taught undesirable lessons. Sometimes these misgivings are warranted. There are older children who abuse and exploit younger ones and teach them undesirable lessons, but older children can also provide a beneficial influence. Certainly they are looked up to and imitated. One reason for the hero status of older children is that their behavior can readily be observed and therefore is easier to imitate than the behavior of grownups at a distant place of work. Our own adult experience underscores the need for models—appropriate models if motivation is to stay alive. A golfer who finds out that a new acquaintance also plays the game immediately inquires about average score. Usually the purpose is to learn how good the other player is. It might be deflating to play with someone who is too skilled. In a similar way the skills of adults may discourage younger children. The performance of older peers may be easier for young children to approximate than the performance of adults. Moreover, older children have recently been little themselves, and the fresh memory of their experience can cause them to be less demanding and more sensitive. Finally, young boys and girls need acceptance from older companions to feel the sense of belonging that goes with being a member of a community.

The Helping Relationship

Some social scientists assert that the USA has the most peer-oriented culture to be found anywhere. Despite the desirable possibilities of peer influence, undesirable outcomes more often receive attention. We hear reports about adolescents who lead their companions to drugs and about elementary-school cliques that reject minority children. Even preschoolers are not spared; they are to be avoided because they teach age-mates words that are out of bounds in many families. It is sometimes easy to resent children's reliance on one another, but the possible value of that reliance should not be overlooked.

In the USA the one-room schoolhouse and peer teaching probably began at the same time. The practice was not always effective, but it did recognize children as capable of teaching peers. For a long time we assumed that the children who were being tutored deserved all our attention. Only in recent years have we begun to look seriously at what happens to the children who tutor. Consider the Mobilization for Youth Project, a massive program in New York City to help elementary-school students who have trouble with reading. Typically, the volunteer tutors in the Project were high-school or college students. One of the project consultants observed that untrained tutors gained significantly in self-concept even when the children receiving instruction did not improve in reading. No matter how well or how poorly the tutors were doing as teachers, they felt good about themselves simply because they were trying to help someone else learn. Adult teachers can well understand this kind of special satisfaction (1).

Similar findings in other studies of peer teaching made it clear to Ronald and Peggy Lippitt at the University of Michigan that tutors must be carefully prepared if they and their students are to benefit. When tutors are properly trained, their sense of accomplishment comes from gains in student performance. They do not have to resort to self-approval for holding noble intentions. The Lippitts have conducted several successful experiments with what they call cross-age helpers. In programs that use cross-age helpers upper-grade students are given preparation to understand young children and reasons why some of them have difficulty in school. The participants learn ways of cooperating with the younger child's classroom teacher as well as techniques for helping the child directly. Cross-age teaching is scheduled several times a week during school hours. There are many programs less sophisticated than the Lippitts'. But, whatever the format, almost all of them appear to be effective. Herbert Thelen, a leader in the peer teaching movement from the University of Chicago, has observed that the benefits do not seem to depend on the subject matter or on the nature of the lesson plan. What does appear important is that the school formally recognizes the helping relationship (2,3).

In some ways children may be better candidates for teaching than we suppose. At the University of Wisconsin, Vernon Allen has studied the ability of young tutors to tell whether lessons are being understood. In one experiment a tape-recorded arithmetic lesson was heard by ten children, each of whom was alone at the time. Because the lessons were either extremely simple or extremely difficult, every child understood or did not understand. A video recording was made of each child listening to the lesson. An excerpt thirty seconds long was taken from each of the ten segments, and these excerpts were made into a single video tape that was shown to observers. It was found that third- and fourth-graders were able to discriminate significantly between the easy and the difficult lessons by watching non-verbal facial cues. A sample of primary-school teachers who were attending graduate classes observed the tape. They could not accurately identify the children who had and those who had not understood a lesson. Certainly the insights of peer teachers, added to our own, would help us diagnose better than we do now. Everyone would benefit if the perceptions of children were properly respected (4).

Motivation and Games

Because play is the preferred way of learning for most boys and girls, play deserves consideration as a method for peer teaching. Parents are convinced that their children need to play with peers outside school. This belief suggests that children can learn by playing with companions about their own age. Teachers daily witness the powerful influence that older children exert on younger ones during recess. For primary students, playing with bigger children is the next best thing to being bigger themselves. One might expect teachers to ask, "What kinds of games ought to be used for peer teaching? What social values can games help us reinforce?" But teachers seldom ask these questions. Teachers are more likely to ask: "How can we cut down on the amount of play in school so that children can get down to the business of learning?" The time scheduled for play during kindergarten and first grade has recently declined in favor of early reading activities. One reason for this change is that teachers do not understand the merits of play well enough to defend its presence in the curriculum. As a result, educators find themselves emphasizing priorities for child development with which they may disagree but for which they are held accountable (5).

At the same time that play is decreasing to make way for other activities in elementary school, play is increasing at the college level. This shift warrants an explanation. A decade ago some professors reluctantly concluded that their traditional methods of teaching about social problems were no longer working. Often the students appeared content merely to verbalize knowledge without acting on it. While searching for approaches that would bring more student involvement, a number of scholars independently decided on games. It seems that while playing games, people become participants in a process different from the usual "learning" experience, a process that includes feelings as well as thought. In these college play sessions the students did learn. Naturally this outcome was disturbing, because university teachers, like the rest of us, have been educated to believe that play and learning don't go together; to link them means a lowering of standards. Most of us can recall being told by a teacher to "quit playing around and get to work." Many professors had long been comfortable with this kind of direction. Time-honored assertions about traditional games—"Football develops character"—did not impress academic faculty. Professors were aware that the assertions are unsubstantiated.

Thus the university attempt to connect games and learning was understandably cautious. It began by conceding that game-like conditions promote learning. However, the frivolous design of commercial games denied players a chance to practice important values. Students needed new games, original at least in their social purpose. About 1970 many new games based on this rationale began to appear. Now there are games for improving police-community relations, games for understanding the elderly and aging, even games for learning to cope as a foreigner abroad. Most of these games come with elaborate directions, lengthy time requirements, and debriefing procedures. Gaming is now accepted as a teaching device by many policymakers, professional planners, municipal administrators, management officials, and professors. So popular has the adult play movement become that in 1973 the University of Michigan School of Education established an extension service to help interested parties better understand and use games, to select appropriate games, and to design games for special organizational needs (6, 7).

In view of the mounting support for play as a way to learn in college, in business, and in industry, perhaps we should reconsider whether gaming also has merit for peer teaching in elementary and high school. Certainly there is no question about motivation. Games are more appealing to the young than to adults. The fact is supported by observation and by retail sales. In addition, games can offer children practice in decision-making. What we surmise about the future suggests that people will need the ability to accept increasing complexity, to cope with more uncertainty, to see alternatives, and to make independent judgments. As we enter what is being called the era of overchoice, children must have experience with decision-making to adopt a set of coherent values. Although most parents and teachers would agree that growing up and decision-making go together, it does not always turn out that way. Adults often justify their take-over of decisions by insisting that children's wrong choices could bring serious consequences. So we are faced with a dilemma: Boys and girls need preparation in making decisions, but the chance to make decisions is often denied them for their own protection. Because children are expected to remain students longer than their parents were, the initial chance to decide for themselves may not come until the stakes are high (8, 9).

One can assume that the only way children can safely learn to make decisions is by being taught. The gaming approach assumes that children can learn by experiencing the consequences of their actions. Through emotional and intellectual involvement, games permit players to try out situations and solutions that are either irreversible or too risky and expensive to test in the real world. Games offer the chance for almost risk-free, active exploration of yet-to-be-experienced social and intellectual problems. Unlike blunders in life, however, the mistakes made in games cost society nothing and for the learner carry the fairly low price tag of ego deflation (10, 11).

If certain conditions are met, games can be an effective means of peer teaching. What matters most is the attitude of the tutor. It is essential that the tutor who is introducing a learning game respect the play style of beginners. If the tutor is not instructed to accept the play style of beginners, the tutor may see the teaching task only as helping a young child understand the rules. From the beginner's view the problem with games is their devaluation of imagination. Before the child was introduced to learning games, he relied on imagination as a guide for play behavior and as a source for sensing power and control. When subject to game rules, some beginners may become frustrated easily, especially when setbacks are imposed such as "lose one turn and go back three spaces." Children make a natural response to the new sense of powerlessness they feel when rules are enforced. Often they request that rules of the game be suspended or at least altered. If we honor the request and before a game invite beginners to make up alternative rules, we can help them keep alive their respect for pretending while gradually raising the priority they assign to rules.

A second problem faces tutors. Beginners at learning games are not sure when they should participate. From their dramatic play children have grown used to moving around, reacting spontaneously, and participating full time. Most board games require that players sit still and respond only when it is their turn. During a group game it isn't surprising to find that some beginners become bored, others don't recognize when it's their turn, and a few assign themselves too many turns. Rather than complain that these children can't follow directions, let's acknowledge that the role of spectator or part-time participant may be unnatural and unappealing to them. It is wise to start with games that have few rules and involve only two players. These conditions minimize turn-taking yet teach it. Above all, the conditions respect spontaneity.

Very young children, more than older children, take pleasure in the activity of play itself. Because they consider play to be its own reward, they do not need to complete an activity to achieve satisfaction. By contrast, older children and adults who play games may find some pleasure in the action but usually look forward to the final score or payoff, which does not come until the game ends and the winner and the loser are determined. With these differences in the timing and the source of satisfaction, to stop a game before completion frustrates some experienced players. They may resort to coercing the beginner who wants to stop playing before a game has ended. Some experienced players hurry the beginner so that the game can be completed. "Go ahead and move," they urge. "No more questions, no moving around, no talking if it has nothing to do with the game." To ensure that both parties enjoy the activity, it's a good idea to alternate between playing games and playing at pretend. This arrangement respects the rules and the competitive orientation of tutors as well as the pretending ability of their younger peers (12, 13).

The results of peer teaching and research on play suggest that the student role should be modified. If students are to teach as well as learn in school, they can improve their influence on others, think well of themselves for being responsible, and experience the respect of a grateful society.

References

1. Alan Gartner, Mary Kohler, and Frank Riessman. *Children Teach Children*. New York, New York: Harper and Row, 1971.

2. Ronald Lippitt and Peggy Lippitt. "Cross-Age Helpers." In *Education for Affective Achievement*, pp. 166–70. Edited by Robert Strom and E. Paul Torrance. Chicago, Illinois, Rand McNally, 1973.

3. Herbert Thelen. "Tutoring by Students: What Makes It So Exciting," *School Review, 77* (September, 1969), 229–44.

4. Vernon Allen. *Children as Teachers: Theory and Research on Tutoring*. New York, New York: Academic Press, 1976.

5. Helen Robison. "The Decline of Play in Urban Kindergartens," *Young Children, 26* (August, 1971), 333–41.

6. Clark Abt. *Serious Games.* New York, New York: Viking, 1970.

7. Frederick Goodman. "Gaming and Simulation." In *Second Handbook on Teaching*, pp. 926–39. Edited by Robert Travers. Chicago, Illinois: Rand McNally, 1973.

8. James Coleman. "Learning Through Games." In *The Study of Games*, pp. 322–25. Edited by Elliot Avedon and Brian Sutton-Smith. New York, New York: Wiley, 1971.

9. Robert D. Horn. *The Guide to Simulations/Games for Education and Training*, pp. 1–16. Volume 1. Cranford, New Jersey: Didactic Systems, 1977.

10. J. Coleman, S. Livingston, G. Fennessey, K. Edwards and S. Kidder. "The Hopkins Games Program: Conclusions from Seven Years of Research," *Educational Researcher, 2* (January, 1973), 3–7.

11. Loyda Shears and Eli Bower. *Games in Education and Development.* Springfield, Illinois: Charles Thomas, 1974.

12. Robert Strom and Guillermina Engelbrecht. "Creative Peer Teaching," *Journal of Creative Behavior, 8* (Summer, 1974), 93–100.

13. Robert Strom. *Growing Together: Parent and Child Development.* Monterey, California: Brooks/Cole Company, 1978.

Sharing Your Impressions

1. How do you feel when a child wants to quit playing a game before it is over?

2. Identify some of the problems faced by young children when they begin to learn games that have formal rules.

3. Why do you suppose children need to play with peers who are their own age? With older kids? With younger kids?

4. Compare the age segregation you observe in children's play now with your own experiences as a child.

5. Think of some advantages that being a peer teacher has over being a classroom teacher.

6. How do you suppose parents and teachers feel about peer teaching at school? Outside of school?

7. Recall your play experience as a younger or older sibling.

8. Describe some games that you feel are appropriate for big and little kids to play together.

9

Learning through Games

James S. Coleman

Playing games is a very old and widespread form of learning. The child first comes to understand the meaning of a rule—that a rule must be obeyed by all—in a game with others where, if the rules are broken, the game does not function.

From *NEA Journal*, January 1967, 69–70. Reprinted by permission of the National Education Association.

Recently, educators have begun devising games for high school and pre-high school students that simulate complex activities in a society. One of the ways that simulation and games were first combined was in war games. Many of the oldest parlor games (chess and checkers, for example) were developed as war simulations long ago, and today armies use war games to develop logistic and strategic skills.

From war games developed the idea of management games, a simulation of management decision-making which is used in many business schools and firms to train future executives by putting them in situations they will confront in their jobs.

The games that I and my associates at Johns Hopkins have developed simulate some aspect of society. There is a Life Career Game, a Family Game, a Representative Democracy Game, a Community Response Game (in which a community responds to some kind of disaster), a High School Game (which is really for pre-high school students), and a Consumer Game (in which the players are consumers and department store credit managers).

Other sets of academic games on topics ranging from international relations to mathematics have been developed and tested by other persons or institutions—Clark Abt, Cambridge, Massachusetts; Harold Guetzkow, Northwestern University; Layman Allen, Yale; and Western Behavioral Sciences Institute, La Jolla, California.

A description of one of the games developed at Johns Hopkins, a legislative game designed to teach the basic structure of representative government, gives some idea of what and how the games are designed to teach. Six to eleven players sit around a table or circle of desks. The chairman deals a set of fifty-two cards, each representing a segment of a constituency and giving the positions of constituents on one of eight issues. The cards a player holds represent the positions of his constituents on some or all of the eight issues: civil rights, aid to education, medical care, defense appropriation, national seashore park in Constituency A, offshore oil, federal dam in Constituency B, and retaining a military base in Constituency C.

The player, as legislator, is attempting to gain reelection, and he can do so only through satisfying the wishes, as indicated on his cards, of a majority of his constituents, For example, if he has 80 constituents in favor of an aid to education bill and 20 against it, he has a net gain of 60 votes toward reelection if the bill passes or a net loss of 60 if it fails.

After a player brings an issue to the floor, a two-minute negotiation session ensues. The negotiation consists largely of an exchange of support among the players. A legislator will offer his support for or against issues his constituents have no interest in, in return for support on legislation in which they are interested. A vote of legislators, with each player-legislator having one vote, is then taken and the session proceeds to an issue raised by the next player. When all bills have been acted on, each legislator calculates his reelection or defeat by adding up votes of satisfied and dissatisfied constituents. The overall winner is the legislator who is reelected by the largest majority. This is the first "level" of the game, which altogether consists of eight levels, each introducing more of the complexity of legislative functioning.

I developed an interest in simulation games several years ago while I was making a study of high school adolescents in Illinois. The study suggested that high schools either did not reward academic activity or rewarded it in wrong ways. In my opinion, the organization of academic work in school acts to keep down the amount of effort and attention a student gives to academic pursuits as compared to extracurricular activities.

The structuring of athletic activity, for example, is very different from the structuring of academic activity. A student making a touchdown for the football team or winning the half-mile at track achieves for both the school and himself, something he can seldom do academically.

It seemed, for this and other reasons, that making use of the simulation techniques of war and management games might be particularly appropriate for schools. First of all, it would make possible a reward structure which would focus on achievement for the school as well as on individual academic achievement. Last spring in Fort Lauderdale, Florida, for example, a number of schools from eight states participated in the "Nova Academic Olympics," playing an equations game, a logic game, and a legislative game in the kind of interscholastic tournament often reserved for athletics.

A more important asset of simulation games is that they constitute an approach to learning that starts from fundamentally different premises than does the usual approach to learning schools. The first premise is that persons do not learn by being taught; they learn by experiencing the consequences of their actions. Games which simulate some aspects of reality are one way a young person can begin to see such consequences before he faces the real actions and the real consequences as an adult.

A second premise underlying the development of these games is that schools find it difficult to teach about the complexity that characterizes modern society, with the result that students have had little or no experience to prepare them for facing a multitude of decisions and problems in adult life. The games we and others have created present the student with an approximation of certain facets of modern society that he will have to face later.

Learning through games has a number of intrinsic virtues. One of these is its attention-focusing quality. Games tend to focus attention more effectively than most other teaching devices, partly because they involve the student actively rather than passively. The depth of involvement in a game, whether it is basketball, Life Career, or bridge, is often so great that the players are totally absorbed in this artificial world.

Another virtue of academic games as a learning device is that using them diminishes the teacher's role as judge and jury. Such a role often elicits students' fear, resentment, or anger and gives rise to discipline problems. Games enable the student to see the consequences of his actions in his winning or losing. He cannot blame the teacher for his grades; instead he is able to understand the way in which his own activity is related to the outcome. The teacher's role reverts to a more natural one of helper and coach.

In developing an appropriate sense of consequences contingent upon action, the amount of chance in a game is quite important. If a game has the appropriate mixture of chance and skill, persons of somewhat different abilities can play together, and success will depend in part, but not entirely, upon their relative skill.

A special value of academic simulation games appears to be the capacity to develop in the player a sense that he can affect his own future. A massive study conducted by the U.S. Office of Education shows that one attribute strongly related to performance on standard achievement tests is a child's belief that his future depends on his own efforts rather than on a capricious environment. Many disadvantaged pupils appear to lack this belief.

Seeing the consequences of one's actions in a game develops the sense of predictable and controllable environment. When a game simulates aspects of a student's present or future life, the student begins to see how his future depends very directly upon present actions, and thus gives meaning to these actions.

Still another virtue of academic games is the range of skills a game can encompass. A teacher's class presentation has a fairly narrow range: Some students fail to understand unless it is very simple; others are bored when it is that simple. Games, however can encompass a much larger range of skills. One example indicating the wide range of simulation games is the successful use of the Representative Democracy Game with high school classes of slow learners and, in identical form, with a group of faculty and graduate students in political science and sociology.

Games of this sort hold the attention of bright students in part because they continue to think of new variations in strategy and in the rules. When the rules are not merely accepted but examined and perhaps modified, possibilities for creativity are opened up that the classroom situation often inhibits. The same game may be played successfully—usually at a less sophisticated level, but not always—by children who perform poorly in school. Several groups in a classroom may be playing the same game at different levels of skill.

When a game is designed to illustrate a general principle, some students understand the principle, while others will not do so without guided discussion after play. Thus games are clearly not a self-sufficient panacea for education, although they are more than simply another educational device.

They can be used in many ways ranging from merely inserting them into an existing curriculum to transforming the curriculum by using games and tournaments to replace quizzes and tests.

In the broadest sense, the development of academic simulation games is a response to two challenges: that posed by a complex, difficult-to-understand society and that posed by children uninterested in or unprepared for abstract intellectual learning. These challenges may be blessings in disguise if they force the development of approaches to learning in school that more nearly approximate the natural processes through which learning occurs outside school.

Sharing Your Impressions

1. How does the role of the teacher change when games are the medium of classroom learning?
2. Think of some advantages of learning about careers in a game situation.
3. How do the benefits of simulation games differ from the benefits of athletics?
4. In what ways has the concept of using games as a teaching method changed since you were a child?
5. Compare your feelings about the rewards received by athletes and the rewards received by scholars.
6. Think of some ways in which students could be rewarded individually for participating on the winning side of a non-athletic team.
7. What are some of the elements in games that help to hold the attention of children?

Chapter 4

Adults as Play Partners

10

Too Busy to Play?

Robert D. Strom

It seems ironic that children are expected to learn the worthy use of leisure time from grownups whose work seldom makes them available for play. Even in their own homes some youngsters are regularly told: "I'm too busy now to play with you—wait until later." This evasion of parent-child play is not a deliberate attempt to frustrate the young. On the contrary, it simply reflects the difficulty most of us have in arranging time with our children. One of the recommendations I am frequently asked to give involves the allotment of time that parents should spend at family play. It is insufficient to point out that since families differ there can be no single set of guidelines. Instead I advise parents to decide for themselves after they have self-directed the following questions:

How long can I remain interested while at play? We need have no doubt about the attention span of children for play. Even a casual observer will notice that whenever young boys and girls are obliged to discontinue their play, they do so with gross disappointment. Our own sustained interest in children's play activities is a different story. Many of us find it difficult to remain interested in play ("pretending") for very long. The typical adult beginner can handle only about ten minutes of fantasy play with a preschooler. This fact means it is unreasonable to participate beyond our point of disinterest, or else we convey the impression that the activity lacks worthwhileness. When it becomes necessary to withdraw, we might tell the child: "I think it's time for me to stop now—I can't play for as long as you can." Most parents find enjoyment in imaginative play after a few sessions. As a result their attention span grows and they become able to play for longer periods of time.

How important is my influence during play? Some parents believe that play with age-mates is sufficient to meet the needs of

From *Childhood Education,* November/December 1977, pp. 80–82. Reprinted by permission of the author and the Association for Childhood Education International, 3615 Wisconsin Avenue, N.W., Washington D.C. Copyright © 1977 by the Association.

children. Mothers and fathers who reach this conclusion do not love their children less than families who play together. But they ought to consider certain of the benefits that are unique to parent-child play, especially the chance for learning conflict-resolution, vocabulary and value development, sharing dominance and approval of imagination. Once informed of these possibilities, a person can still suggest that the amount of time spent with children is less important than the *quality* of time. This excuse fails to recognize that play without practice is bound to be of low quality, coercive or concession-oriented. Moreover, all skill development, whether it be golf, basketball or imaginative play, requires repetitive practice, which in turn takes time. In short, parents are unlikely to achieve a quality relationship with children unless they invest time. Then, too, children often base their sense of worth on the amount of time and degree of parental involvement in their activities. Thus, it is not surprising that the most accessible parents, those who play the most with their children, are also the ones with the most appropriate childrearing expectations and child responsiveness. These people have taken seriously their own question: How much time is my child worth?

How comfortable am I during play? A majority of grownups report a feeling of silliness when they first enter the realm of child play. This sense of embarrassment reflects a belief that childhood is the only justifiable time for pretending. Unless inhibition can be reduced, the parent will have less access to imagination than is needed for fantasy play. Whether a parent feels uneasy can also depend on how the interaction is seen. If the younger player is viewed as a competitor whose creative behavior must be surpassed, then probably the adults will undervalue themselves and withdraw altogether. Only when the child is seen as a partner does the parent cease to engage in unfavorable self-comparison. In a partnership the strength of each member is to the advantage of both parties. Therefore, during imaginative exchange no one loses because success is mutual. Actually, the parent who feels comfortable at play has learned to teach respect by modeling. Essentially respect means that the other person's strength is allowed to influence relationships rather than to lock them into a subordinate role by interacting only on our terms. Grownups can respect the creative strength of children by sharing dominance with them during play.

Am I willing to set aside a time for play? Many of us seem unable to schedule play. Consider the growing number of people whose employers allow them to work at home. Often these parents are perplexed about how to handle the continued interruption by children. On the one hand, they feel guilty about not responding to the child's appeals for play; and at the same time they are angry because conditions are such that they cannot be productive. Reluctantly the decision may be to go back to the office. One alternative is to set aside a time for play that the child is aware of and can depend upon. Given this intention, a father says to his four-year-old son: "I'll be in my study from 9 to 11 and must not be disturbed. But at 11 I'll come out and play with you. If I'm not out when mother says it's 11, you come and get me."

The chance to withdraw is seldom an option for housewives who remain at home with small children. They report a need to be surveillant most of the time and a high frequency of interrupted activity. Some of them learn to incorporate sessions of pretending into their daily chores. Others plan the day so that a child can count on spending a regular play time with mother and a time by him/herself with access to her.

A somewhat different problem is experienced by people who have to leave home for work. When they return tired or late, the tendency is to excuse themselves from parent-child play until the weekend. That this decision is unfortunate can be shown by the child's continuous need to share intrafamily dominance and also the short attention span of parents for fantasy play. A better plan might be to amend the family schedule so that two periods of at least ten minutes can be devoted to parent-child play. We can be sure these daily sessions include some of our best minutes of insight and energy rather than our least tolerant moments, the time of fatigue. In addition, we can try to recognize when unscheduled play is necessary. On some occasions almost every child will make demands or give other clues that extra attention is needed. In such cases, a few minutes of play may well avoid punishment or an all-day argument.

What will happen if I avoid family play? Parents differ in the value they assign to conversations with young children. Some of them view the exchange as a delight, while others regard it as an unwelcome distraction. Later, however, when the same children reach adolescence, some parents reverse themselves by complaining that they cannot get their teenagers to talk to them. Usually this loss in communication is explained as though it represents normal development, a natural change indicating a greater reliance on peers and the quest for independence. The fact that some parents continue to enjoy access to the feelings of sons and daughters once they become teenagers and continue to be sought after for advice is often interpreted as a stroke of luck. The truth is that at every age we share ourselves most with whoever has demonstrated willingness to spend time with us. For example, psychologist Daniel Brown reports a study of 300 seventh- and eighth-grade boys who kept a diary of the time their fathers spent with them. They noted that during an average week the typical father and son were alone together a total of seven minutes. Parents can establish themselves as a lasting source of guidance only if they make it a practice to participate in activities that interest their children.

How worthwhile am I as a model for leisure? In a society of increasing leisure, a child should observe parents at leisure to learn what adults enjoy. Youngsters cannot do this if parents say, "I'll relax later when you're in bed" or, "I'm sacrificing my spare time in order to provide you all the things I never had." What parents can share with children is more valuable than the things they can give them. Certainly happiness is one of our most elusive goals. When we show our children how to achieve satisfaction during adult life, the young are rich if not affluent beneficiaries. But if in the attempt to provide our family with a higher income we insist on holding two jobs or avoiding the pursuit of our own pleasure in the children's presence, we fail to convey how satisfaction can be attained. In my own profession, I know many teachers who assign themselves too much homework. Usually they see themselves as dedicated persons whose evasion of time with the family is justified by their example of hard work. The fact remains that, unless such parents also illustrate for their children how to find joy and contentment during adult life, the young must discover it by expensive experimentation with immature peers.

Many parents live for tomorrow. Perhaps they look forward to the freedom and economic advantage that should come after their children grow up. Some look ahead to leaving the job, to retirement and its leisure options. But in the anticipation process, many of us fail to enjoy our children now, our jobs now, our lives together now—and then later, when the date for retirement arrives, we regret that the children are gone, we resent the loss of vocational role, and we painfully face our failure to establish intimacy. To enjoy the future, we must learn to cope with leisure in the present. Moreover, at school and in the home we have an obligation to teach the young how this can be done.

References

Strom, Robert D. *Growing Together: Parent and Child Development.* Monterey, Ca.: Brooks/Cole Publishing Co., 1978.
_____ . *Parent and Child in Fiction.* Monterey, Ca.: Brooks/Cole Publishing Co., 1977.

Sharing Your Impressions

1. What are some of the things you recall doing with your parents that you really enjoyed?
2. When you were a child, how did your parents spend their leisure time?
3. How does the amount of time you spend playing with your children compare to the time your parents spent playing with you?
4. Make some guesses about how your child views you as a model for leisure.
5. How do you respond when your child asks you to play?
6. Think of some benefits that play with your children has for you.
7. What do you think is the effect on the children when parents play with them out of a sense of duty rather than for fun?

11

Parents and Teachers as Play Observers

Robert D. Strom

Many parents and teachers underestimate their influence in the role of observer. Maybe this fact helps explain why most of us are poor observers of play. Some people disagree, however, and suggest that we are too interested in observing play. After all, an increasing number of men watch television athletics so much each weekend that they run the risk of disrupting their marriages. Apart from ignoring wives in favor of "Wide World of Sports," these game minded fathers are also accused of having a poor influence on their children. The Saturday-Sunday-Monday routine of television football allows little time for family interaction; and in some homes only occasional grunts are heard from the father, who insists on silence except during the commercials. Another group of adults have been warned by physicians against observing sports too much because, unlike the athletes they watch, the excited fans cannot release the emotion of game stress. As a result they enlarge their risk of heart failure. Surely these kinds of circumstance suggest that being a play spectator is an accepted role in our society.

The same conclusion is reached when we record the preferred focus of grownups who visit the zoo. Young and middle-aged adults alike apparently prefer the monkey facility to all others. Perhaps the reason

From *Childhood Education,* January 1975, pp. 139–141. Reprinted by permission of the author and the Association for Childhood Education International, 3615 Wisconsin Avenue, N.W., Washington, D.C. Copyright © 1975 by the Association.

primates are so popular is that they resemble people but have furry tails; they love to chase, wrestle, swing and jump. It is fascinating to watch them play. For a child, monkeys invite a sense of wonder; for an adult, the longing to be agile and carefree again. We speak a language that includes many references to their play—"monkey business," "monkey shines," "monkeying around"—all referring to a spirit of mischief.

Given the wide appeal of being a play spectator, why do we consider the play activity that once occupied most of our time as a child and gave such pleasure no longer to be worth watching? Is observing child-play less satisfying or less important than watching organized athletics? Surely preschoolers want to be watched; their constant appeal is "See me!" "Look!" "Watch this!" They gain obvious satisfaction from being observed. Well, then, why can we not find the time to look at little boys and girls as they engage in imaginative play when we will travel miles to watch our pre-teenager participate in a Little League contest? Why are we so quickly distracted as we witness a four-year-old at play? Is it because we don't know what to look for, what to find pleasing, how to identify success, what to say about a form of play that has no rules, no hits, no runs, and so cannot be scored? Why is it that I can invite friends to see my ten-year-old son Steven take part in a hockey game but, if I ask them to stop by for half an hour to watch four-year-old Paris play, they decline and ask "Why? Has he a special trick? What does he do?"

Whatever prevents our becoming serious and regular observers of preschool play, I believe we are lesser guides to young children lesser parents and teachers because of it. Do you remember the law of effect? Simply stated, this law of learning suggests that behavior that is satisfying tends to be repeated. We know that preschoolers like to pretend; they also desire the approval of their parents. So, when pretending brings parent disapproval, indifference or inattention, it predictably begins to wane, to decline, to drop off. If by seldom observing child drama we give boys and girls an impression that imaginative play is unimportant to us, that original thinking does not merit our attention, that fantasy is not worth watching, that we respect only nonfictional play—then we should expect that a child's wish for parent affection will lower the priority the child attaches to his own imaginative behavior.

Maybe our difficulty lies in holding too narrow a definition of "achievement." Many of us agree that creativity will be crucial for adults in the future; yet play, the dominant form of creativity during childhood, receives infrequent respect, is too little observed, and in some cases is not even allowed. Perhaps we need to shift the focus to ourselves and compare our play encounters with children of different ages. Playing games like football and baseball, activities in which motor skill, rules and judgment have a higher priority than imagination, seems to present little problem for most parents. These types of play please us and we can spend hours being involved. On the other hand, most of us have trouble spending even a few minutes playing with or watching a preschooler play. Our adult attention span appears to be in question. When we stop-clock parents at play with children or observing their children, the parents usually estimate their length of involvement to be three or four times greater than the actual amount of lapsed time.

By watching a child at play we can communicate a confidence, a belief, an approval of his ability. By watching him at play we accept him as he is. Conversely, to ignore his play can mean he will find it more difficult to like and accept himself. He must feel he is worth the time for us to bother watching him before he can believe his imaginative play is important enough to retain.

My advice to parents is that, if you believe in reward, do not underestimate the reinforcing influence of your observation. Since observation requires time, watching represents approval. In my judgment, giving time can be a far more authentic reinforcement than is verbal praise. To give time requires an investment of self, whereas no personal investment is required to momentarily acknowledge a child's appeal for observation by announcing that his play product is "good" or "wonderful." To put it another way, observation is a more effective form of reward than is verbal comment.

In this connection, I am always disappointed by the parents who tell me that when their child has visited the grandparents he is difficult to live with because he has been spoiled. I don't think that reaction is a fair assessment of the influence of many grandparents. What in fact often happens is that when children visit grandparents who do not have jobs, who are able to spend more time with them than parents are, the grandparents watch the children a lot and play with them. The children come to expect the same response when they return home. Instead we pronounce the child's higher expectations of us as a fault engendered by grandparents; in short, the children have been spoiled.

Actually, one of the best ways to show respect for someone is to watch him "do his thing." And it follows that, if we avoid spending time in the child's arena of play, we pass by a valuable chance to share power with him, to share dominance with him, to acknowledge his strength and respect him. By respect, I mean allowing the other person's strength to affect our relationship rather than keeping him always in the position of subordinate.

As you know, most observation systems are used to improve the behavior of the person being observed. This is not the case for the child at play. Instead, by watching him, we automatically reinforce the importance of who he already is and the creativity he owns. Somehow more of us must learn to value in our children what we would have them retain beyond childhood. I believe the philosopher Montaigne said it best: "The play of children is their most serious business." I propose that we make the observation of this serious business a larger part of the parent experience.

Sharing Your Impressions

1. How does your behavior as a play spectator influence the children you observe?
2. How does fantasy help you cope with your present problems?
3. What factors cause children to abandon their predisposition to fantasize?
4. Why do you suppose play and learning are so often viewed as opposites?
5. Compare your readiness to watch organized youth sports with your readiness to watch the play of preschoolers.
6. To what extent should praise be used by adult observers of child play?
7. What are your reactions to the assertion that play observation is participation?

12

Observing Parent-Child Fantasy Play

Robert D. Strom

There are few observers of parent-child fantasy play. Maybe this is because we feel the interaction would be hindered by a witness. After all, the best observation occurs in a natural setting where spontaneity is allowed and contrived behavior is minimal, when people feel relatively comfortable and are not threatened by evaluation. Fantasy play seems natural for the preschool child and somewhat unnatural for his parents. Also, some observers avoid the parent and child at play because the observer feels uncomfortable especially about the interpretation of play content. It seems fair to question the need for the reliable recording of play content if its meaning is to remain unknown. Obviously, the most common explanation for the low interest in parent-child play is that it simply isn't worth watching. Instead, persons who wish to see the dynamics of imaginative play are counseled to observe children in their peer groups.

From *Theory into Practice*, October 1974, *13*(4), 287–295. Reprinted by permission. (This paper was presented to the annual meeting of the American Psychological Association in New Orleans on August 30, 1974.)

Each of the reasons for ignoring parent-child play could as well be seen as reasons for observing it. If fantasy play with preschoolers seems unnatural for many parents, perhaps, by observation, we can learn how to help them feel more comfortable. If the recording of play content does not yield to interpretation, maybe we can find meaning by redirecting our attention to the play process. Finally, if we believe that parent-child play is a less worthwhile focus than peer play, maybe our comparative observation can reveal the differential benefits for each of the two conditions.

We must recognize that most popular observation systems were developed to describe non-play conditions (Simon & Boyer, 1967). Therefore, much of the needed research on parent education awaits the design of a coherent process-oriented play observation system. To elaborate the possibilities, I wish to share some categories of behavior we have found useful in our research at the Parent-Child Laboratory of Arizona State University.

Play Observation Categories

Attention Span

The readiness of preschoolers to sustain attention while at play can be timed. This ability to pay attention is for the process of play rather than any among the discontinuous events or plots on which process may focus.

Many children have a short attention span for adult-preferred activities. For example, boys and girls alike find the process of window shopping a low interest activity. Typically they ask mother to end the shopping well before she is ready to do so. They also exaggerate the amount of time spent shopping. What the children may complain of as having been "a long time" is of course recognized by mother as being only a few minutes. We find this relative disability of attention span reversed in the child-preferred activity of play. During play it is the adult attention which is in question. Most of us have trouble spending even a few minutes playing with a preschooler. When we stop-clock the play or play observation of parents with four-year-olds, the grownups generally estimate their involvement to be three to four times greater than the actual amount of lapsed time.

The great breadth of child focus during play is usually considered as an indication of short attentive ability. But perhaps the preference of the child for wide focus facilitates an inventive orientation by bringing together otherwise mutually remote ideas. From this perspective it would appear that parents need to enlarge both the length and scope of their attention in order to participate in fantasy play.

Delays of Closure

The preschoolers' ability to successively engage in play events without their serial completion illustrates the delay of closure. Persons of this ability demonstrate a tolerance for incomplete events and the consequent tension of ambiguity.

The greater need of parents than children for closure accounts in part for parent frustration during play. Whereas the child proceeds from one focus to another and back again without revealing a need for completion, parents sense tension unless the play themes reach some type of conclusion. Most parents who need play closure also show a preoccupation with rules. They tend toward the opinion that before any fantasy play can take place, it is necessary to decide the rules and define the boundaries which will govern behavior. This press to eliminate ambiguity by determining limits for players is not an antecedent for peer play between preschoolers. We have not determined the exact age when the change happens. However, I am often disappointed in observing nine- and ten-year-olds who find it necessary to spend most of their play time trying to decide about rules. Some teachers regard this daily scene at recess as evidence for the beginnings of democratic behavior; it could also be that the observer is witnessing the decline of creativity.

Peer play does not require closure. Since no rules are set forth and the reward is continuous rather than terminal, the child is not obliged to complete play. To him, play is a never-ending and all important task. On the other hand, parents who often approach fantasy play as though it were a competition sense a need to finish one thematic event before starting a new one. That is, their satisfaction lies in the outcome rather than in the process of play. This difference in the locus of satisfaction attributes to the cognitive style preference of preschoolers and their elders. Children and highly creative grownups show a stronger preference for perceiving (becoming aware) than for judging (reaching conclusions). Conversely, most grownups prefer judgment. While a judging person emphasizes the control and regulation of experience, the perceiving individual is inclined to be more flexible and spontaneous, more curious and receptive to experiences both of the world within and outside the self (Strom, 1969).

It is important to recognize that we live in a world of early deadlines, a period when the time for reaching conclusions and for finishing tasks is continually compressed. Researchers and students alike complain about being expected to produce reports before their project is well underway. Indeed most of us are disappointed with the environmental forces that dictate our accelerated closure. Yet we impose the same conditions on children when every play event must have a conclusion. The more closure conscious we as a society become, the less likely we will be able to tolerate delayed closure when we meet this characteristic in children. Yet the stubborn fact is that creativity and the ability to delay closure are inextricably related.

Expression of Emotion

The preschooler's relative absence of inhibition accounts for the verbal and nonverbal intensity with which he expresses emotion. This readiness for self disclosure includes sanctioned and disapproved emotion.

It is common for parents who witness excited children simulating sounds for trucks and trains to caution "not so loud." The noise of child play which reflects the intensity of involvement is sometimes perceived as an indicator of hearing loss. A more reasonable assessment is that the young train conductors are doing what is required in adult life—and therefore in role playing—shouting above competing engine noises! If a mother were aware, she would know how foolish it is to announce in a whisper, "All aboard." In one such case, minutes later the mother credited herself with blowing up a bridge without making a lot of noise. Much to her dismay, the young play partner continued to cross the bridge refusing to acknowledge its demolition since he had not heard the dynamite charge.

Granted there are many families who live in densely-populated apartment complexes. Mindful of paper-thin walls and neighbor complaints, parents in these circumstances feel obliged to minimize the sound of child play. The petition of urban parents for more play space in their neighborhood is seldom successful. Although teachers urge more play space for school, they are relatively unconcerned about the children's need for territoriality outside of school. Apart from the restriction that lack of space imposes on play during early childhood, there are serious losses in the possibilities for affective identification.

Recognize that at age four a child is modeling emotion—what his parents feel and how they express their feelings. It is fair to say that grownups who suppress or fail to show emotion represent poor models of response. Paradoxically, such parents are both less and more influential than they intend. On the one hand, parents who neglect to show emotion offer a limited repertoire to their child. Studies by Hoffman (1971) have shown that when tired or uninterested parents dutifully read and tell stories to their preschoolers, the monotonous presentation (as assessed by facial expression, speech inflection and emotional tone) has a negligible educational benefit for the child. By comparison, parents who read with feeling and express emotion in the telling of stories to their children register an appreciable impact.

From another perspective, parents who undervalue emotional expression have a great, if unfortunate, influence. When adults invest too little of themselves in situations, their children can adopt the same coping response. For instance, if parents fail to show fear, grief or excitement about a play fire, toy accident, or death, the child may learn this reaction to disaster. Today it is fashionable to blame television for blunting the emotional reaction of children. But to what degree are we as injurious while at play? To what extent do we, by trying to depress the noise level of child play or by failing to show feeling during play, contribute to the decline of emotional expression? At least there is emotion on television; I am less certain it can be seen in parent-child dyadic play.

Acceptance of Imagination

Preschoolers show a willingness to acknowledge without discount the fantasy experience of others. This acceptance of imagination is demonstrated by allowing its products to influence the play situation.

It is one thing to lack the power to pretend and quite another to be unaccepting of that power in someone else. When five-year-old Greg wanted to drive his toy truck to Africa to join a safari, his grownup play partner did not react with enthusiasm. Instead she dismissed the venture by reminding Greg that Africa is across the ocean and trucks cannot travel by water. A similar discount of imagination is likely to occur when children voice relationships between toys that adults do not recognize. Steven did not feel that his account of what was happening had to be plausible. However, his explanation that a man in a crash between two toy trucks was not hurt because he wore a brick coat was immediately dismissed by the parent who wanted to use the occasion to urge the value of safety belts.

The parent preference for realism and an unwillingness to accept divergent thinking combine in Maria's record. Her mother felt compelled to remove the policeman from a group of cowboys because "He doesn't fit." Young Maria perceived the matter differently and so kept the officer in the group on the premise that since the fort was already surrounded, the cowboys would be unwise to exclude a possible ally just because he wore blue. I wonder if we unwittingly teach children prejudice in the name of classification. Grownups often ask preschoolers to decide: "Which one doesn't belong in the group?" Usually the choice is among objects, animals and persons. The unintended lesson is that the different should be isolated because they do not belong. If integration is an American goal, the "unlikes" will have to go together. Maybe we can start by teaching recognition of differences without insisting that the different be excluded.

The greater readiness of children than adults to accept imagination attributes to a basic difference in cognitive style. Preschoolers prefer to become aware of their world through intuition, an inventive orientation which consistently emphasizes the possibilities of an idea or situation Most grownups prefer to perceive by sensation, the tendency to experience things only as they are without recourse to imagination. For them, the world of actuality is considered a sufficient source of experience without seeking impressions from the realm of what is unseen. In consequence, most adults are less inclined than children to question and to wonder about the inherent mysteries of situations. The difference between preferring intuition or sensation as the dominant mode of perception is more than a matter of academic interest. Studies of highly creative adults at the University of California Institute for Personality Assessment yield estimates that 75 percent of all men in the general population might classify as sensation types with a focus on what is immediate and with attention devoted to life's givens; 90 percent of the creative grownups assessed by IPAR classify as preferred intuitives (child-like), not bound to the present but oriented to what may be rather than what is (MacKinnon, 1965).

How do children who begin life with the same preference for intuition as creative adults gradually relinquish it in favor of an orientation which depreciates imagination? The assumption that decline in creativity is genetic or a function of age has been dismissed by cross-cultural research. While Anglo-American cultures show a drop in creativity beginning at about age nine, this is not the case in cultures like those of Western Samoa and India. It appears that parents and teachers have an important influence in determining the continuity of creative development. In this connection, Torrance's (1965) concern about the preservation of the creativity among children led him to examine the "ideal pupil" concept as perceived by approximately 1000 teachers representing several countries. Each of the teachers from Germany, India, Greece, the Philippines, and the United States were presented a list of 62 student characteristics all of which were included because of their previous reliability in discriminating persons of high and low creative ability. The educators were obliged to indicate the characteristics describing the kind of person they wished to see their students become. Conversely, the characteristics they felt ought to be discouraged were to be indicated. All five cultures seem to have values which undermine the growth of creative process. For the United States sample and more specifically in the realm of "accepting imagination," it was learned that, as a group, our teachers believe the following characteristics should be discouraged: (1) being intuitive; (2) being a good guesser; (3) regressing occasionally; (4) being a visionary; and (5) always asking questions.

Acceptance of Spontaneity

Preschoolers are willing to tolerate disorder in the process of inter-action. The greater acceptance for spontaneity than for turn-taking is shown by the routine sanction of interruptive speech.

Most of us, at some time, have been counseled against interrupting a speaker. The stated reason is that courtesy requires peers to take turns so everyone has the respect of being heard. For conversations between preschoolers and adults, the rules are even more restrictive. In this type family dyad, age is commonly believed to bestow a privilege of dominance. There are many homes in which guests can expect to find normally exuberant children comparatively silent during their visit. Such children are less often described as controlled than as well-behaved—meaning the young do not question an imposed imbalance of speech. I am unsure as to how old some children must be before they are accepted as persons in their own home, that is, someone whose feelings and speech can be expressed at any time without permission.

Certainly we can take pride in the fact that fewer parents than ever before believe "children should be seen and not heard." Then too, fewer boys and girls are told, "Don't speak unless you are spoken to." Still there are a great number of youngsters who hear "Be polite and wait for your turn to talk." That admonitions like these may be an inadequate guide to maturity is shown by the behavior of most elderly people who, like preschoolers, can carry on a conversation speaking and listening at the same time. Next time you encounter an old couple, notice their unashamed manner of mutually talking to you at the same time they elaborate or disagree with each other. It would seem that those of us between early childhood and old age are the least able to demonstrate this ability. A poor response is to make our disability an obligation for everyone. Rather, if we cannot listen and speak concurrently, let's learn from the children and elderly who can.

Among themselves, preschoolers are unbound by an established order or procession for speakers. When deference occurs at all, it is to those who exhibit a readiness to say something. This basic difference between the rules of child conversation and the rules of adult conversation tends to disturb parents when they begin play. Whereas children find it acceptable for players to talk at once, most beginning adult players can accept only one voice at a time. For grownups, the custom of turn-taking is sacrosanct. Unlike children who interrupt a companion without reluctance, many parents and teachers politely wait for a turn supposing that, out of courtesy, their child partner will eventually allow them an entry. Our observations reveal that open moments seldom happen, leaving some grownups to conclude either that their prospect is hopeless or that their child partner needs instruction in etiquette, a lesson in how to behave. In my judgment, the adult preference for ordered speech stems from a competitive training in which conversations are seen as debates; a verbal exchange is expected to produce a winner and loser. Unless spontaneity is accepted in play, the possibilities are lost for both parties. The spontaneous nature of play makes the ordering of its expression an impossibility. Therefore, we must decide what kind of speech we want to encourage—the predictable or the spontaneous. Many early childhood programs produce predictable speech; too few programs aim for spontaneous speech.

Allowance for Reflection

Preschoolers feel that their questions deserve serious consideration. As a result, they are willing to refrain from anticipating the speech of others. They also refrain from restating questions which are not quickly answered in favor of allowing the time needed for reflection.

Some parents complain about the noise a child makes during play. When the same child is reflective, we feel uncomfortable about his lack of noise. For those of us who undervalue deliberation, its silent process in others is assessed as a sign of their misunderstanding. Men and women of this impression often amend questions or resort to cueing. However well intended, attempts to press a partner for premature answers disrespects his pace of decision making or what is called cognitive tempo. The term "cognitive tempo" refers to the speed at which an individual typically processes information, reaches judgment, and solves problems. Whereas reflective cognitive tempo serves as an antecedent to analytically-oriented thinking, persons of an impulsive tempo make more errors in inductive reasoning because they do not pause to evaluate the quality of their inferences. Although two individuals of different tempos may have the same intelligence, they do well at different types of intellectual tasks. The trait of cognitive tempo seems to become stable at about age four and appears related to early mother-child patterns of interaction. Hock (1967) conducted a tempo study of inner city children using Kagan's Matching Familiar Figures Test. The greater maternal reliance on a restricted code rather than an elaborated code of communication was revealed by the high proportion of low income children who classified as impulsive types.

Perhaps the differential is best illustrated by contrasting how children of different tempos respond to different types of television programs. Wright (1973) examined the content and audience of Sesame Street and Mister Rogers' Neighborhood. These two programs were chosen as extremes because Sesame Street is fast moving, sharp and brisk. It is geared for the low income, urban child and incorporates much street knowledge. Mister Rogers is softer, more benign, slower paced, and cross-references most of the content. The following measurements were taken of both programs under lab conditions. Segments of programs lasted 70 seconds on Sesame Street and 140 seconds on Mister Rogers' Neighborhood; six special effects occurred per 30 minutes on Sesame Street—two per 30 minutes on Mister Rogers. On Sesame Street there were 18 dialogue shifts per minute compared to two per minute in Mister Rogers. Cartoons were involved in 39 percent of Sesame Street shows and one percent of Mister Rogers. The depth development of characters on Sesame Street was assessed as "shallow," and Mister Rogers as "deep." Wright's results suggest that since impulsive (fast and inaccurate) children tire faster of some stimuli, perhaps they should be taught the same concept by different approaches such as those offered by the format of Sesame Street. On the other hand, Mister Rogers may be better for reflective (slow and accurate) children who can be taught by using highly familiar situations, people, and places over and over again to teach different concepts. In my estimate, play should be considered among the most promising means for improving the reflective potential of impulsive children (cf. Egeland, 1974).

Sharing of Dominance

Preschoolers usually satisfy their need for interpersonal power by a division of dominance. The process of sharing control during play takes the form of constructive conflict in which assertion and compromise serve as the prominent responses.

Peer play is usually conflict play with participants sharing dominance. By contrast, parent-child play seldom includes the conflict dimension. Since they are unable to conduct conflict, some parents attempt to pacify their child by docile behavior. However well intended, this strategy of total concession avoids the interaction the child needs and prefers. In such cases the child typically may even demand active participation from the parent to the result that the parent becomes upset and feels the need to discipline the youngster. The opposite and less frequent parent tack is to attempt complete control of the play from the

outset by excluding spontaneity. In this instance, the child may ultimately become disconcerted with the attempt at parental dominance and
discontinue in favor of solitary play.

We should realize that the child's need for power and conse-
quent assertion of self has a place in parent-child play. Unless we define
play as an escape from the real world, it is appropriate to view conflict as
an essential part of the play process. Many adults can play with children
for only a short period because they can't stand being dominated for a
long time. The same reason describes why some children cannot tolerate
certain school classes. The child who is continually dominated, no matter how kindly, will cease in some measure to grow because his power
needs remain unexpressed and unsatisfied. Identity requires self-
assertion—yet when children assert themselves with playmates, the
usual result sequence is adult intervention, reprimand, and guilt. By
contrast, when preschoolers play with parents, they do not feel guilty
about assertion. Instead, the typical consequence of child assertion during parent-child play is parent concession. When we ask four-year-olds
whom they prefer to play with—playmates or parents—almost always
they choose parents and give as their reason, "Then I can be the boss."
The power possibility also seems to explain why preschoolers prefer to
play alone with the parent rather than to include a sibling. Older siblings
are less able to accept the dominance of younger brothers and sisters
because they have a more narrow scope of power than their parents. In
other words, the fact that preschoolers prefer a less competent partner
like a parent to a more competent player like a peer or sibling suggests
that the child desire for play with parents is partly to redress their imbalance of interpersonal power.

In a culture of increasing leisure, diversity, and crowding,
more of us will need to learn how to conduct constructive conflict. At the
moment our societal responses to conflict tend to be self-disabling. One
has only to look at the size of domestic court dockets or the incidence of
litigation between neighbors to confirm that withdrawal is the dominant
reaction to disagreement. For many other people, conflict is generally accompanied by guilt and the need to conceal disputes from children,
peers, or parents.

The most unfortunate result of these common reactions is that
they effectively prevent us from growing up and from developing
respect for others. One criterion for a mature relationship is that the
other party be seen and regarded as a separate person whose perceptions
and judgments may vary from our own. Given this condition, we can
ask, "Is it reasonable to educate for divergent thinking and then lament
divergent expression?" If there cannot be a worthwhile relationship
where one party is always subordinate, should we sponsor guilt as the

price for self assertion? Can we advocate the development of alternative lifestyles and yet concurrently insist that we will only live near people whose choices and background resemble our own?

To enable children to develop in a conflict culture, it would seem wise to legitimize self assertion at an early age. Because the need for power and the development of conscience occur simultaneously, the preschooler is susceptible to frequent self-recrimination if adults discourage him from becoming a separate person. To avoid the destructive emotion of guilt, some children elect to drastically reduce their level of aggression. The tragedy here is that there can be no freedom of lifestyle choice if aggression is eliminated, since aggression is necessary to some degree to favor or oppose anything. Because children who lack a sense of power can find security only via dependence, gaining power is important to their growth and independence. Certainly the sense of potency is only one aspect of maturity but if it is to grow, the small beginnings need to be accepted.

It has been said that power corrupts. However, we can as easily demonstrate that power humanizes if its use and responsibility are learned at an early age. Even small children should have some power in order that its larger attainment will not assume a coercive form. Perhaps too few adults realize that it takes most of us as long to learn the wise use of power as it does to obtain power. Moreover, if we do not educate children for power, we invite them to a life of impotence. Learning to sense power and to share dominance are important ingredients for mental health and can best begin with parent-child play for there the conditions allow a wide range of possible conflicts, consequences that are non-punitive, and a better-than-random positive model.

All of the categories described thus far represent strengths which are more readily observed in the play behavior of preschoolers than of their parents. Before considering several less desirable behaviors which appear prominent among beginning adult players, it is appropriate to comment on the availability of free lessons. I have found that parent-child play and peer play are most alike in homes where parents have recognized the wisdom of reciprocal modeling. To recover the creative skills required for optimal intra-family play, parents must perceive children as teachers and themselves as learners (Strom, 1974a,b).

Speech Imitation

An imitator repeats the speech of a partner verbatim or in paraphrase. The greater preference for reiteration than for reaction avoids the play process and supposes the partner to need correction or reinforcement.

Whenever we do not know what to say or lack the skills to act, it is helpful to watch and behave like others of greater experience. Unfamiliar situations often require that we imitate in order to quickly adapt, to remain inconspicuous, or to physically survive. Granting the adaptive merit of imitation, it is wise to also recognize that sustained imitation can prove maladaptive. Unless one moves from just copying the behavior of others to incorporating the process which generates the copied behavior, an incomplete adaptation remains fixed. If in learning from a preschooler, the parent limits her speech to imitative reiteration, she unwittingly avoids interaction and hence entry to the arena of play.

Some parents rationalize their imitative speech by suggesting that it provides immediate corrective feedback of a child's expression. This greater preference for correction than interaction is defensive. Apart from the obvious problem that a child at play is less interested in an echo than a partner, the possibilities for speech development actually decline. Children improve language more by interacting with persons of greater verbal ability than they do by listening to an adult replay of themselves. Indeed by subconsciously imitating adult speech, children recognize our greater verbal ability. It is doubly unfortunate to refuse a child's strength and simultaneously ignore the possibilities of our own. Yet this is what happens when we imitate a child's less mature speech and consequently refuse a reaction to his imagination. The differing strengths of parent and child warrant a mutual response in order that each party can share the role of teacher and learner.

Use of Praise

The partner who relies on verbal reward does not view play as a process offering intrinsic satisfaction. The motive of assigning greater priority for praise than for acceptance is to control rather than reinforce creative behavior.

Children seek recognition, but I believe it is less the recognition of praise than the recognition of acceptance. Because the person who is accepted can remain who he is without risking a loss of affection, he does not have to change to continue being valued. In this sense, acceptance is the greatest reward we can offer children for they can then retain their imagination into adult life. Although praise is generally well intended, it is often used to shape behavior in ways that deflect a child from normal development. Normal development would be the continuation rather than the decline of creative behavior. If praise sustains creative behavior, schools would not influence its decline because most teachers spend a great deal of the time praising the children. Farson

(1971) has suggested that, "It is when we want to develop initiative, creativity, and problem solving that praise fails us most. To liberate these qualities in people, we need to rely on internal motivation—we need to make people feel they are free of our control" (cf. Torrance, 1973; Wallach and Kogan, 1971).

An observer of play among children will note that children experience the intrinsic satisfaction of play and so seldom praise one another. Boys and girls attempt the control of playmates and playthings, but praise is not their tool nor does the scope of power include the partner's way of thinking. However, by contrast, the praising adult seems oblivious to the intrinsic satisfaction of play and insists on being a judge (not a perceiver) whose function is to verbally reinforce selected behaviors. If parents found pleasure in play, they would not have difficulty sustaining attention. The law of effect states, "Behavior which is satisfying tends to be repeated." If one finds play dissatisfying, it will usually show up in terms of a short attention span and the use of praise, an extraneous reward system.

Because the praising adult is easily distracted from play, he frequently lapses into a pattern of near constant praise. Four-year-old Harvey was playing a submarine plot with Jill, the grownup partner. When Harvey announced they were getting close to an island of monsters, Jill replied, "O.K., you keep watching the controls." Almost immediately Harvey exclaimed, "Oh, oh, we're out of gas." Without delay Jill said, "Good, keep going." Harvey, who was the only person involved in this play theme, then declared, "Good, what do you mean good?" Many children at play could ask Harvey's question of their distracted parent partners who substitute praise for involvement, who use praise as an excuse for not investing attention or time.

Embarrassment

The player who senses embarrassment feels self conscious, silly, uneasy, awkward or out of place. Although the player himself is the best judge of whether these obstacles are experienced, there are overt indicators like facial blush, a reliance on joking and overdependence on the partner.

Unlike preschoolers, many parents are embarrassed to engage in fantasy play. Probably this is because most of us were taught to conceal weakness, to avoid situations in which we lack competence. Often the result has been to postpone play with children until their interest includes the nonfiction games which require our skills. Naturally this background makes us uneasy when educators urge that we engage children in fantasy play. Perhaps the decision rests on how we choose to view the strength of our children. We tend to feel self-conscious about the greater strength of someone when we regard our interaction with them as competitive. Our studies show that it is better to view the parent-child dyad as a non-competitive union, a partnership in which the strength of each member is to the advantage of both members, an arrangement in which no one loses because success is mutual (cf. Torrance, 1971).

Unless parents feel comfortable about the greater play competence of their children, they may severely judge themselves and withdraw. This tendency to unfavorably evaluate oneself as a play teacher occurs even among middle-grade children. Our studies with fourth graders who were trained to toy teach kindergarteners have shown the necessity to enlarge the usual teacher criteria for self-judgment (Strom and Engelbrecht, 1974b). Teacher uncertainty can best be overcome by providing feedback about changes in student self-concept. When play teachers of any age recognize that their tolerance for creativity and their willingness to reduce control are the attitudes that result in student gains, then teacher self-evaluation is more satisfactory. For example, the priority put on their imagination and play increased the enthusiasm and eagerness of kindergarteners who participated in our cross age teaching program. Over an eight-week period their percentage of undesirable perceptions about the teaching-learning process dropped from 46.9 to 3.1. This desirable transition suggests that the fourth grade child teachers achieved a most important lesson—namely, as play teachers they believed in creativity and helped kindergarten students gain confidence in their recourse to imagination.

The conclusion for parents might be stated as an admonition: don't be embarrassed about your inability as a player. Be embarrassed about your reluctance to learn. Better yet, get down on your knees—and play.

References

Egeland, Byron. "Training Impulsive Children in the Use of More Efficient Scanning Techniques." *Child Development* (45) 1974, 165–171.

Farson, Richard. "Praise Reappraised," in *Teachers and The Learning Process,* edited by Robert Strom. Englewood Cliffs: Prentice-Hall, Inc., 1971. pp. 25–32.

Hock, Ellen. "The Relation of Culture to the Reflection-Impulsivity Dimension." Unpublished M.A. thesis. Columbus: The Ohio State University, 1967. 54pp.

Hoffman, Earl. "Prekindergarten Experiences and Their Relationships to Reading Achievement." *Illinois School Research,* Fall 1971, pp. 6–12.

Kagan, Jerome. "Reflection-Impulsivity and Reading Ability in Primary Grade Children." *Child Development,* 1965 (36) 609–628.

MacKinnon, Donald. "Testing to Identify Creative People." Speech delivered at The Ohio State University, Columbus, Ohio, February 19, 1965.

Simon, Anita, and E. G. Boyer. *Mirrors For Behavior.* Philadelphia: Research for Better Schools, Inc., 1967. pp. 1–24.

Strom, Robert D. *Psychology For The Classroom.* Englewood Cliffs: Prentice-Hall, Inc., 1969. pp. 109–116, 204–270.

Strom, Robert D. "Play and Family Development." *The Elementary School Journal,* March 1974a (74)(6), 359–368.

Strom, Robert D., and Guillermina Engelbrecht. "Creative Peer Teaching." *Journal of Creative Behavior,* Vol. 8, No. 2, 1974b.

Torrance, E. Paul. *Rewarding Creative Behavior.* Englewood Cliffs: Prentice-Hall, Inc., 1965. pp. 221-234.

Torrance, E. Paul. "Stimulation, Enjoyment and Originality in Dyadic Creativity." *Journal of Educational Psychology,* 1971, (62)(1), 45-48.

Torrance, E. Paul. "Does Evaluative Feedback Facilitate Creative Thinking?" Unpublished paper prepared for educational psychology students at the University of Georgia, 1973. 4pp.

Wallach, Michael, and Nathan Kogan. "Creativity and Intelligence in Children's Thinking." *Teachers and the Learning Process,* edited by Robert Strom. Englewood Cliffs: Prentice-Hall, Inc., 1971. pp. 350-360.

Wright, John. "Cognitive Tempo: Matching the Pace of Communication to that of the Child." NEA: Elementary-Kindergarten-Nursery Educators New Notes, April, 1973, (3)(1), p. 4.

Sharing Your Impressions

1. Identify the most frequent problems you have when playing with young children.
2. What do you remember about your parents playing with you during childhood?
3. Speculate about the benefits of parent-child play.
4. How do you react when children at play destroy something they've made?
5. How do you think being a play partner at home differs from using play as a teacher at school?
6. What strengths do preschoolers show during play?
7. Suggest some ways for parents to become better play partners.

Chapter 5

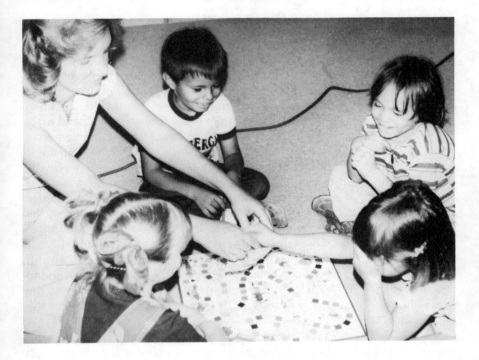

Teaching through Play

13

What Happens When a Child Plays?

Bruno Bettelheim

"How is play important for a child?" asked a woman in a recent mothers' discussion group. She knew that play means as much to children as significant adult activities do to her, but she wasn't sure how or why. She also wondered whether television deprives children of play experience. This mother could remember how, as a child, she had delighted in taking care of her dolls. But her children seem to spend most of their time watching TV. She wondered whether watching someone else's stories is the same as making up your own stories with your toys.

Play, said Freud, is the language of the child. Through play he makes his first cultural and psychological achievements. Most parents are convinced that play is important for their child and they encourage him in it. But how many parents know the grammar and syntax of the language of play? How many can speak it freely with their children? Many a mother remembers the elaborate fantasies she acted out with her dolls. So she buys her daughter a doll, and perhaps even sews beautiful doll clothes. But if she is a typical modern mother, she does not spend much time playing dolls with her daughter. And she isn't aware of the stories her child invents about her dolls, or the kinds of experiences the child makes them undergo.

One important, often overlooked aspect of all play is the companions involved. It is one thing for a child to play with an adult. It is quite another to play with other children as directed by adults—as in a nursery school setting. And different from both these experiences are playing with other children with no adult companion, and playing alone. Most children get lots of play experience with other children, but very little experience of playing with an adult who remembers his own childhood play experiences.

The more people involved in play, the more structured it tends to become. Group activity is more frequently game than play. There are some important distinctions between the two: In play, as in fantasy, everything is possible—reality can be and frequently is entirely

From *Ladies' Home Journal*, November 1971, *88*(11), pp. 34–35. © 1971 LHJ Publishing, Inc. Reprinted with permission of *Ladies' Home Journal*.

disregarded. Games, on the other hand, require playing according to rules.

It is normal for the growing child to move back and forth from the freedom of unstructured play to the more rigid demands that games impose. When all is going well he can do justice to a game, but he reverts to play when things become too difficult. A child may be able to play checkers pretty well, for example, until he suddenly realizes that he is losing. Then the checker, which he previously accepted as a marker within the prearranged rules of the game, suddenly becomes a very personal missile to be hurled off the board—or even at the winning opponent. The opponent may recognize what is going on and say, "Don't be such a baby!" Other children intuitively realize that under great stress their companions can revert from game to play. Unfortunately, some parents have a hard time understanding these normal relapses. They are too anxious to have their child act mature before he is ready.

When the child throws the checker away and disrupts the game, he is preventing defeat at a time when defeat would overwhelm his self-esteem. By reverting to play for a time, he becomes the powerful king who can jump all opponents. As that restores his confidence, he will again try to play the game according to its rules. But if he is prevented from reverting from game to play, he may lose all interest in games, because of the pressure they put on him.

Both play and game serve important but different needs for a child. Each belongs to a different developmental stage, and experience with both is necessary for growing up well. Play must come first, however. The more a child has a chance to enjoy fully all the richness and free-floating fantasy of play, the more he will later be able to gain through the experiences games offer. Children lose out on a great deal if watching TV, or even studying, prevents them from having wide experience with both play and games.

For example, the game, "Go to the Head of the Class" reinforces the school experience. But it does not help the child to master that experience. On the other hand, the child who plays "school" imaginatively is trying to repeat in play, and thus to assimilate more fully, what has happened to him in class. He might play at being teacher to his stuffed animals all arranged in a row, or to his preschool siblings. In doing so he now actively masters what he has been passively subjected to during the school day. Acting out the teacher's role makes her more understandable and acceptable as a person, and as an imposer of discipline.

Thus play makes it easier for the child to accept being taught in class and to use all his school experiences positively. And here the parent, playing his child's eager pupil, can be a great boon. As is well known, one learns something most easily by teaching it to someone else—preferably someone who seems to learn it.

Through play, more than anything else, the child achieves mastery of the external world. He learns how to manipulate its objects as he builds with blocks, makes sand castles, etc. He masters body control as he skips and jumps and runs. He learns to deal with his psychological problems as he reenacts in play the difficulties he has encountered in reality. He also begins to master social relations as he learns that he must adjust himself to others if group play is to continue.

Many of life's experiences, even those that seem commonplace to the adult or the older child, are overwhelming to the young child because they are entirely new and unexpected. This is why a child repeats again and again in his play any event that has made a great impression on him in reality. Through repetition he tries to become familiar with it. Also through play, which does not have to conform to reality in all details, a complicated real experience can be broken into manageable segments. Each segment can then be relived—and thus understood and mastered—without undue anxiety.

It is quite important to the child to be able to change an experience in which he was the passive subject into one in which he is in charge of what goes on, such as when he plays school. For our well-being, all of us need the conviction that we are to some degree masters of our fate. The child is no exception to this; he, too, needs that conviction in order to feel that he has an important stake in the world and that he can shape his own life in it to some degree. This the young child can hardly do in reality, but in play he can. Since the line between reality and fantasy has not yet been clearly and definitely drawn, the process works for him. Therefore he can master in fantasy even those events that have clearly been inflicted on him.

Purpose of Play

Until fairly recently, parents played with their children the same way their parents had played with them, and there was an almost automatic, nearly unconscious understanding between adult and child as to the purpose of the play and why it was both meaningful and enjoyable. Fortunately, this is still true for the earliest, most primitive and most important play activities of the infant. When the baby tosses his rattle out of the crib and mother hands it back to him, she need not realize the psychological dimensions of this new achievement in order for both of them to enjoy it. But in fact her infant is unconsciously exploring several all-important questions: Can I exercise influence over my objective environment without dire personal consequences? Can I safely manipulate objects without having to suffer because of my effort to assert my will? Can I let go of a thing for a while and get it back?

The mother's response answers these questions. A positive response applauds the action and guarantees its repetition by returning the object to the crib. But a negative answer makes him feel that such active dealing with objects is naughty. Consistently not returning the object teaches him that to manipulate the world leads to permanent loss—an objective loss because his rattle is not returned and a subjective loss because his activity brings about interpersonal frustration. The questions the infant asks about the world through his play are so crucial that he has to put the same query innumerable times to feel sure of the answer. Hence the persistent, repetitious nature of his play.

In his own way, the child deals with the deepest questions of individual philosophy: Is there such a thing as a Me? How can I feel sure about my existence? What is the intention of the world toward me? The child investigates and partially answers such issues through play.

A game such as peek-a-boo shows the child that even if he is temporarily out of sight, his mother—and other persons—will not forget him but will look for him and find him. On the strength of this knowledge, the child learns that he need not cling to his mother at all times but can afford occasionally to lose her from his sight. Other play gives the child a sense of the safety of all parts of his body and their importance to his parents. Within this category falls play involving touching and naming parts of the body, such as "This little piggie went to market. . . ." Such play conveys to the child that his body is in good shape, that nothing in it is missing or overlooked.

Hide-and-seek, like peek-a-boo, assures the child that even though he is not visible, he is not forgotten. Indeed the game—and in the transferred sense, life—cannot go on without him. This is the reassurance such games can confer.

Today adults and children rarely play together with equal enjoyment. It still happens in sports such as baseball, or when father and son are both avid fishermen. But these are activities of later childhood, when play is no longer so crucial. For an adult to engage in play chiefly because it is important to the child is not the same as playing together, and the youngster can discern this. The adult wishes to understand, guide, educate; he does not really wish to play.

Take Play Seriously

Our current need, then, to understand children's play, and to organize play and nursery schools, stems from the fact that our adult world has become too separated from the child's world. For the same reason it is difficult for us to take children's play seriously, despite our best intellectual efforts at recognizing its importance.

The modern parent must learn to take her child's play as seriously as her child does. If the parent can do that, her own life will be enriched with respect to exactly that which is so often missing from the world of adults: the enjoyment of free-floating fantasy. This enjoyment and appreciation can only be gained by having direct empathy with your child's play, by making up his bedtime story as you go along, instead of reading it from a book. Then you will begin to grasp the seriousness of "child's play."

Sharing Your Impressions

1. What are your reasons for playing with young children?
2. What function do you think repetition serves in children's play?
3. Recall a time when you or another person demonstrated social immaturity in not complying with the rules of a game.
4. What happens to play as more people become involved?
5. Compare your method of coping with losing a game with that of a child who loses.
6. Why do you think hide-and-seek and peek-a-boo remain ever-popular games?
7. Why do you suppose children and adults rarely play together with equal enjoyment?

14

Teaching Children as They Play

Dorothy Anker, Jackie Foster, Joan McLane, Joyce Sobel, and Bernice Weissbourd

Play as an avenue for social, emotional, and intellectual development has been recognized by educational philosophers for well over 100 years. More recently, Isaacs, Almy, Biber, and Peller—all experts in the field of early childhood education—have delineated the many benefits, and most especially the intellectual benefits, inherent in spontaneous play. While some have added the concept of an "enriched" or "planned" environment, many educators remain committed to the

Reprinted by permission from *Young Children*, Vol 29, No. 4 (May 1974), pp. 203–213. Copyright © 1974, National Association for the Education of Young Children, 1834 Connecticut Avenue, N.W., Washington, D.C. 20009.

concept that children should engage in activities of their own choice, and that children learn through meaningful interaction with their environment.

Other educators, however, attracted by America's desperate call for instant education, have developed a vast array of recipes guaranteed to provide immediate results in reading and arithmetic. Many teachers are drawn to "cookbook" education for a variety of obvious reasons. Other teachers understand and appreciate the potentialities of spontaneous play, but are not certain what children learn through play and how teachers teach through spontaneous interactions. They are concerned that the children will not be able to survive the "testing threat" unless subjected to constant drill of subject matter assumed to be essential for later school achievement.

Those who are committed to a model which values learning through spontaneous play feel that children use play to work through their internal and interpersonal conflicts. In the process, they become freed to attend to intellectual and cognitive tasks. They become more able to pursue the skills necessary for later learning. Children who are permitted to engage in activities of their own choice gain a sense of autonomy and effectiveness; become motivated to mastery; develop such attributes as self-direction, trust in themselves, self assurance, and a feeling of self-worth. When a child sets himself a task it is, by and large, developmentally appropriate. As opposed to this, programmed curriculum superimposes a learning event without regard for the great variation in individual interest or readiness.

If we are concerned with intrinsic motivation, then we must be equally cognizant of the type of reinforcement we provide—is it that which arises from within the child and leads to a sense of personal accomplishment, or is it that which results from a teacher's praise and leads to a reliance on recognition by authority figures? As teachers, we face broader issues regarding the role of educators. Are we interested in enabling children to develop self-reliance, initiative, creative thought, and self-esteem, or do we see ourselves as perpetuators of a system which values submission, conformity, and dependency?

And so, a group of teachers, in an effort to reinforce the child development approach and counteract the pressures for early rote learning, describe some specific cognitive learning events which are embedded in the spontaneous play of young children.

The design to be described is not intended as a total curriculum plan. We recognize that a single narrow methodology is not appropriate for all children; that some children are unable, for a variety of reasons, to engage spontaneously in play; that some children need an environment containing the least possible amount of stimulation.

Most children, however, will readily respond and integrate

new material which is directly related to their momentary concern or interest, and the teacher can "intrude" with an appropriate casual, but thoughtful, word, thought, or question which would expand the child's learning opportunities. The learning would occur in relation to the activity in which the child is already engaged—in his "life space"[1]—and the participatory intrusion would take a variety of forms, involve any range of time (depending on the interest stimulated in the child), and include the development of numerous cognitive and mental abilities.

For example, if we agree, as current research indicates, that most children have a strong need to investigate their environment, perhaps we can be somewhat more trusting of children's desire to make sense out of their world. Given only a mud puddle, children will seek it out, poke sticks into it, swirl, pat, plop, mash, and mess with it. On their own, children will discover that mud drips through fingers, sticks to hands, can be thickened (and thereby given shape), or thinned (and made more runny). They discover the "feel" of mud and its qualities. They experience the release of certain emotions and the joys of "messing." Words and explanations can be offered (language development), questions can be raised (problem solving), creative thought can be encouraged. Add any five articles, and teacher and children can begin to consider such concepts as size, shape, color, mass, volume, numbers, similarities, prepositions, etc., within the framework of "playing in a mud puddle." They can engage in higher levels of thought involving the nature of change, discrimination, problem solving, hypothesizing, memory, etc. The point is that an enormous range of learning experiences can be accomplished by means of a mud puddle. Concepts and thought processes can be integrated into what might be called a self-selected activity.

Luckily for some teachers, mud is not the consuming interest of all children, nor is it the medium through which all learn best. Given a choice of activities, children will gravitate to those areas which, for unknown reasons, trigger their particular interests or needs. The problem of motivation and investment (for most children) evaporates. The teacher's energy, formerly devoted to seducing children to be interested in her program, is now freed to engage in different—though perhaps more difficult—pursuits.

The Teacher's Role

Providing for the growth of each individual within a spontaneous play model can be difficult and time consuming. Inherent in this approach is the need for staff members to function spontaneously and

---

[1]Life space refers to the child's social, emotional, and intellectual experience at a given moment in a particular place. It is the child's present activity.

creatively in relation to the ever changing play engaged in by children. At the same time, the teacher needs to be aware of individual learning patterns, plus each child's ability to function on various levels of conceptual thought. She is constantly called upon to respond to a number of variables and must focus not on teaching *per se*, but on the process of learning which belongs to the child.

It is absolutely necessary for the adults in the classroom to work together as a team, sharing observations, ideas, and evaluations so as to keep the total child clearly in view. This team must be able to work together with creativity, knowledge, and sensitivity in order to set priorities and plan carefully. They must be able to accept a momentary lack of response or interest and find other appropriate ways of involving children. The teachers must let the children know which behaviors are acceptable (investment in learning, constructive use of equipment, respect for other children, etc.) and clearly define the routines of the classroom.

The Program

In planning the program, the teachers develop curriculum ideas, sequence concepts and activities, and purposefully structure the environment in a number of interest areas of a typical preschool setting—for large blocks, unit blocks, doll corner, and art activities. It soon becomes apparent that the same content or cognitive learning tasks arise in all areas. As the teachers become more skillful in their ability to interact with the on-going play of the children, they become able to evolve similar learning experiences in each of the above mentioned areas, though the activities are vastly different. For example, categorizing, sorting, and number concepts can be taught equally effectively in the housekeeping corner (around foods, dishes, doll clothes, etc.) or in the art section (around collage materials, crayons, pictures, etc.) or in the block area.

For purposes of this paper, we will focus on play in the block area while reminding the reader that many of the same responses can occur in other areas of the classroom. Observation of children's block play leads one to assume that children, on their own, learn something about size, shape, sorting, balance, and spatial relationships. Unit blocks are designed with inherent mathematical qualities, lend themselves to varied uses, and children naturally involve themselves frequently in block play. If we think of a small group of children building with blocks, we are aware that they have made some tall structures and what appear to be streets or roads. They have included some toys which are near the block area—toy people, animals, small and large trucks, etc. How can the teacher intervene to make specific information available to the child, and how can she expand the learning possibilities inherent in the situation? What concepts can be learned? What manipulations, what language, what focus should be introduced to provoke learning?

Simple Encounters and Learning

The following are merely a few examples of the infinite variety of possible encounters (This description of learning is somewhat arbitrary and should be viewed as a way of looking at the cognitive experience involved.):

"This block is square." (labeling, mathematical concept)

"You've used all rectangles in your building." (classifying by shape, labeling)

"Can you find another block just like this one?" (matching, classifying according to size and shape)

"Let's see how many round blocks we can find." (labeling, number concepts, classifying by shape)

"How can you make this road as long as that one?" *"How can you make this side as high as that one?"* (language development, measurement, defining spatial relationships, problem solving)

"Here, this truck will fit through your garage door." (language development, measurement, size discrimination, spatial relationships)

"I wonder what would happen if we put this block here." (experimentation, testing)

"How can we connect these two blocks?" (problem solving, language development)

"Look, two square blocks are as long as, or equal to, one rectangle." *"This rectangle is half as long as this rectangle."* (fractions, measurement, spatial relationships, language development, labeling)

"When you put these two triangles together, they make the same shape as the square." (mathematical concepts, language development, experimenting)

"Which block feels heavier?" *"Do these blocks weigh the same?"* (weight concepts, language development)

"Let's put the big blocks on this shelf." (classifying by size and shape during clean-up)

"This is not a big block." *"This is not a square block."* (the concept of "not" in classifying)

"Could we build a house with round blocks?" (hypothesizing, problem solving, classifying by shape)

Often children build enclosures with no doors or windows: *"How will the people get into your house?"* (language development, problem solving)

"Does your road have a curve or is it straight?" (language development, shape distinction, spatial relationships)

"Which is the shortest way from the house to the store?" (measurement, spatial relationships)

"Let's make a bridge over the road." (expanding possibilities, new ideas, developing abstract concepts)

"Will the car go under the bridge or over the bridge?" (language development, prepositions)

"You used a lot of blocks." "He has only a few blocks." "He needs five more blocks." (number concepts, language development, comparison of quantity)

"What would you do if he closed the road?" (problem solving, verbalizing alternatives, experimenting with ideas)

"You made it balance." "Let's balance this block with another one on this side." (language development, structural relationships)

"Will it fall down if we put this large block on top?" (concepts of balance, gravity, relationship of base to height)

"My foot is five blocks long. How many blocks long is your foot?" (concepts of size, numbers, measurement)

"Let's see if this tower is as tall as you are." (height size comparison)

"Is there room enough for that big truck in your garage?" (spatial relationships, language development)

"John's road has a pattern. Let's make his road longer using the same pattern." (discrimination, sequencing, imitation)

"How does it feel when you walk down the inclined plane? When you walk up?" (language development, gravity, force)

"How will the car (the rubber animal, the handkerchief, the crayon) go down (or up) the ramp?" (language development, concepts of force, gravity, motion)

Thus, a statement or question introduced by the teacher as the children are engaged in block play can lead to expansion of such concepts as size, shape, sets, measurement, weight, patterns, categorization, classification, spatial relationships, language expansion, prepositional phrases, directionality, mapping, gravity, symbols, and discrimination.

Dramatic Play and Learning

Yet another way in which the teacher can intervene to promote self-motivated learning for children is through expansion of the normal role-playing or dramatic play of the children in the block area.

The teacher can encourage the use of dolls, vehicles, animals, etc., in conjunction with blocks. Ropes can be used for gas lines, for tying objects together, for making cranes, and for measuring. Pulleys provide yet another use for ropes. A few large planks can be added, and the children will combine them with the large blocks to make larger structures into which they can fit; they will make them into bridges to be crawled under, walked over, etc. Large planks can be used for inclined planes and levers. By observing how the children use such additions, the teacher can expand their learning of concepts involving movement, weights, measures, gravity, and leverage.

There are many themes around which children center their play in the block area. Some of these themes are seen more frequently than others, but all lend themselves to broader concepts and a wide range of learning opportunities.

The following are only a few of the possible themes around which children often build their spontaneous play activities. Inherent in this play, assuming some intervention by the teacher, are opportunities for the development of science, math, geography, and social studies concepts; opportunities to engage in mapping arrangements, sign making, recognition of symbols and words; and opportunities to enrich language and thought processes. The teacher can plan to expand learning opportunities in some of the following ways.

Themes with Trucks and Cars:
  a. sign making: directionality—using one- and two-way streets, traffic lights (combined with art activities)
  b. following directions, police, accidents, ambulance, medical supplies
  c. mapped out roads, cross walks (tape on floor)
  d. fix-it men: tools, jobs, pulleys, mechanics
  e. gas station: pumps, workers, car wash

Themes around Stores and Restaurants:
  a. different stores and their purposes (classifying, conceptualizing)
  b. money, goods, colors, labeling, signs and symbols (counting, categorizing)
  c. drive-in, sit down eating places, foods
  d. people who work: salesman, customers, waitresses, cooks (appropriate interactions, exchange of services involving language, math, memory, etc.)

Themes around Bus, Train, Airplane Trips:
  a. tickets, money (counting, symbols)
  b. people who operate vehicles, provide service, tasks, roles
  c. short trips: routes, stops, safety
  d. long distance trips: packing, eating and sleeping, distance, measurement, climate

e. gas stations, train and bus depots, airports, services

f. maps, directionality, signs, places

Themes around Firemen:

a. going to fire, relaying of information, preparations, maps, directionality

b. at fire: equipment needed—ropes for hoses, ladders, water, pumping, hoists, protection

c. other helpers: police, ambulance—functions and roles

d. people involved in fire: safety, problem solving, escape, fears, care of injured, saving one's treasures

e. after fire: clean-up of equipment, rebuilding structures

Themes involving Construction Activities:

a. planning a structure, blueprints, maps, measurements

b. excavations, tunneling, foundations, bridges, gravity

c. constructing, tools, materials, people, tasks, balance, pulleys, levers, spatial relationships

d. build a group block structure: each child adding a block at a time—when completed, each take his off to show how parts go into making a whole.

Planning the Environment for Specific Learning Events

Some teachers prefer to describe the concepts that children need to learn and then plan the environment in a variety of ways to insure that the necessary learning occurs. For example, preschool children are usually developmentally ready to attend to shapes, sizes, quantity, numbers. They are in the process of learning to classify according to similarities, differences, color, shape, etc.; to categorize according to function and role; to deal with patterns, balance, directionality, etc.

The teacher may decide to spend a certain amount of time on a particular concept such as shape. Her intervention can focus on labeling the different shapes of the blocks, pointing out the relationships between the blocks (i.e., two squares equal a rectangle, or that half a square is a triangle), that cylinders roll but cubes do not, etc. The teacher may wish to deal with some of the following concepts:

Measurement: In relation to height, width, length, depth, weight, time, comparisons, spatial relationships.

Quantity: In relation to amounts (a lot, a few, many, some, more, less), counting, ordering, fractions, whole/parts, sets.

Categorizing and Classifying: With regard to similarities and differences (by color, shape, size, feel, taste, sex, age, function, pairs, sets).

Sequencing or Seriation: Of amounts (few to many, tall to short), of events (cooking experiences, growth and development of plants and animals), of time (before, after, yesterday, tomorrow, school routines), of stories (sequencing the events).

Process of Change: Chemical changes (dissolving, mixing substances, effects of water, oxidation, heat, cold on various substances); physical changes (due to force, gravity, magnetism, pressure, electricity); temporal changes (day, night, seasons); biological changes (body changes, growth, decay, birth, death).

Adaptation: In relation to problem solving, experimenting, finding alternative solutions, memory, flexibility in thinking and action.

Children can be exposed to an enormous number of concepts simply with a word, a question, or a momentary interaction provided by the teacher. Since the teacher is responding to the observable play in which the child is engaged, she can provide just that learning experience which could conceivably be integrated. Similarly, if a teacher feels more comfortable delineating the types of cognitive development which she would like to see occur in her classroom (assuming she has evaluated the children, their capabilities, and intellectual stages), it is possible to structure an environment which would tend to stimulate such learning events. By permitting self-selected activities within the structure, the teacher will be free to respond to each child's individual competence within the prestructured learning environment.

A good teacher functions as a model for young children. If she values autonomy, self-motivation, social interactions, exploration and experimentation, flexibility, and the acquisition of skills, then she will reinforce such behaviors as she interacts with the children.

Whether such attributes can be enhanced in rigidly structured and exclusively cognitive programs is indeed questionable. The necessity for encouraging the development of such attributes is a high priority for most educators though the methodology for their attainment may vary. It is our contention that a program of spontaneous, self-directed play provides a vehicle for achieving both the goals of self-enhancement and competence for learning and achievement.

Sharing Your Impressions

1. In what ways do you succeed and fail as a model for children during play?
2. Recall how your teachers spent time with you during periods of play.

3. Explain why you would prefer to use a teacher-determined or child-chosen play activity as the basis for curriculum planning.
4. How does the teacher's role change when the play activity chosen by children becomes the medium for learning?
5. Think of some ways to expand learning when children use a boat theme for play.
6. In what ways can high school teachers serve as leisure models for their students?
7. Recall some of the adult roles you preferred to play as a child.

15

Learning to Play with Preschoolers

Robert D. Strom

Parents of preschoolers have a difficult teaching role, because they must accomplish certain goals primarily through play. Using play as a medium for instruction may not seem demanding until we recognize that the parents (the teachers) have a much shorter attention span for fantasy interaction than do their children (the learners). Then, too, the children also possess greater imaginative strength. Given these conditions, it is clear that parents can succeed only if they regard themselves and their children as partners in play. In a partnership there is no competition; the strength of each party is used to the advantage of both. But how can this kind of collaboration be established within the context of family play? What assets do parents bring to the merger, and how can these be combined with the strengths of children? How can family members best use their time together for mutual benefit? Mothers and fathers realize that complete answers to these questions may not yet be available. Nevertheless, they are eager to apply whatever is known about learning to play with young children.

My own motivation to study parent-child play grew from dissatisfaction. As a father of two sons, I had searched in vain for advice about how to join them in their favorite activity. Most of the research literature seemed to ignore the human variables. Instead, play was usually described as though players were interchangeable, and had a uniform influence. Intuitively, I felt that different benefits could be

Presented to the European Conference on Parents and Bilingual Education at the University of Munich, West Germany, February 22, 1980. Reprinted with permission from the *Journal of Creative Behavior*, Volume 14, Copyright 1980 by the Creative Education Foundation, Inc.

gained when children played with parents, with peers, with grand-parents, and alone. To test these assumptions, a setting for experimenta-tion was needed. With the help of the Rockefeller Foundation, various toy manufacturers, and a group of creative student architects, a colorful, spacious laboratory was constructed. Soon thereafter, other private foun-dations and a continuing cadre of doctoral candidates began to provide assistance with what has become a large-scale project involving families at play throughout the world. Looking back over a decade of research, I find that I initially underestimated the possibilities of teaching and learn-ing through play. Let me tell you something about our exploration, our mistakes, and our progress.

Play Needs and Preferences

One of our first observations was the preference of young children for repetition, their need to recreate certain play situations over and over again. By contrast, most grownups are quickly bored in repetitive settings. Thus, when four-year-old John asks his father to play soldiers, he may hear Dad say "But Johnny, we just played that yester-day. Let's do something else, something different." Since grownups are quickly bored in repetitive settings, few of us can play with preschoolers for long periods of time. Indeed it is fair to say that, during parent-child fantasy play, it is the adult who has the shorter attention span.

The difference in the attention spans of parents and children suggests an incompatibility of play styles. And after all, why should they play together anyway? When it comes to play, what children need is other children—at least this is the common impression. Perhaps we can better appreciate the play needs of children by examining our own recreational needs. What kinds of games do we consider the most excit-ing, the most fun to watch? Generally, adults agree that they like a close game, one in which the outcome remains doubtful until near the finish. When a football team outscores another 60 to 0, the spectators may be heard to complain that what they saw wasn't a game at all. By this they mean that the imbalance of power eliminated the uncertainty and conse-quent excitement about who would win. Indeed, when our team runs away with the score, we may even begin to encourage the opposition to score and find pleasure in their success. The pro draft was initiated just so that power would not become the exclusive realm of one team in the league. Sports promoters realize that, whenever power is unilateral, fans will conclude "Why watch?"

Some parents experience a similar motive when they play games with young children. The parents recognize that they are too com-petent for the child to win the game, perhaps even too powerful for the youngster to feel any satisfaction in playing at all. Thus, in a game of checkers, when the child begins to complain, threatens to quit, or seems ready to cry, the parent must decide what to do. Why do some parents decide they should cheat in favor of their young opponent? Certainly it isn't to teach the child dishonesty. Isn't it to make the child feel powerful? The fact that young children are so often powerless in games oriented toward adult rules means that these are not the best play activities for intrafamily encounter. There is a better and more authentic way to respect small children and become involved in their lives—through fantasy play.

In the Parent-Child Lab at Arizona State University, we decided to run a simple check of our hunch that preschoolers need play with parents in order to share dominance. A group of middle-class, suburban couples were obliged to engage their four-year-olds in fantasy play for ten minutes each morning and evening. This schedule was followed for a week. During the succeeding week, the parents were instructed to avoid any participation in play. Throughout the experiment, each of the two dozen families kept its own daily record of child misbehavior. As a group, the family records showed an incidence of misbehavior six times as great for the non-play days as for the "child power" days. The fact that there was less misbehavior on days when parents played with their children suggests that certain power needs are met during family play. In addition, we have found that parents who play with their youngsters more often than most other parents have more appropriate childrearing expectations.

Parent Use of Play Themes

To return to the issue of preferences in play, it seemed to us that we had to find out just how the children's need for repetition could be reconciled with the expressed need of grownups for diversity. With this in mind, we began to examine the range of topics or themes that preschoolers prefer to play, noting those receiving the highest frequency of attention. The favorite themes involved such toys as doctors and nurses, action-figure dolls, trucks, airplanes, soldiers, boats, and prehistoric animals. In playing with the children, we discovered that it was possible to accept repetition without experiencing monotony by playing a single theme and revising it a bit each time. For example, during play with doctors and nurses, we were able to extend our own attention span by using subthemes like these:

- We must find the dog that bit the little boy.
- The witch doctor wants to work at the hospital.
- The Martian has never been to a doctor's office before.

- Nurse, the hospital is full of noises, and I can't sleep.
- His family can help him get well.
- The patient is hiding around here somewhere.
- I want my dog with me at the hospital.
- The girl has decided not to have her tonsils out.
- Animals make the best animal doctors.
- Let's help the elephant have her baby.
- Let's visit sick people in the hospital.

It became clear that children want familiarity but will accept incremental variety. Thus, the parent's need for novelty can be met without giving up the child's favorite theme. But how does one learn to improvise, to think quickly of subtheme variations? Most of the adults we watched, including preschool and primary teachers, were extremely poor at generating alternative subthemes. Yet it was obvious that somehow we needed to extend the adult attention span—to make it long enough so parents could enjoy fantasy play, and so use it as a medium for teaching, without experiencing boredom. Clearly, a teacher who could not pay attention for very long could hardly be an effective teacher. How could we provide ideas for players who needed more novelty than they themselves were able to generate spontaneously?

Initially we tried brainstorming lists of subthemes and giving them to parents during observed play periods. To illustrate, for the general theme of "The airplanes are ready," we provided a list of 50 alternatives like these:

- Planes can make it rain for the farmer.
- All passengers must be checked for weapons.
- The people want to go to San Francisco, but the skyjacker says Mexico.
- Our suitcases didn't come on the same plane.
- We found someone hiding on the plane.
- This airplane will have animals for stewardesses.
- Children are working in the control tower.
- There is not enough food on board for everyone.
- Will we get our puppy back when we land?

By providing this kind of structure and access to resource ideas, we hoped to help more parents avoid the polar responses that typically characterize their play with children—coercion and concession. On the one hand, some people mistakenly suppose that, so long as they are using toys in teaching children, a coercive interaction can be called play. On the other hand, some parents ask the children what to do and how to move because they have no ideas of their own. But there is no sharing of dominance in concession, either. What children need, of course, are interactive partners, not echos.

Our lists procedure seemed to be helpful, but it did have certain limitations. The incidence of coercion and concession was reduced, but some adults were overwhelmed by the wide range of content choices. Other parents with a high need for closure felt frustrated when a child moved back and forth between subthemes, thereby preventing the couple from covering all the subthemes during a single play setting.

At that point I decided to discontinue the use of lists and instead represent each of the subthemes by figures. Surely this change would better meet the adult need for variety. In addition to many subthemes there would now also be a diversity of shapes. To illustrate, Figure 1 shows the types of dinosaurs we make from colored construction paper. By including only one subtheme on each dinosaur, we can present fewer subthemes to parents so that they will not be overwhelmed. We soon learned that parents and children are less distracted when parents manipulate a colorful paper figure on which a play subtheme is written than when the adults frequently refer to a list of subthemes. Again, the purpose of putting subthemes on each paper dinosaur is to provide the parents with a continuing source of ideas for sustaining their play involvement. Paper figures resembling boats, soldiers, or airplanes are given to parents when the corresponding toys are found to be of greatest interest to their children. In all cases the couple play with actual toys rather than the construction paper figures, which are intended solely as a guide for parents. This approach has proven to be very successful as a way of structuring resource ideas for family play. And make no mistake about it—adults need structure.

Before parents can effectively use subthemes during play, they need to feel comfortable with this means for achieving their childrearing goals. We start by orienting them to the possibilities for teaching values. For example, dinosaur play is introduced like this:

> *This is dinosaur country.* Most of us do not realize just how hard it is to be a dinosaur today. The fact is, except for young children hardly anyone pays attention to them. I got to thinking that maybe things would be better if somehow the dinosaur population could grow, if they weren't such a small minority group. After some persuasion, the 25 dinosaurs you see on the wall behind me agreed to come here today on the premise that you'll help them increase their numbers and start the population boom they need.
>
> As you might expect, dinosaurs are not all alike. I've found that the best way to tell them apart is by the values they represent. These differing values are shown by separate colors. For example, it seems that regardless of their shape, all the pink ones feel the most important thing to learn is the constructive use of power. The blue dinosaurs believe that

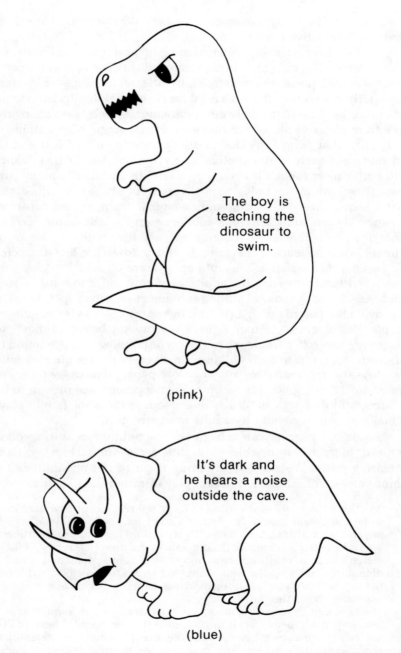

FIGURE 1. Examples of Dinosaur Cutouts

(yellow)

(green)

FIGURE 1. (*continued*)

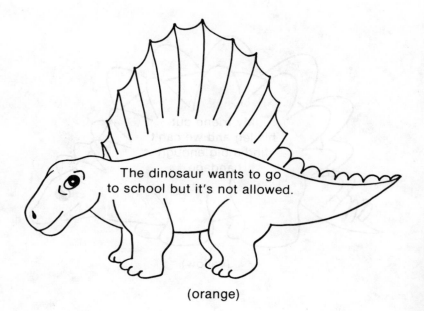

(orange)

FIGURE 1. (*continued*)

sharing fears and anxieties deserves the most attention. Green dinosaurs indicate that understanding the needs and feelings of others deserves greatest consideration. Yellow dinosaurs emphasize collaborating with others and orange ones give priority to expressing differences verbally.

All the dinosaurs will now be taken from the wall and placed in colonies according to color. I'm asking each of you to join the particular colony whose values you wish to support. In addition to the figures with subthemes, your group will also receive two dinosaurs that have nothing written on them. Bear in mind that to become a member of any colony as well as add to the total dinosaur population, each of the unmarked dinosaurs needs to acquire a subtheme. So, during the next few minutes, your group task is to recommend two subthemes from a longer list of possibilities you brainstorm first.

Play Theme: This Is Dinosaur Country

Affective Objective: Constructive Use of Power (Pink Dinosaurs)

The boy is teaching the dinosaur to swim.
We can cross the river on the dinosaur's back.
Let's ask him to be a wrecking machine and tear down old buildings.

Tell the dinosaur family that the hunters are coming.
The biggest dinosaur got stuck in the mud.

Affective Objective: Sharing Fears and Anxieties (Blue Dinosaurs)

It's dark, and he hears a noise outside the cave.
It's an earthquake, and all the trees are falling down.
She woke up crying from a bad dream.
She got lost on the way home.
People are running to hide from him.

Affective Objective: Understanding the Needs and Feelings of Others (Green Dinosaurs)

My best friend is moving away.
She's sad because she can't fit on the merry-go-round.
He's not chosen for the animal parade.
She needs to make lots of noise, but it bothers people.
He needs to play, but no one will let him out of his cage.

Affective Objective: Collaborating with Others (Yellow Dinosaurs)

My friend cut his leg, and we can't find a big enough bandage.
This is the world's only dinosaur circus.
He can help us at the school playground.
Let's climb his tail so we can pick fruit from the trees.
Teach the dinosaur how to cook so he won't be hungry.

Affective Objective: Expressing Differences with Others (Orange Dinosaurs)

The dinosaur wants to go to school, but it's not allowed.
He's friendly, but only the children know.
The cave people are mad.
He wants to watch television all day.
The little dinosaur tells his parents he'll run away.

After the parents collaborate in generating alternatives, they are each provided five subtheme figures of their choice to take home for a trial. The only recommendations given at this stage are:

1. Play with your preschooler for a few minutes every day during the upcoming week.
2. Schedule all play sessions at a time when you are fresh rather than fatigued.
3. Record your reflections in the notebook following each play period.

Generally, parents report that using subthemes enables them to interact longer with their children. As the group members share their experiences, most parents acknowledge their discovery that children are the best models for learning how to play. Once this understanding is attained and the corresponding respect for children is evident, parents are ready to assume a more influential teaching role.

What are the instructional benefits of the subtheme approach? First, it is well known that helping children perceive alternatives is important because it displaces either/or thinking, the my-way or your-way type of mentality. The philosophy that there are two sides to every issue is usually a gross underestimate in a heterogeneous society. Instead, if each of us can come up with a number of ways of seeing a single situation, our chances of being able to conciliate, get along, share dominance, and live with one another even though we are different are considerably improved. Children need to develop an ability to see many possibilities in a situation if they are to do well in problem solving and conflict resolution, areas of achievement in which too few people excel. What we have in the subtheme approach is a way to increase the duration of parent-child play, a way to encourage practice in sensing alternatives, and a way in which the child can learn to use assertion as well as compromise. Unlike a child's immature peers, parents can offer a more mature model of how to express differences.

Second, we should take advantage of the identification phase of early childhood more than we do. Using play subthemes colored according to personality (affective) objectives allows parents to assume certain positive roles that daily affairs may prevent them from modeling. Some of the values parents hold dear ordinarily are displayed in response to situations that seldom occur when children are present. Some children could follow their parents around for weeks and never observe some of the values that the parents consider to be most significant. By contrast, play offers a unique opportunity to invent situations that permit parents to demonstrate values consistently.

The illustration of parental values has more effect on children than does the imposition of values. Consequently, I recommend that, instead of settling for a random positive model of our values, we choose a deliberate, consistent model. The affective objectives combined with a subtheme approach allow us to do so during play. The single limitation of this method, which we refer to as Toy Talk, relates to the age of the children. Until boys and girls are three and a half years old, they lack a sufficient language base and the concentration necessary to sustain thematic interaction. Parents report mutual gains throughout the primary grades. The upper age limit for Toy Talk appears to be 11, when soldiers and futuristic space toys serve as the final dominant themes.

Play and Language Development

When parents learn to enjoy play, as shown by their increased attention span to a minimum of 12 minutes, and to use it for affective modeling, we concentrate next on using play to share language with the child. In terms of deciding what vocabulary to offer, we're interested in sharing context-relevant language. This means respecting parents' own vocabulary choices and home circumstances rather than prescribing "appropriate" words for them. We include a choice of words for each of the various subthemes.

Play Theme: This Is Dinosaur Country.

My friend cut his leg, and we can't find a big enough bandage.
accident   hurt   cooperate

Tell the dinosaur family that the hunters are coming.
afraid   dangerous   warn

The dinosaur wants to go to school, but it's not allowed.
alone   different   unfair

For each of the words parents choose, they receive suggestions about enacting the definition in context. Consider several of the words you have just encountered.

Accident: something that happens not on purpose
a. The caveman fell off the mountain. He had an *accident.*
b. The caveman cut himself with a rock. It was an *accident.*

Afraid: scared, frightened
a. This little dinosaur sees a big mean dinosaur coming toward her, and she feels *afraid.*
b. The caveman is running away from the big dinosaur.
He is *afraid* of the dinosaur.

Alone: without company, by oneself
a. The baby dinosaur is sleeping *alone* under the tree.
She is all by herself.
b. The caveman took his friends with him to swim in the lake. He did not want to swim *alone.*

Similarly, during the course of a ten-minute "flight" with airplane subthemes, the parent might introduce and try to define terms such as *destination, passenger, skyjacking, search, weapons, altitude, afraid, negotiate, rescue, and reunion.* Or, while on a submarine voyage to find treasures, the child might learn the meaning of *buried, search, submerge, surface, depth, pirate, survive, float, unknown,* and *sink.* Whatever the play theme, parents can enlarge a child's basic vocabulary by defining words in context. Usually we recommend focusing on a small number of words each week and discourage the introduction of too many words in a single session.

By the time school age is reached, there is already a great disparity in word power among children. In terms of sentence structure, it is estimated that a child's spoken language reaches 90% of its mature level by age six; a first-grader uses every part of speech and form of sentence.[1] Toy Talk is one way for parents to meet the responsibility these data imply for contributing to their children's language development. Toy Talk is a play activity in which children are given the chance to learn at least one meaning for each of a number of words and to use the words in a relevant setting. At the same time, Toy Talk is a way to build positive attitudes and values through play.

Although it is possible to communicate feelings and thoughts with a minimum of vocabulary, the more words at one's command, the richer and more exact the speech. Each person needs language facility to express ideas, to label thoughts, to urge the consideration of feelings, to describe emotions, and to compare experiences. Everyone has experienced trying to convey an idea when the appropriate words seemed fugitive. The problem is more acute for persons whose speech has developed in settings where a minority linguistic system or a restricted language is prevalent. People from these backgrounds often find themselves less able to understand and to make themselves understood than peers who come to school with facility in the language of the dominant culture. The greater the access to vocabulary, the less frequently all these frustrations occur.

Before parents can start teaching language through play, we must help them learn to assess their child's vocabulary. Otherwise, they have no way of knowing whether they've taught the child anything the child didn't already know. Here it is important to underscore the self-concept of the parents as teachers. The ability to confirm the effectiveness of their own teaching can help offset parents' feelings of insecurity in the role of teacher. Figure 2 shows the vocabulary-assessment procedure we have devised. Note that the pre/post questions parents ask children are the same for each word but that the pictures used differ. The children are asked to identify, explain, and finally elaborate the meaning of each word. This broad procedure enables a more accurate assessment of

[1]Many parents are concerned about their children's mastery of speech sounds. By three years of age, children usually master B, P, M, W, and H sounds. At four, most children can pronounce D, T, N, G, K, NG, and J sounds; at five, F, V, TH, SH, L, and CH sounds. Z, S, R, and HW ("when") sounds may not be mastered until six or seven years of age. In terms of language-skill development, making three-word sentences, telling stories, sharing ideas, and telling first name, last name, and age are skills that develop at two to three years of age. Three- to four-year-olds make sentences of four to five words and ask many questions. Four- to five-year-olds define common words, count to 20, and enjoy looking at books.

PRETEST

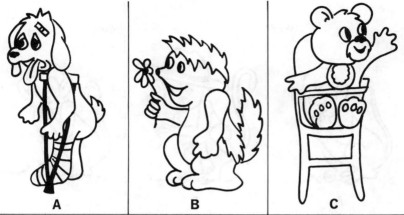

HURT: to injure, to ache.
1. Which picture shows someone who is hurt?
2. Why did you choose that one?
3. What can hurt you?

POSTTEST

HURT: to injure; to ache.
1. Which picture shows someone who is hurt?
2. Why did you choose that one?
3. What can hurt you?

FIGURE 2.

PRETEST

DIFFERENT: not alike.
1. Which picture shows someone who is being different?
2. Why did you choose that one?
3. What do you do to be different?

POSTTEST

DIFFERENT: not alike.
1. Which picture shows someone who is being different?
2. Why did you choose that one?
3. What do you do to be different?

FIGURE 2. (*continued*)

comprehension than is common in vocabulary testing. By the way, over 90% of three-year-olds indicate comprehension of the pictures.

Summary

Many adults need help in learning how to pretend with young children. Some people regard play as a relatively unimportant activity that is appropriate only for children. The fact is that play contributes to mental health at every age. Play is an especially powerful tool on which parents can rely for teaching their children values and language facility. Furthermore, playing with young boys and girls requires creativity, and adults regularly need experience in the exercise of imagination!

A final reminder is in order. The concern that most deserves attention is not whether the trained parent has become a better player—that is, more childlike—but whether the relationship between child and parent has improved. In other words, we are more concerned about gains in the family relationship than about the quest of some adults to "succeed" as players or to become better competitive performers. As a competitor in play, the parent is destined to forever finish second out of two. Although all of us are accustomed to adult models, the best models for learning how to play are children. Clearly if we cannot learn from children merely because the children are younger, we cannot teach them how to respect others. To use Toy Talk we must be able to tolerate teaching in a setting in which the learner's performance often surpasses our own.

References

Strom, Robert D. "Toy Talk: The New Conversation between Generations." *The Elementary School Journal, 70*(8), 1970, 418–428.

Strom, Robert D. "Play and Family Development." *The Elementary School Journal, 74*(6), 1974, 359–368.

Strom, Robert D. "Education for a Leisure Society." *The Futurist, 9*(2), 1975, 93–97.

Strom, Robert D. "The Parent as a Teacher Inventory." In Johnson, O. (Ed.), *Tests and Measurements in Child Development*. San Francisco: Jossey-Bass, 1976. Pp. 829–833.

Strom, Robert D. *Growing Together: Parent and Child Development.*Monterey, Calif.: Brooks/Cole, 1978.

Strom, Robert D., & Engelbrecht, Guillermina. "Creative Peer Teaching." *Journal of Creative Behavior, 8*(2), 1974, 93–100.

Strom, Robert D., & Greathouse, Betty. "Play and Maternal Self Concept." *Theory into Practice, 13*(4), 1974, 296–301.

Strom, Robert D., & Hill, Jane. "Childrearing Expectations of Hopi and Navajo Parents of Preschoolers." *Journal of Instructional Psychology,* 6(3), 1979, 15-27.

Strom, Robert D., & Johnson, Aileen. "Assessment for Parent Education." *Journal of Experimental Education,* 47(1), 1978, 9-16.

Strom, Robert D., Rees, Roger, Slaughter, Helen, & Wurster, Stanley. "Role Expectations of Parents of Intellectually Handicapped Children." *Exceptional Children,* 47(1), 1980.

Strom, Robert D., & Slaughter, Helen. "Measurement of Childrearing Expectations Using the Parent as a Teacher Inventory." *Journal of Experimental Education,* 46(4), 1978, 44-53.

Sharing Your Impressions

1. Describe some of the strengths parents can rely on during fantasy play with children.
2. Why do you suppose grownups have such a short attention span for pretending?
3. Identify two of your child's favorite play themes. Then generate some subthemes and relevant vocabulary.
4. Describe some values you would like to model and reinforce for your child during play.
5. Compare your readiness to play the part of villain versus your readiness to play heroic characters.
6. Make some recommendations for parents who want to know how to play with preschoolers.
7. Suggest some ways of encouraging a parent not to give up in learning how to play with preschoolers.

Chapter 6

Play and Sex Roles

16

From Cheerleader to Competitor

Mariann Pogge

Historically, the American woman's place in athletics has been much the same as her position in the working world. The stereotypical success story for a teenage girl was to be a cheerleader or the steady girlfriend of a football star. Continuing this role into womanhood, the successful female was one who had captured a man with a promising future. Since the late 60s many women have rebelled against being man's cheerleader. Consequently, today's woman is more likely studying to be a doctor, lawyer, or business executive than looking to marry one. This trend has currently spread to school-age girls. Many teenage females are trading their pom-poms for basketballs.

Woman's invasion of man's athletic sanctuary, like her entrance into the working world, proceeds slowly and often with difficulty. The female athlete must contend with centuries-old prejudices which have become institutionalized in the educational system. This article will examine women's historical place in sports, discriminatory practices against female athletes in schools, and progress made towards surmounting these obstacles.

Centuries of myths, traditions, and beliefs support the relegation of women to spectators of sports rather than participants. Muscles and physical strength were admirable in males but ugly and undesirable in females. Female fashions reinforced this premise. During the 1800s women poured themselves into waist cinchers which constricted their internal organs and made them prone to genteel fainting spells at the slightest exertion. Spike heels and tight skirts of the 1950s kept the average woman at a careful pace.

The delicacy of the female sex was not only a social but also a medical belief. In an 1840 lecture to students at New York's College of Physicians and Surgeons, Dr. Chandler Gilman stated,

> In women, inferiority of the locomotive apparatus, the apparatus of physical labor, is apparent in all parts . . . the brain is both absolutely and relatively smaller than in men. Women have an abundant supply of soft and semifluid cellular tissue which creates softness and delicacy of

From *Update on Law-Related Education*, Fall 1978, *2*(3), 15-18, a publication of the American Bar Association. Reprinted by permission.

mind, low power, non-resistance, passivity, and under favorable circumstances, a habit of self-sacrifice.

Even those who supported women's athletics held prejudices about the adaptability of the female temperament to competitive sports. Ethel Perrin, Chairperson of the Women's Division of the National Amateur Athletic Federation in 1928, stated,

> Girls are not suited for the same athletic programs as boys. Under prolonged and intense physical strain, a girl goes to pieces nervously. A boy may be physically so weak that he hasn't the strength to smash a creampuff, but he still has the will to play. A girl is the opposite.

Discrimination in Schools

These myths and beliefs have been institutionalized, particularly in the educational system, where most children receive the bulk of their athletic training and attitudes. Boys are provided with equipment, coaches, and most important, encouragement for the development of their bodies. As Brenda Fasteau points out in her article "Giving Women a Sporting Chance" (*Ms. Magazine*, July, 1973), girls from early childhood on are discouraged from taking pride in active and strenuous use of their bodies.

Evidence of sex discrimination in schools ranges from lack of media coverage to unequal financial support and allocation of equipment.

One high school teacher complained, "In the latest edition of the school paper, there were five articles on football and no mention at all of the girls' tennis team, which had won its last three matches." And consider these instances of sex discrimination in college athletics.

- At a Southern state university, female students could not take coaching courses for credit, with the result that they were not qualified to coach teams.
- At one Ohio institution, a woman could not use the handball courts unless a male signed her up.
- Men but not women in one school could receive academic credit for participating in intercollegiate athletics.
- At another school, female teams had to pay for their own transportation and meals, while the university footed the bill for first class air fare for the men's football team.

Differences in financial allocations for men's and women's teams are often enormous. One large university spent over $2.6 million for its men's intercollegiate athletic program and allotted not one cent for the women's program. In 1973 the University of Washington allotted only $18,000 of a $2.6 million athletic budget for women's sports.

A problem must be recognized before it can be corrected, and women as a class are beginning to realize what Edward Bellamy stated over 100 years ago:

> Be it remembered that until woman comes to her kingdom physically, she will never really come at all. Created to be well, and strong, and beautiful, she long ago sacrificed her constitution. She has walked when she should have run, sat when she should have walked, reclined when she should have sat . . .

In a 1974 *Sports Illustrated* article, Bill Gilbert and Nancy Williamson remarked, "An explosion of female participation in athletics has been noted (with varying degrees of pleasure and alarm) by virtually every sports administrator in the U.S." Women are breaking out of their delicate stereotype. Though the average man is larger, stronger, and heavier than the average woman, the gulf between them is rapidly shrinking. According to Ann Crittenden Scott in her article "Closing the Muscle Gap," the difference in strength between trained male and female athletes is far less than between average or untrained men and women. In addition, differences of strength *within* either sex are far greater than differences between them. Dr. Jack Wilmar of the University of California asserts that the vast superiority of male over female strength is probably more an "artifact of social or cultural restriction imposed upon the female . . . than a result of true biological difference in performance between the sexes."

Women are beginning to demand their rights as athletes, and the law has been involved at every turn. Major avenues have been court action, legislation, and the passage of Title IX prohibiting sex discrimination in education.

Court Action

Lawsuits or the threat of legal action have led many schools to accept girls on boys' teams, especially in noncontact sports. Before the passage of Title IX, female athletes challenged rules barring girls from boys' athletic teams with the constitutional argument that such rules denied women equal protection under the 14th Amendment.

Challenges to segregated athletic programs arose in two main types of situations: girls who wanted to participate on boys' teams where no girls' teams were provided, and outstanding female athletes who wished to compete on boys' teams where there was a girls' team because the male team offered them an opportunity to make better use of their athletic ability.

One of the first cases to deal with the issue of mixing male and female athletes was *Hollander v. Connecticut Interstate Athletic Conference* (Super. Ct. of New Haven Co., Conn., March 29, 1971). No track team was provided for women, and Ms. Hollander argued that the 14th Amendment promise of equal protection to all U.S. citizens applied to education, of which athletics was a part. However, the court refused to overturn a rule forbidding girls to participate on the boys' track team. The court found partial justification for the rule forbidding girls in that it reflected the customs and traditions of sports. The court also asserted that competition between males and females would probably produce psychological damage to members of both sexes:

> The present generation of our male population has not become so decadent that boys will experience a thrill in defeating girls in running contests . . . With boys vying with girls in cross country running and outdoor track the challenge to win, the glory of achievement, at least for many boys, would lose incentive and become nullified. Athletic competition builds character in our boys. We do not need that kind of character in our girls, the women of tomorrow.

The court in *Haas v. South Bend Community School Corp.*, 289 N.E. 2d 495 (Ind. 1972), recognized the absurdity of this position. In this case, a proven female athlete challenged a rule of the Indiana High School Athletic Association which prohibited mixed teams in interscholastic and intraschool athletics and also forbade matches between male and female teams. No female golf team was provided at this school, and though Ms. Haas shot a qualifying score she was not allowed on the male team. The trial court upheld the rule, but the Supreme Court of Indiana reversed the decision by a narrow margin. The court pointed out that the rule mandating separate teams was reasonable in the sense that if girls were permitted to try out for boys' teams, boys should logically be able to try out for the girls' team. Since males as a class possess a higher degree of skill in traditional sports, males would probably come to dominate both male and female teams, thus excluding females from sports. In the present case, however, where no separate team was provided for females, the rule was discriminatory. Thus where separate male and female teams existed, the school had reason to restrict mixing. Where there was no team for females, a woman should be allowed to try out for the male team and be judged solely on her athletic ability.

Bucha v. Illinois High School Association, 351 F. Supp. 69 (N.D. Ill. 1972), is one of a small number of athletic discrimination cases in which teams were provided for both sexes. *Bucha* was a class action suit challenging the association's rules which forbade mixed interscholastic competition. The girls bringing the suit were both outstanding athletes who asserted the right to equal educational opportunity and the right to equal treatment regardless of sex when trying out for athletic teams. However, the court resolved the case in favor of the association, arguing, as the court did in *Haas*, that allowing mixing of teams might result in male domination of both teams.

The States Act

Legislative change has been precipitated by court cases in some areas. For example, in one case two high school girls in Michigan, Cynthia Morris and Emily Barrett, filed suit against a rule preventing them from participating in interscholastic tennis matches. In the case of *Morris v. Michigan High School Athletic Association,* the U.S. Court of Appeals for the Sixth Circuit agreed that girls may not be prevented from participating fully in interscholastic noncontact athletics.

The suit probably helped pass a new law. Shortly after the complaint was filed, the Michigan Legislature enacted a law guaranteeing that all female pupils be permitted to participate in noncontact interscholastic athletic activities and to compete for positions on the boys' team even if a girls' team exists. According to the American Civil Liberties Union, suits or the threat of suits prompted at least five other states—Connecticut, New Jersey, Indiana, Minnesota, and Nebraska—to integrate noncontact sports in their high schools, and New York and New Mexico now have regulations which call for the integration of the sexes in all noncontact sports whenever there is a high school team for boys but not for girls.

The Key Law

Title IX is the most far-reaching response to women's demands for athletic rights. Suits based on the 14th Amendment led to some advances for women, but progress was slow because the cases were so different and because, as we have seen, judges did not agree on how the amendment applied to women's sports. Progress through changes in state laws was also piecemeal, with laws differing greatly from state to state. Passage of Title IX by the federal government was a giant step forward—it deals directly with women's rights to equality in sports and affects every school receiving federal funds, which is virtually every school in the country.

The main provision of Title IX is an absolute prohibition against discrimination: "No person in the United States shall, on the basis of sex, be excluded from participation in, denied benefits of, or be treated differently from another person or otherwise be discriminated against'' in any athletic program at an institution receiving federal funds. The Department of Health, Education and Welfare subsequently issued regulations which govern the interpretation of this act. Probably the most controversial of these regulations were those dealing with equal athletic opportunities for men and women in competitive sports. Athletic associations around the country said that equal opportunity was impossible in male and female sports. Many claimed that a strict application of Title IX would destroy collegiate athletics as it is known today. As a result, HEW's final regulations fall far short of the absolute proscription of sex discrimination which Title IX asserts.

The regulations essentially give women's sports ''separate but equal'' status, greatly undermining the Title's prohibition of different treatment according to sex. The educational institution may operate separate single-sex teams in such contact sports as basketball, football, wrestling, and ice hockey. Schools can also offer separate teams for noncontact sports, such as tennis, golf, swimming, and track. If, however, a school fields only one team in a noncontact sport, the excluded sex must be permitted to try out for the single-sex team.

Thus it is conceivable that the female who excels in tennis may try out for the men's team if there is no separate women's team, but the girl who wants to be a football player is out of luck if there is no women's team. The only check on the discrimination permitted by this section is a general requirement that the schools provide equal athletic opportunity for members of both sexes. Thus the female football player's only recourse would be to gather enough women to form a team, which the school would be bound to support.

Regulations governing financial support also fall short of Title IX's absolute prohibition against sex discrimination, permitting unequal expenditures for members of each sex or unequal expenditures for male and female teams, as long as all teams receive ''necessary'' funds.

Supporters of this regulation argue that unequal support is justified because even after opportunities are equalized, fewer girls will participate in competitive athletics than boys. In addition, some sports are more expensive to equip than others. If one sex predominates in such a sport (football, for example), total expenditures will be unequal.

One author who disagrees with this position points out that past discrimination may be a major reason why girls are not as interested as boys and will not come out for competitive athletics. If throughout their school years girls have had no training, no access to gyms and equipment, and no encouragement to participate, it is hardly a justification for unequal expenditures that at the age of 16, girls are not as interested in sports as boys. In addition, though a warning has come through that equal expenditures would change the face of intercollegiate athletics, a major purpose of Title IX is to prevent the tuition, fees, and tax dollars of female students and taxpayers from being used to benefit only men.

The separate but equal doctrine which the HEW regulations prescribe has had both positive and negative reactions. In "Giving Women a Sporting Chance," Brenda Fasteau points out that, as a class, men have the potential to perform better athletically than women as a class. The very best male athletes—ones who enter the Olympics—are still better than the very best women. Even in professional sports it is debatable whether Billie Jean King, at one time the best female tennis player in the world, would even make the top 10 if male and female professional tennis players competed against each other.

However, if women are allowed to try out for men's teams, men should, in all fairness, be allowed to try out for women's teams. The result would probably be an overwhelming majority of men on both teams. This new form of exclusion for female players would destroy Title IX's purpose of giving females equal opportunity to achieve their athletic potential.

Several other writers agree with this position but point out that males and females have equal athletic capacity in their pre-high school years. Medical evidence that girls aged 9 to 12 are at least as strong as their male peers convinced the New Jersey Supreme Court that girls of that age must be allowed to play little league baseball (*N.O.W., Essex County Chapter v. Little League Baseball,* 127 N. J. Super. 22, 318 A. 2d, 33 [1974]). For this reason and for the purposes of healthy male-female contact in a competitive situation, several authors assert that athletic segregation of the sexes before junior high school is neither justified nor desirable. Since the regulations on Title IX permit (but do not require) integrated male and female teams, even in contact sports, they argue that sports should be integrated on the pre-high school level.

Brenda Fasteau suggests other guidelines which would assure compliance with the spirit of Title IX.

1. Coaches of women's teams should be paid as much as those for men's teams.
2. Scholarships must be equalized for men's and women's sports.
3. From first grade through college, girls and boys should have gym classes together and equal access to athletic facilities and instruction. Students, regardless of their sex, should be encouraged to perform to the best of their individual ability.
4. Because girls have not enjoyed the same physical and psychological opportunities as boys to develop athletically, resources should be made available for at least two teams per sport, one for boys and one for girls.

A Law That Works

The growth in women's sports since the passage of Title IX is remarkable. In high school, girls' participation in interscholastic sports has increased dramatically. In 1971, 7 percent of high school athletes were girls, but today almost 30 percent are female. The same trend is clear in college sports. In 1974, only 60 colleges offered women's athletic scholarships; in 1978, 500 colleges offered grants. And some real money is now being made available to women's sport. For example, the Berkeley campus of the University of California spent only $5,000 on women's sports in 1972 but now spends $500,000 a year.

When women's athletics are taken seriously, the results can be striking. In Iowa, for example, girls' basketball draws bigger crowds than boys'. Women's basketball is a matter of state pride. Consequently, high school and college women in Iowa are able to try out for teams without the amusement or disdain frequently encountered by female athletes.

If women are going to continue their struggle from cheerleader to participator in life, they will need the "character" which the *Hollander* court restricted to men. As Simone de Beauvoir proposed in 1949:

> Not to have confidence in one's body is to lose confidence in oneself . . . It is precisely the female athletes, who being positively interested in their own game, feel themselves least handicapped in comparison with the male. Let her swim, climb mountain peaks, pilot an airplane, battle against the elements, take risks, go out for adventure, and she will not feel before the world that timidity.

Sharing Your Impressions

1. Why do you suppose "tomboys" are more socially acceptable than "sissy" boys?
2. How have the concepts of masculinity and femininity changed since you were a child?
3. How are children's sex roles influenced by play?
4. How do you feel about girls playing on teams that have traditionally been open only to boys?
5. What kinds of sports do you remember girls being involved in during your childhood and adolescence?
6. Forecast some of the benefits of equalized spending on sports programs for boys and girls.

17

Raising Boys Who Know How to Love

Dorothy and Jerome Singer

Increasingly in recent years there have been great changes in what girls growing up expect for themselves and from their lifestyles. Largely as a result of the women's movement, the old masculine ideal of the happy housewife, cooking, cleaning, caring for children—and keeping Daddy happy—is obsolete. Girls today expect to grow up to be true and equal partners of the men they marry—if they marry. Most will, of course, and will want to have children, too, but in a new kind of family life—equal partners with their husbands not only in their sexual lives, but in the daily routine that makes up 95 percent of human relationships.

Are the boys being reared today to prepare them for the reality of the new women with whom they will spend their lives? We think they are not.

As parents, we ourselves recognize in how many ways we have failed our sons by not preparing them to face many of the realities of the new man-woman relationships now emerging. And as we watch young women and their small children, we see that so many mothers are still fostering differences between the sexes that don't bode well for future, equal relationships.

Psychologist Jean Humphrey Block in California has collected ample evidence that attitudes and expectations of fathers and mothers today toward their sons and daughters are very different. By the age of two-and-a-half, the make-believe play of girls—which is encouraged by their mothers—is nurturant, protective, providing, while that encouraged in boys is adventurous and aggressive. Our own observations of nursery school children point up the same very striking differences. Even the structure of the physical plant of nursery schools—with the doll corner for girls and the more aggressive toys for boys—still fosters longstanding differences in style. Boys are not being taught the nurturing behavior that their future wives will expect of them, and that they themselves may well want to be able to perform in a natural way.

A research study, involving 290 eleven-year-old children, shows that traditional sex stereotyping is very strong by fifth grade. The boys in the study wanted to be craftsmen, engineers, scientists, doctors, lawyers, dentists, sportsmen and pilots. The girls wanted to be teachers,

From *Parents Magazine*, December 1977, *52*(12), 32, 40, 54, 60. Copyright © 1977 Parents Magazine Enterprises. Reprinted from *Parents* by permission.

artists, stewardesses, nurses and veterinarians. Close to 90 percent of the children in the study thought of boys as fighting more, and about 75 percent of the boys and 85 percent of the girls described girls as more gentle. In setting down their expectations for the future the eleven-year-old boys—in sharp contrast to the girls—made no mention of family activities and domestic life.

Though some people claim these kinds of sex differences are inborn, we're convinced that constitutional differences play only a small role in the development of the very specific attitudes we observed. Many attitudes are clearly modeled on parent behavior, and the kind of response given by parents to boys and girls in various situations. Rarely, for example, would a girl who had come crying to her mother after having been hit by another child hear the words, "Go back and stick up for yourself. Don't be a sissy." Boys, however, are very often encouraged to fight.

In most homes girls—but not boys—are still being enrolled quite early as "little helpers." They are still being raised in what might be called a highly socialized, really, a "civilized" fashion. That is, along with their new opportunities, they are also still encouraged to be sharing, caring, and cooperative, and to learn household management skills.

But why should boys be deprived of these most human and needed of skills? Most particularly, since girls are also now learning to develop skills to prepare them for a great variety of occupational roles hitherto closed to them, boys have a double need to "catch up" as it were.

Research studies of the play behavior of children between three and five show dramatically how feminine roles are expanding. Professor Brian Sutton-Smith of the University of Pennsylvania has documented changes in preferred toys for groups of boys and girls over the past half century or more. What has happened is that girls have increased the range of their interests in toys from those exclusively related to child-care and domestic activities to include the more adventurous and warlike toys always favored by boys. But the boys have shown no increased interest in the toys girls have always played with.

Our own research studies of play behavior of nursery school children and studies carried out by Dr. Mary Ann Pulaski at the City University of New York show that girls are now attracted to toys such as play garages or airplanes or cowboy sets. Boys, however, act as if they would sooner be without any toys at all than play with dolls, tea sets, or even school-teaching and other child-care props.

Clearly the young boys now growing up are not only being short changed in an education for nurturing and caring, they are also largely still unaware of what the girls growing up alongside them will be like when they reach womanhood, and what they will expect of their men.

For the most part, the women boys see in the movies or on television are housewives or sex objects. Even when women are presented as having special skills or careers, they still relate to their husbands in most of the popular media by being the cooks and housekeepers when the couple gets away together or sets up its love nest. Boys are continuing to expect, therefore, that the women they grow up to marry (though they will be intelligent), will also be super-homemakers and sex goddesses.

While certainly the role of the father cannot be minimized in its influence on the aggressive or *macho* characteristics of boys, it is more likely that mothers are even more central to the problem. We have carried out numerous interviews with mothers, as well as observations of mother-son and mother-daughter interactions. We have also surveyed the reactions of mothers to the kind of television fare to which children are exposed. Our experience suggests that the persisting aggressiveness of boys, their refusal to try out in play the care-taking roles that society will later require of them, and the very origins of their sense of male superiority, are actually fostered by their mothers. Women, then, are contributing to the serious problems their young sons will have when they grow up and set about looking for a mate among the newly liberated females of the species.

Moreover, men in our society are still not encouraged to move into a whole host of professions for which they might be quite well suited. An obvious example is dance. Very little in the early training of young boys makes it possible for them to contemplate careers as dancers. Indeed, such a role choice tends all too often to be made late in life by young men and is frequently accompanied by considerable concern about sex role. And yet, dancing is a genuine kind of athletics, and a profession in which men can reach outstanding heights of competence and esthetic quality.

The early childhood play of children also doesn't provide boys with any orientation toward cooking. Again, we know that the greatest chefs have been men, but this has been in a very specialized way in certain countries.

Within our own society, the need is not so much for gourmet cooks, but for men who enjoy cooking in the kitchen—not just at the barbecue grill—and who like it enough to be willing to share this responsibility equally with their wives. It is in this dimension that the young boys reared today are being let down. A few high schools are beginning to consider offering cooking as a course for boys. Again, these are just the very first glimmerings of what must be done.

What is needed is a major revolution in our overall concept of masculinity and femininity. Consciousness-raising groups for women, alone, cannot meet the need. Men need to be included in these groups as equal partners so that they can begin to examine some of the limiting and soon-to-be impractical premises on which their own self-concepts are based. Women will have to be helped along with the men to recognize that true manliness involves the fullest development of a man's capacities, including the capacity to feel—and express—tenderness. True manliness involves commitment and responsibility for others, a sense of sharing and a willingness to risk something for a full family relationship.

From an early age, boys will have to be allowed from time to time to run away from battle; they will have to be allowed to cry. They will have to be given a chance to play with dolls or to engage in make-believe play as nurses or teachers. Fathers will have to be willing to accept some softness in their sons and, indeed, to set examples in their own behavior of men sharing in child care and household tasks.

Women, too, are going to have to face up to some of their own myths about what a real man is so they can allow their sons to develop more broadly. They will also have to overcome their inhibitions about helping their husbands learn to share equally in a great variety of domestic duties and to be available to the children on equal terms. Every family may not involve such complete sharing, since people will always differ in talents and skills, but more options must be provided.

This does not mean that vigorous sports should be downgraded for boys—or for girls. Sports provide both sexes with opportunities to develop strength, endurance, agility, intelligence. They also provide, better than any tranquilizer, peace of mind and relief from tension.

However, we believe there ought to be a shift in emphasis in the kinds of sports now encouraged in schools for both boys and girls. Rather than focusing on the especially talented athlete, encouraging him—or her—to master a specialized sport, we might do well to place greater emphasis in encouraging all boys and girls to develop several sports skills which will last them throughout their lives, sports that will include opportunities for husband-wife participation. Activities such as mountaineering, hiking, bicycling, skiing, swimming, tennis and golf—all lend themselves to lifelong, shared participation. These are the kinds of activities that should be taught in our schools and encouraged by parents.

Parents are undoubtedly the key in helping to develop a new relationship between the sexes. Nevertheless, much of what they hope for can be undone unless they actively promote a change in the pattern of education and in the broader demands of this society in relation to sex attitudes.

One step that seems necessary is the availability of male

models in the nursery school, kindergarten and early primary grades. Until recently it was believed that young children were more comfortable in the company of women, because they were used to spending their days with their mothers at home. But this notion seems to be merely a reflection of the differences in child-care orientation that have prevailed in most societies. The poor pay and exploitation of women in education have also accounted for some of the failure of men to move into the early training role with children. Our observation of male figures in nursery schools and in the open classroom settings of the early primary school years has convinced us that the male in the school setting with very young children has an exciting and important impact on the children.

All too often, boys in school have been treated by women teachers as ruffians subject to scolding. At the same time they have been subtly encouraged to continue their aggressive activities. The availability of male teachers can redress some of this imbalance and provide the boys with encouragement toward self-control and decorum, which will help them develop the reading skills essential for schooling. Our observations of children in the early primary grades suggest that boys (who, as we know, are far more likely to lag in the development of reading skills) suffer by comparison with the girls because they simply aren't used to sitting still long enough to organize the contents of the reading material.

It is entirely possible that the academic superiority of girls over boys during the early school years may not reflect intrinsic differences between the sexes, but differences in socialization and identification with the teacher.

A major impact of the women's movement, in our opinion, is the fact that it has exposed many of the false assumptions underlying much of our educational and social points of view. In discovering how much has been left out of women's education and out of their opportunities to develop, we have also exposed how much has also been left out of the upbringing and education of boys. We are at the threshhold, then, of a great chance to recast our whole conception of child rearing and development.

We issue a call to young parents. Help your daughters to try their muscles and to be daring and adventurous in thought and action. Help your sons to be more tender and loving, to care for each other and to curb aggression. Then, when the boys and girls of this new generation grow up and find each other, as inevitably they will, they will be prepared for a life of mutual trust and sharing, and a new level of human loving.

Sharing Your Impressions

1. Compare the societal expectations of boys today with those that were prevalent when you were growing up.
2. How do you feel about boys who exhibit behaviors once considered to be feminine?
3. What types of traditional sex-role behavior do you find yourself perpetuating in boys?
4. What kinds of situations in most homes tend to perpetuate sex stereotypes?
5. What alternatives can parents and teachers offer the child whose peers call him a sissy?
6. Suggest some ways for parents to help boys become more loving and caring.
7. In what ways do toys influence a child's concept of sex roles?

Chapter 7

Sports and Spectators

18

Parents and Kids' Sports

Sandy Hotchkiss

While some 20 million kids across the country are playing some sort of organized sports, a handful of researchers have chosen sides on just how those games should be played.

For starters, Gary Fine thinks that nostalgia for sandlot baseball and backyard football may be coloring the current controversy around "adulteration" and competition in children's sports, and, after three years of studying Little League baseball, the University of Minnesota sociologist is in a position to know. More than 80 percent of the boys he got to know in Rhode Island, Boston and Minneapolis/St. Paul said they liked Little League "extremely much." That seems to be backed up by the fact that only two of the 91 players left their teams during the first two years of his study. The parents Fine talked to were also generally satisfied with the program and did not feel that there was too much emphasis on competition. Their biggest gripes were with the condition of the field and whether their sons got to play enough.

Well-behaved folks. But were the parents competitive? Only when their kids were on winning teams, says Fine. Parental attendance was better for such teams, although it's not clear whether parents have more enthusiasm for winners or whether enthusiastic parents promote those winning ways. In either case, Fine says that problems arose when two good teams squared off and everybody on both sides—parents, coaches and players—expected to win. On the whole, he rated the parents as "reasonably well-behaved." They directed their hostilities at the umpires rather than at the boys.

Nancy Forbis, who earned her PhD from nearby University of Michigan by studying the behavior of parents at children's hockey games, agrees that parental behavior varies according to a team's standing. "Spectators who viewed their teams as winners were inclined to be more competitive than parents on the lower-ranked teams," she reports. "The rivalry was particularly intense among those whose teams were in first and second place." Also, aggressiveness and excitement ran higher when parents sat close together.

From *Human Behavior*, March 1978, p.35. Copyright © 1978 *Human Behavior* Magazine. Reprinted by permission.

While Fine found that parents of boys on losing teams tended to accept the situation and emphasize fun rather than competition, Forbis's parents preferred instead to transfer their sons to a winning team. "Winning," she says, appeared to be "an ultimate goal," and one with the power to influence behavior and thinking.

Learning from losing. As a coach, a team manager and a mother, Forbis feels that pint-size sports have another purpose—to encourage human growth and development through the learning experiences of both losing and winning. "Athletic settings have to promote an atmosphere, for both spectators and participants, wherein persons may learn to be less intensely and more constructively competitive," she urges.

Sharing her views are two other researchers, Keith Henschen of the University of Utah and Leon Griffen of the University of New Mexico. They conducted a less than complimentary study of Little League football in Salt Lake City. To answer charges that the sample was too small and unrepresentative, they repeated the study in Albuquerque. The findings were the same. On the basis of this, Henschen and Griffen have come up with some ideas on how to improve Little League.

Parents, they advise, should not be allowed to attend practices and there should be no spectators at games. "Parents are the predominant cause of the pressures on both coaches and players," they insist. About a quarter of the boys and over a third of the coaches in both samples said that parents were the reason kids played Little League. In contrast to Fine's observations, over half of Henschen and Griffen's players said that their parents "chewed them out" when they played poorly; a third admitted they were affected by their parents yelling at games.

Public pressure. "A fundamental law of learning," the researchers remark, "is to practice in private and once you have mastered the skill, then perform in public."

Asked whether they would rather play a lot on a losing team or sit on the bench with winners, 75 percent of the boys said they would rather play than win. (Parents concurred, but to a lesser degree.) Although 90 percent of the players like the idea of trophies, Henschen and Griffen feel that such extrinsic rewards are unnecessary.

By the same token, they would eliminate postseason competitions and expensive trips for the champions. "Take the same money and purchase more and better equipment; field more teams so additional boys can participate; or maybe sponsor clinics for your coaches," the researchers recommend.

Everyone should play. On the Albuquerque teams studied coaches included all players for at least five plays of the game, and they considered it important for all boys to play whether the team was winning or not. Salt Lake City coaches had no such requirements and were more intent on winning; they also had more problems with parents. Henschen and Griffen conclude that the Albuquerque policy should be universally adopted, along with attempts to put boys on teams with others of their same age, weight and ability.

Sharing Your Impressions

1. In what ways could youth sports be changed to allow children more opportunity for decision making and control?
2. As a child involved in sports, to what extent did you make decisions about when, where, and how to play?
3. How do you feel when a parent spectator yells critical remarks to her or his child? To someone else's child?
4. How does your child feel about your presence at youth sports contests?
5. Give a brief description of yourself as a spectator.
6. Make some suggestions for parents about how they can learn to become better spectators of youth sports.
7. What kind of attitude or approach do you expect of your child's coach?
8. Why do you attend your child's games?

19

Is Winning Essential in Youth Sports?

Jerry Thomas

"Win—some: the first half of a phrase uttered by a loser."[1]

Is this a true indication of the post-game emotions of youth athletes? How important is winning and losing in youth sports and to whom is it important? What is the effect of winning and losing on children's perceptions about themselves? In a recent survey of youth football, 72% of the children said they would rather play regularly on a losing team than sit on the bench of a winning team.[2] It's not that winning and losing are unimportant to kids (nor should they be), but their

From *Journal of Physical Education and Recreation*, March 1978, *49*(3), 42-43.

perspective is quite different from that of adults. Adults are conditioned to view the outcome as the most important variable in a contest. They've been conditioned by college and professional coaches that "winning is the only thing." Why can't a good performance be "worthwhile" instead of "wasted" in a loss?

Certainly the outcome of the contest is important to children. Data on youth baseball has recently been reported which support this.[3] It was found that teams that consistently win games attribute winning to high ability levels, a loss to bad luck, and expect to win games in the future. However, teams that lose consistently attribute losing to low ability levels, a win to good luck, and expect to lose on subsequent occasions. In essence, winning causes children to view themselves as having high ability while losing results in ascriptions of poor ability.

Can we afford to let children's expectations about their ability and future performance be based on the desires of parents and coaches for a winning team? I don't believe so. Youth sport should be controlled so that no child loses all the time. In addition, we must help children deal with winning and losing in the proper way. In many sports a small change in perspective will accomplish this result while other sports require a structural change.

For instance, suppose points in age group track or swimming were based on improvement in the child's average performance (based on some number of previous trials). That is, all children swimming in an event who reduced their average time by more than 2 seconds receive two points, anyone ± 2 seconds receives one point, and anyone slower by more than 2 seconds receives no points. The emphasis is then upon every child doing her/his best, yet the contest could still be won or lost.

Of course, this formula is difficult to apply to some sports, for example, baseball; but suppose children were randomly assigned to teams after every four games. It seems unlikely that any child would be on a team that lost all the contests. What has been changed is not the outcome of any individual contest, but the emphasis upon winning and losing, i.e., who wins the league, state, national competition is no longer the point of reference. Only coaches and parents have much concern about that anyway. If coaches want to test their skill, let them take 15 new players every few weeks and mold them into a winning team. Then the won-lost record will be the coaches' responsibility rather than that of the players.

Certainly the above suggestions are not the *only* or best solutions to the overemphasis upon winning, but they do get at the real problem: *stressing contest outcomes above the benefits that should be derived by the players.* Children are not miniature adults in physical, motor, psychological, or emotional development. We should not force adult standards of success and failure on young children.

What are the effects of competition on children? The answer depends on how the situation is structured. Frequently, children enter sports because of the need to feel self-controlling in their environment. If children are competent and feel in control of what happens to them, psychologists say their "locus of control" is internal. However, if children feel their environment controls their action, then the source of control is external. Certainly we want children to increasingly feel they are gaining control over what happens to them. Yet we frequently structure sports situations so that the children make few if any of the decisions about their behavior and thus feel little control or responsibility over the outcome of contests. The coaches make every decision, including who plays and where, when and how long the team will practice, what the game strategy will be, etc. Why can't children be involved in some of the decision making processes?

Most frequently an "information seeking" hypothesis is suggested to explain children's needs and desires for competition in motor skills. That is, since motor skills play an important part in children's development, they seek to evaluate these skills through social comparison with peers of similar ability levels. Since state anxiety is usually increased in social comparative situations, research generally indicates that a winning situation relieves tension and decreases state anxiety, while losing increases state anxiety.

Some interesting insights into children's competitive behavior were offered in a recent report which found children, regardless of previous contest outcomes, sought opponents near their own ability level.[4] This finding supports the "information seeking" hypothesis in youth sports since children probably learn more about their own performance from competitors with similar skills. That is, when players spend a lot of time and effort in preparation for competition, they want to obtain the maximum amount of information about their performance; thus they seek players with comparable skills.

A last point seems particularly important. We should make every effort to avoid undermining children's intrinsic motivation for sport. Children enter sport for various reasons, but seldom in order to obtain the rewards associated with winning. Yet, by rewarding children for something in which they were intrinsically interested, we may be teaching them to associate their reason for participating with an extrinsic value, i.e., the reward. Substantial evidence[5] indicates that expected extrinsic rewards decrease the intrinsic motive for participation and result in a decreased interest in the activity if the reward is not present. However, rewards based upon the quality of a child's performance seem to increase intrinsic motivation for the task as long as the reward is within the child's capacity. Thus, we should probably decrease the number and monetary value of rewards in age-group sports and base the remaining rewards upon the quality of the individual child's performance relative to his/her ability level. The practice of providing a reward for every child regardless of the quality of his/her performance may be the worst possible way to motivate children to continue as participants in activity programs.

I'm particularly fond of the reward system used by an acquaintance of mine who coaches age-group flag football. One example is the "banana" award for the most improved player. He writes the name of the award on the banana skin, calls the child up and presents the award. Then the child must peel and eat the banana because success in sports is analogous to eating a banana; you have to win it every time out because of its short-term value. Doing your best is not a trophy you keep, but something to be achieved on each occasion.

Like James Michener, I'm not against youth sports, competition, or a reasonable emphasis upon the values of winning a contest. But we as physical educators should be opposed to ". . . highly structured leagues run by hypertensive adults, urged on by over-enthusiastic fathers and mothers."[6]

However, opposition does not mean withdrawal. We've done that for too long. Youth sports are here to stay and history has indicated that no amount of criticism on the part of its antagonists will diminish their popularity. There are many values to be gained for children and their families.

As professional educators, let's become active in our local youth sports groups. They are seeking leadership and direction. We know much about desirable behavior in sport. We have knowledge about children's growth and development, effects of exercise on children, how children learn skills, and the social-psychological considerations in youth sports. If we sit by and criticize local and/or national youth sport groups because of over-emphasis on winning, we are not providing a solution to the problem. Become involved in your local youth sport groups and lend your talents to the provision of enjoyable, safe athletic competition for all who wish to participate.

[1]From cartoon "B.C.," 3/24/77, *Hattiesburg American.*

[2]Cooper, W.E. Winning isn't everything nor is it the only thing. In J. R. Thomas (ed.), *Youth Sports Guide for Coaches and Parents,* Washington, D.C.; AAHPER, 1977.

[3]Roberts, G. C. Win—loss causal attributions of little league players. In C. Bard et al. (eds.). *Actes du 7e symposium canadien en apprentissage psycho-moteur et psychologie du sport.* L'Association des professionals de l'activite physique du Quebec, 1975.

[4]Scanlan, T. K. The effects of success—failure on the perception of threat in a competitive situation, *Research Quarterly 48,* 144-153, 1977.

[5]For example, see Thomas, J. R. & Tennant, L. K. Effects of rewards on changes in children's motivation for an athletic task. In F. Smoll & R, Smith (eds.). *Psychological Perspectives in Youth Sports.* Washington, D.C.: Hemisphere Publishing Co., 1978.

[6]Michener, James. *Sports in America.* New York: Random House, 1976, p. 106.

Sharing Your Impressions

1. Suggest some ways for changing youth sports to put less emphasis on winning and more emphasis on other benefits.
2. Give your reaction to the often heard statement "It's not whether you win or lose but how you play the game."
3. What do you feel society's role should be in supporting outstanding athletes?
4. Why do you suppose so many adults have become armchair athletes?
5. Identify some of the advantages and disadvantages of children's participation in out-of-school sports organized by adults.
6. What changes would you anticipate if youth sports were conducted without trophies, championship titles, and won/lost records?
7. How do you define a "good sport"? A "poor sport"?
8. When your child wins or loses, how do you help him or her interpret the experience?

20

Kid Sports and Moral Development

Rainer Martens

Parents naturally are concerned about the well-being of their children in sports—and in sports such as "pee wee" football and "midget" hockey physical injury is a legitimate worry. But parents today are even more concerned about the psychological well-being of their children when participating in sports.

According to journalists, in increasing numbers kids are turned off, burned out and hung up after participating in sports. Impressionable kids are learning by example how to swear, cheat and fight. Despite the criticisms, parents see a great deal of good in youth sports. Youth sports programs continue to flourish with boys and girls alike participating in greater numbers than ever. As a result concerned parents

An address given at the National College of Physical Education Association for Men conference held in Hot Springs, Arkansas, Jan. 8-11, 1976. Reprinted by permission of the author.

are in a dilemma: they want their kids to participate but they are uncertain as to whether youth sports create sinners or saints.

Obviously, youth sports programs can facilitate moral development when conducted correctly and also can facilitate the development of immoral or amoral behavior when conducted incorrectly. The more pregnant question is, what experiences in youth sports enhance moral development and what experiences contribute to immoral development? I will seek to answer this question, at least in part, from existing knowledge in social, developmental and sport psychology.

My objective in this paper is to suggest how psychological research can be applied by youth sports coaches in helping to develop moral standards among young athletes. In the sections to follow I first consider the three progressive phases of moral development. Next I discuss several social learning principles that may be used by coaches to facilitate the child's development of moral standards. And finally I suggest a perspective for youth sports programs—a perspective that creates an environment where not only moral development is likely to be nurtured, but the total development of the child is enhanced.

Moral Development

In 1908 William McDougall wrote "the fundamental problem of social psychology is the moralization of the individual by the society." Through the process of moralization all the major phases of social development arise and are resolved by one means or another. Moral development is the development of the conscience or superego. A child's conscience is developed from experiences with his environment, providing him with opportunities to internalize society's standards. Successful moralization of the child eliminates the necessity for constant surveillance and threats of punishment by society. Moral behavior within a sport context is called sportsmanship.

Psychologist Lawrence Kohlberg (1969) demonstrated that a child may move through three distinct phases of moral development. Each phase emerges out of and subsumes its predecessor and is more cognitively complex than the one before it. *Premoral hedonism* is the first phase of moral development; the child behaves simply to avoid punishment. "You scratch my back and I'll scratch yours" expresses the child's conception of morality in this phase. From premoral hedonism, the child's conscience develops into a phase where his moral behavior is guided by what he believes others will approve of and by an increasing concern for external rules and sanctions. This phase is known as the *conformity* phase. In the final phase of moral development the individual places greater reliance on internal moral principles. A person enters what is known as the *internalization phase* of moral development when he has learned that external rules which lead to absolute judgments must be tempered by internal moral principles. It is a morality based on the need for harmony between persons rather than inflexible conformity to rules (Sutton-Smith, 1973).

Socialization through Sport

Philosophers, psychologists and physical educators have eulogized play, games and sports as a means not only for developing morality in children but socializing them to many facets of society. According to these academicians games may act as a buffer, permitting children to learn the realities of life without sustaining the total impact of negative consequences. But do not for a moment believe that play and games are not serious business to children. Through the eyes of a young boy, failure to learn to ride a bicycle is just as serious as his father's failure in business.

Play may be a source of self-discovery, a means for learning new social roles, a medium for parent and child to communicate. Games and sports may permit a child an opportunity to learn how to cheat in the process of learning the meaning of fair play. But just as play, games and sport have the capacity for positive socialization, they also may breed deceit, hatred and violence. Thus it is not the game, the play or the sport that automatically determines the worth of these activities for the child; it is the nature of the experiences within these activities. It is the interactions with parents, teammates and coaches that determine if sports help the child develop morally or immorally. In the next section some examples are presented of how reinforcement principles and modeling can be used by coaches to make sport an experience that enhances moral development.

Reinforcing Moral Behavior

Through popular psychology it is easy to obtain the impression that the application of reinforcement principles in modifying behavior is straightforward. We simply reward moral behavior and punish immoral behavior. But the use of reinforcement principles with humans is not as easy as Skinnerians have led us to believe because people are not pigeons or rats (at least not most of them)!

Bad Billy. Seven-year-old Billy, a goalie with the Buffalo Bombers of the midget hockey league, becomes entangled with teammates and opponents in a skirmish around his net. Billy is hit and dazed, but is uncertain by whom or what. In his anger Billy retaliates by punching the nearest opponent in the nose with a solid right. The referee throws Billy out of the game and his coach punishes him by sitting him out of the next game. As a result Billy may hesitate to hit an opponent again in a similar situation to avoid punishment, but he may not understand why he should not. If, on the other hand, the coach explains that it is wrong to hurt people, Billy may also hesitate to punch other children when he is off the ice.

The point in this example is that the things coaches say to a child are of particular importance to the internalization of moral standards because they help form thoughts that the child associates with rewards and punishments. When a coach tells a child why he is being punished, he may provide the child with a general rule that helps him control his own behavior in a variety of situations.

Understanding the Golden Rule. In the hockey game Billy retaliated because he was hurt. He was unconcerned whether the other players intended to hurt him or if the hurt was accidental. Children younger than seven or eight years of age seldom show concern for the intent of the act. With cognitive development, occurring in part from maturation but more through learning experiences, the child becomes aware of other persons' intentions by developing the ability to place himself into the role of the other person. Role-taking, which normally develops in the 8-12 year age span, is an essential skill for the development of morality. The Golden Rule, "do unto others as you would have them do unto you," has no significance for the child unless he can take the role of others.

Youth sports provide valuable opportunities to develop the role-taking ability. Sport is a social situation and the role-taking ability can only develop in social context. The more social experiences and interaction—that is, the more opportunity for social learning—the greater the role-taking opportunities available to children. Role-taking is very susceptible to reinforcement and modeling influences (Sutton-Smith, 1973). Coaches, parents and other involved adults have unique opportunities through sport to develop children's role-taking capacity. The coach especially can do much to teach his aspiring paladins to look beyond the act and understand the intent of the actor. In brief, through sport the coach with empathy strives to teach his players empathy.

Undermining moral development. Another hazard in the use of rewards and punishments is that extrinsic rewards may undermine the development of intrinsic motives (Greene & Lepper, 1974). Too often in youth sports the child's intrinsic interest in the sport is decreased by inducing him to engage in that sport as an explicit means to some extrinsic goal such as a trophy, a trip or a state championship. When these extrinsic rewards for playing are removed the child may lose all intrinsic motivation to participate in the sport. In some cases this may generalize from a specific sport to sports in general.

Using extrinsic rewards to undermine intrinsic motivations was put to clever use in the following story.

> [An] old man lived alone on a street where boys played noisily every afternoon. One day the din became too much, and he called the boys into his house. He told them he liked to listen to them play, but his hearing was failing and he could no longer hear their games. He asked them to come around each day and play noisily in front of his house. If they did, he would give them each a quarter. The youngsters raced back the following day, and made a tremendous racket in front of the house. The old man paid them, and asked them to return the next day. Again they made noise, and again the old man paid them for it. But this time he gave each boy only 20 cents, explaining that he was running out of money. On the following day, they got only 15 cents each. Furthermore, the old man told them, he would have to reduce the fee to five cents on the 4th day. The boys became angry, and told the old man they would not be back. It was not worth the effort, they said, to make noise for only five cents a day (Casady, 1974).[1]

Analogously, the stringent extrinsic control of moral behavior will not foster the development of internalized moral standards.

If the child's conscience is to develop fully, if moral standards are to become internalized, as the child matures rewards and punishments must slowly be withdrawn and replaced with increasingly complex reasoning to help him form rules of behavior. When a person has internalized the moral standards of society, he will forego external rewards and punishments to behave in socially acceptable ways, even in private.

Psychological punishment. Parents inevitably must decide how they will punish their children. Among the most significant findings in the child development field is the discovery that children punished psychologically, using love-withdrawal or approval-withdrawal and reasoning, develop stronger consciences and are more susceptible to guilt feelings than children punished physically (Berkowitz, 1964). Children disciplined mostly by corporal punishment tend to display substantially more overt hostility.

---

[1]From "The Tricky Business of Giving Rewards," by M. Casady, *Psychology Today,* 1974, *8,* 52. Copyright © 1974 by Ziff-Davis Publishing Company. Reprinted by permission.

Subsequent research (see Hoffman, 1970) has shown that love-withdrawal is not as critical a factor in shaping the conscience as the reasoning given to the child for the withdrawal of love. As we observed before, reasoning with a child encourages him to take the role of others and it helps the child internalize moral standards by providing him with thoughts that he associates with rewards and punishments. If the reasoning with a child is overly complex, however, it may be of little value because it will not be understood. What is important in the moral development of the child is that he have experience with moral judgments more advanced than his own, but not so advanced that he cannot understand them. A child in the premoral phase will not understand the use of advanced reasoning, helpful for internalizing moral standards, but instead the child will learn more from teammates and adults who talk in conformity terms. On the other hand, corporal punishment inhibits internalizing moral standards because it engenders hostility, modifies behavior only because of fear, and often leads to rebellion.

A parent's or coach's threat to use psychological punishment obviously will not be overly upsetting to a child who has no love for his parent or respect and admiration for his coach. A coach's threat to withdraw his approval becomes an effective reinforcer only when the child is concerned with what the coach thinks; the child must have respect for his coach. It is not a coincidence that adults who are unable to obtain respect from children are the same persons who rely most on corporal punishment to control children's behavior. Obviously they must!

Pygmalion and sport. My final observation about the use of rewards and punishments for moral development concerns the powerful effects that *expectations* can have on the behavior of young people. Popularized recently as the Pygmalion effect, but more aptly described as the self-fulfilling prophecy, social psychological research has shown that kids sometimes become what we prophesy for them. If a coach has the expectation that a child will not be a good athlete or that he is immoral (and irrevocably so), the child may sense his coach's expectation and act to fulfill it.

Rosenthal (1973) reports that a coach's expectations may influence the child's learning of skills and moral standards through one or more of four factors. The coach may create a warmer social-emotional mood around his "special" athletes; he may give more feedback to these athletes about their performance and behavior; he may teach more material to these athletes; and he may give his special athletes more opportunities to participate and question events.

I suspect as kids we all have been in situations where we

sensed that others felt we were inferior. Kids with self-confidence usually confront such expectations as a challenge to be proven wrong. Kids lacking self-confidence, however, may simply accept their lot and behave to fulfill their coach's negative expectations. The process, of course, may function in reverse. Coaches' positive expectations may help motivate kids to achieve what they otherwise thought could not be attained. What coaches must remember is that expectations can reinforce both positive and negative behavior and that these expectations are communicated not only knowingly but often unknowingly.

Modeling

Kids learn moral behavior not only by being rewarded and punished, but by observing other people behave morally and immorally (Bandura, 1969). Learning by observing is pervasive in children. They imitate mom and dad in their games, mimic their siblings and peers in play and model themselves after their sport heroes. But kids do not instinctively imitate everyone in their environment. Children are likely to imitate those who command resources or have access to desirable goals. The coach who controls the child's participation in sports and games often commands an important resource or goal for the child. Thus it is no surprise that kids often imitate their coach.

Kids may not only imitate specific behaviors of their coach, but may strive to become exactly like him. Known as *identification,* this complete imitation of an emulated person has a profound influence on the development of the child's self-concept. To the extent the child perceives that his attributes match those with whom he identifies and that the culture regards these as good, he develops a positive self-concept.

Superficialness. Children show less development of strong moral standards when they grow up with adults who reinforce only the surface appearance of their behavior. Adults who serve as models for kids can create, by overly assertive and domineering behavior, the attitude that an immoral act is only immoral when it is detected and punished (see Aronfreed, 1969). Coaches in particular may easily give the impression that cheating is not really wrong unless it is detected, and then only to the extent that it hurts the chances of winning. When coaches promote immoral behavior to attain victory youngsters may conclude that ''the-end-justifies-the-means'' attitude is a proper code of morality.

Adult aggression. It is not surprising that social psychological research discovered that kids physically punished for aggression later behave more aggressively than kids who are psychologically punished (Bandura, 1969; Hoffman, 1970). Adults who physically punish kids for aggressive behavior provide a model for that very behavior. Moreover, the coach who displays hostility toward the officials and contempt for the other teams' coaches and players may wittingly or unwittingly reinforce his behavior as appropriate.

Hypocrisy. One of the difficulties in working with kids is that we want them to be better than we are ourselves. Too often we preach one thing and practice something else; or one day we do one thing and the next day we do the opposite; or one parent says one thing and the other does the opposite.

These inconsistencies must be resolved by the child if he is to form a stable conscience. Does he do as we say, or as we do? Does our preaching or our practice have a greater influence on our children's moral behavior? Recent evidence showed, for example, that when generosity was modeled by adults, kids increased their own generosity, but exhortations to be generous did not prompt increased generosity (Bryan, 1969). More important, hypocrisy did not affect the children's generosity; that is, kids were as generous when observing a generous model who preached avarice or stinginess as those who practiced and preached generosity. If we dare to generalize from these findings, our conclusion must be that actions speak louder than words.

This is to the chagrin of American religious, educational and sport institutions who have had great faith in the value of precepts in moral education. Reciting such precepts as "love thy neighbor as thy self" or "honesty is the best policy" or "cheaters never win" has little to do with the moral development of our children (Berkowitz, 1964). Instead if we want our kids to mature morally, the bellwethers of sport must be paragons of virtue.

Putting It into Perspective

Although brief and oversimplified, I have discussed a few social learning principles that may help the young athlete enjoy and benefit from his experience in sports. But implementing these principles, as well as knowledge from other sport sciences, into positive coaching behaviors is impeded because of (a) the lack of an effective delivery system for communicating what is known to adults working with young athletes and (b) inadequate means for motivating these adults to use this knowledge when coaching. The latter problem is particularly vexing. So often we know what is right for our kids, but we do something less than what is best. We know that screaming derogatory remarks at a child when he makes a mistake does not help him, but in the midst of the contest we sometimes forget. We repress the child's needs for ours. We lose our perspective. But these problems are surmountable—we can develop an effective delivery system and we can help coaches maintain their perspective. Let's consider next some facets of youth sports that the critics say are not in perspective.

Competitive Stress

Undeniably there is at times an overemphasis on winning in youth sports, but no one knows for certain the magnitude of the problem. Among the major criticisms of the winning-is-everything philosophy is that it places too much stress on kids. Critics impute that the resultant fear of failure leads to competitive stress equivalent in some cases to the stress manifested by soldiers in combat. When the fear of failure outweighs the fear of detection, immoral behavior such as cheating is more likely to occur unless the child has a well-developed conscience. Consequently it would be helpful to know precisely how much stress kids can handle for each of the three phases of moral development.

To understand the proper dosage of competitive stress we need to examine further the complexities of competitive stress. First we must consider whether the stress to excel in youth sports is unilaterally detrimental or whether there are occasions when this stress may be beneficial. Some experts tell us that we should seek to eliminate all sources of stress for our children or at least keep them to a minimum; kids will have enough stress in adult life and they do not need to be burdened with it as a child. These same experts tell us that youth sports are entirely too stressful; they should be eliminated and children should be encouraged to participate only in unstructured play.

Other experts believe kids must learn the harsh realities of the world and coping with stress is one of these realities. Learning the hard knocks of life as a youngster will prepare the child better for a successful adult life. These experts usually promote "miniaturized" big league sports programs; they encourage extremely competitive, highly organized programs because they build character.

Stress research and common sense suggest a position between these extremes. We can, no doubt, over-stress our kids: we can burn them out, damage their self-concept, and retard their moral development. On the other hand, kids raised in sterile environments who have little opportunity to learn to cope with stress have significantly greater problems in adjusting to adult life. Children need opportunities to learn to cope with increasing degrees of stress.

Youth sports provide many opportunities for learning to cope with moderate stressors, but they are equally amenable to placing too much stress on the child. The key to whether youth sports are opportunities for learning to cope or jungles where a high degree of coping is essential to survive, is dependent upon the objectives emphasized by parents, coaches and sport organizers. When the predominant emphasis is toward the child's physical and psychological development and not just on winning, the chances increase that competitive stress will be in perspective.

More on Winning

To discuss the issue of winning further we need to consider what the objectives are of youth sports in our society. Minimally we want youth sports to be fun without having negative consequences on the child's development. Optimally they are to be fun while contributing to the physical, psychological and social development of the child. Most adults involved in youth sports will tell you that winning is not the important goal, but their behavior sometimes defies their words.

Critics of youth sports are the first to point out that all too often these developmental objectives conflict with adults' desire to win. Competing to win, however, is not necessarily a negative goal; striving to achieve can foster personal growth. In fact it may be that moral development is nurtured more when moral decisions come into conflict with winning. Walter Kroll (1975) in an impressive paper on sportsmanship made this point vividly. He writes:

> Perhaps we need to inspect the notion that noteworthy acts of sportsmanship seem always to involve sacrifices of success strategy in favor of a decision guided by moral criteria. Success is not easily relinquished when it is so highly esteemed, but the conduct prescribed by a code of moral behavior can—and often does—compel the individual to forego the rewards of success. . . . Unless winning is important, putting success in jeopardy in favor of conduct compatible with a moral code fails to qualify as a noteworthy event. Such a proposition really needs to be considered by those harsh and outspoken critics of athletics who lambast the emphasis upon winning, who urge that cooperation replace competition [p.22].

Competition as a process of striving for a valued goal is unjustifiably maligned by critics intending to say something else. Competition is not a den of iniquity nor is cooperation utopia. Competition and cooperation are not antithetical, but complementary. What the critics intend to say when they attack competition and extoll the virtues of cooperation is that winning is *over-emphasized* and the cooperative emphasis will bring winning back into balance.

The crux of the problem then is knowing when winning is over-emphasized. Actually it is not as difficult as it may appear to detect the win-at-all-cost philosophy. We can with some accuracy infer coaches' motives by observing their behaviors. When coaches play injured youngsters, when they leave players sitting on the bench the entire season and when they routinize practice so that it becomes a complete bore, over-emphasis is indicated. When in the frantic race to be first, the developmental objectives blur into the background, winning is out-of-bounds.

Conclusion

Youth sports are not inherently evil nor are they inherently good—they are what we make them. Youth sports are more likely to build character when coaches with character have some knowledge of social learning principles and apply them. A coach cannot permit himself to repress his players' needs in order to satisfy his own need to win. A moderate degree of competitive stress, created by an environment where winning is prized and losing is not scorned, is more likely to be helpful than harmful in the moral development of the child.

To enhance the probability that youth sport participation will help the psychological and social development of our children they need an environment that is warm and friendly, where adult behavior is firm but consistent, and where opportunities are ample to make decisions within their cognitive capacity. How the environment we create can influence our kids is succinctly expressed in these words:

> If a child lives with criticism, he learns to condemn. If a child lives with hostility, he learns to fight. If a child lives with fear, he learns to be apprehensive. If a child lives with encouragement, he learns to be confident. If a child lives with praise, he learns to be appreciative. If a child lives with approval, he learns to like himself. If a child lives with recognition, he learns to have a goal. If a child lives with honesty, he learns what trust is.[2]

References

Aronfreed, J. The concept of internalization. In D.A. Goslin (Ed.), *Handbook of socialization: theory and research.* Chicago: Rand McNally, 1969.

Bandura, A. Social-learning theory of identifactory processes. In D.A. Goslin (Ed.), *Handbook of socialization: theory and research.* Chicago: Rand McNally, 1969.

[2]Abridged from a "Great Cities Project Report," which was reprinted in the *Baltimore Bulletin of Education*, 1965–66, 42, No. 3.

Berkowitz, L. *The development of motives and values in the child.* New York: Basic Books, 1964.

Bryan, J.H. How adults teach hypocrisy. *Psychology Today,* 1969, 3(Dec.), 50-52, 65.

Casady, M. The tricky business of giving rewards. *Psychology Today,* 1974, 8(Sept.), 52.

Greene, D. and Lepper, M.R. Intrinsic motivation: how to turn play into work. *Psychology Today,* 1974, 8(Sept.), 49-54.

Hoffman, M. Moral development. In P.H. Mussen (Ed.), *Carmichael's manual of child psychology* (3rd ed.), Vol. II, New York: Wiley, 1970.

Kohlberg, L. Stage and sequence: the cognitive-developmental approach to socialization. In D.A. Goslin (Ed.), *Handbook of socialization: theory and research.* Chicago: Rand McNally, 1969.

Kroll, W. Psychology of Sportsmanship. Paper presented at Sports Psychology meeting, National Association for Sport and Physical Education (NASPE), AAHPER National Convention, March 14, 1975, Atlantic City, New Jersey.

Rosenthal, R. The Pygmalion effect lives. *Psychology Today,* 1973, 7(Sept.), 56-63.

Sutton-Smith, B. *Child psychology.* New York: Appleton-Century-Crofts, 1973.

Sharing Your Impressions

1. Recall how your parents reacted to your wins and losses in youth sports.
2. Explain your preference between having a child play seldom as a member of a winning team and having the child play often on a team that usually loses.
3. Compare the benefits of winning and losing in sports.
4. What did the coaches you had as a child do to promote moral development?
5. How can coaches and parents determine whether a child is experiencing too much stress?
6. Describe the qualities of an ideal coach of children's sports.
7. React to the familiar assumption that "sports build character."
8. How do you react to the umpire's decisions when they are unfavorable to your child's team?

Chapter 8

Places to Play

21

Making Playgrounds Safe for Children and Children Safe for Playgrounds

Joe L. Frost and Michael L. Henniger

Children's outdoor play spaces are in a state of transition. Exciting environments are being developed to replace the traditional concrete and asphalt-paved playgrounds equipped with jungle gyms, merry-go-rounds, swings, and slides. An example of such an environment is the *creative playground* (Frost 1978; Frost and Klein, forthcoming). This type of play space is constructed creatively from existing commercial equipment, a few purchased materials, and a wide variety of donated "junk" materials such as old tires, utility poles, railroad ties, and cable spools. It is often planned and constructed by parents, teachers, and children with the help of a playground specialist. Such an environment encourages a wide range of creative play from the children who use it.

A second example of an exciting play environment that is gaining popularity in this country is the *adventure playground*. Imported from European countries where it has been a huge success, the adventure playground is a highly informal play environment where tools, a wide range of scrap building materials, and modifiable climbing structures are provided for children to use in freely expressing themselves. In addition, the best adventure playgrounds in Europe accommodate a variety of farm animals and full-time adult play leaders to support and encourage children's play.

The American Adventure Play Association (Vance 1977) cited the following advantages for adventure playgrounds: (1) they are used by more children than conventional playgrounds; (2) they are maintained less expensively; and (3) the community participates more actively through donations. In addition, other sources indicate the adventure playground stimulates a wider variety of play (Frost and Campbell 1977), a broader range of language, and more originality in play themes (Hayward, Rothenburg, and Beasley 1974).

As these new types of playgrounds gain popularity in this country, concerns are frequently expressed about their safety. Can such play environments, constructed from junk and surplus materials by parents, teachers and children, be as functional and safe as the traditional commercially-equipped playgrounds? The data now available show that traditional playgrounds are unduly hazardous. Accidents and injuries are encouraged by slipshod equipment manufacturing, improper installation, and lack of maintenance.

Traditional American playgrounds are also inappropriate for the wide range of developmental play needs of children. Our personal observations and those of playground colleagues in North America and Europe make it clear that many American children are unsafe for any playground because they spend too little time on playgrounds of sufficient challenge and variety to allow optimal development of perceptual-motor skills.

Playground Hazards

What kinds of hazards exist on typical American playgrounds? (See Vernon 1976; Wilkinson and Lockhart 1976; National Recreation and Park Association 1975; McConnell, Parks, and Knapp 1973; Bureau of Product Safety 1972.) The most serious hazard is the *surface* under and around children's play equipment. Hard-packed earth, rocks, asphalt, and concrete are commonly found beneath swings, slides, and climbing structures. Children falling from equipment onto this type of ground cover can receive bruises, sprains, broken bones, concussions, or even a fatal injury.

Exposed bolts, sharp or rough edges, and protruding corners on outdoor equipment are a second common source of injuries. Cuts and scrapes, many of which require more than just a bandage to repair, are a frequent result. The *openings and angles* found on certain pieces of equipment present another hazard for children playing outdoors. Some of these openings allow children to get their fingers, hands, feet, or heads trapped in the equipment. In addition to the discomfort and fear of being unable to move a limb, serious injuries can result from such entrapments.

Improper installation and infrequent maintenance of playground equipment create additional hazards for children. Installation of equipment with inadequate footings, weak braces, and minimal surrounding play space can lead to a variety of unnecessary injuries. Without periodic examination and maintenance of moving parts, bolts, screws, ropes, paint, wood, and metal, other potential hazards gradually develop.

A less obvious but potentially dangerous situation is created on many playgrounds when the available equipment is *inappropriate for the developmental levels of the children* using it. A frequent problem arises when kindergarten and preschool children are enrolled in schools where the play equipment is designed for older children. Another serious problem exists when children have thoroughly mastered all of the equipment available to them. It is then that they begin experimenting and using the equipment in ways for which it was never designed. The risk of injury in such situations increases markedly.

Hazards such as these can be dramatically reduced. They are not an inherent part of any playground and should never be used as an excuse for avoiding the outdoor environment or for not providing a challenging playground. With careful planning, the hazards described can be reduced far below their present intolerable levels as evidenced by statistics on the extent and seriousness of playground injuries.

Playground Injuries

Although data on playground injuries are incomplete, British researchers (International Playground Association 1977) have estimated that as many as 150,000 children a year are treated by doctors and hospitals for playground-related accidents in their country. These researchers indicated that the leading cause of injuries was the surface onto which a child fell.

The Consumer Product Safety Commission (CPSC 1975) has reported playground injuries in the United States. The National Electronic Injury Surveillance System (NEISS 1977) data, taken from a statistically selected sample of hospital emergency rooms, revealed that an estimated 118,000 playground-related injuries were incurred during 1974. Seventy-eight percent of the injured children were under ten years of age. The injuries, reported in rank order, included lacerations, contusions, abrasions, fractures, strains/sprains, concussions, and hematomas. Twenty-four death certificates were issued from July 1973 to October 1974 for fatal injuries related to playground equipment. Thirteen of the injured chidren were between the ages of five and nine.

More recent statistics from the Consumer Product Safety Commission (Desbordes 1976) indicate that an estimated 125,000 playground-related injuries occurred during 1975. During the twelve-month period ending November 1977, an estimated 150,773 injuries related to swings, slides, seesaws, and climbing apparatus resulted in emergency room treatment in the United States (NEISS 1977). An in-depth analysis of these statistics has yet to be completed.

The Consumer Product Safety Commission (1975) also analyzed the causes of playground injuries and deaths. As in England, falling from a piece of equipment was found to be the leading cause of accidents. Other major causes, listed in rank order, included being struck by a moving piece of equipment, entrapment of an extremity, and contact with rough edges and protruding bolts. The leading cause of deaths on public playgrounds was falling onto hard surfaces; hanging was the leading cause of home playground deaths.

The statistical analyses to date have many shortcomings. One is the lack of any serious attempt to compare the number and severity of injuries on different types of playgrounds. Because of the commonly held belief that the more creative, stimulating play environments such as adventure playgrounds are more dangerous than traditional playgrounds, this is an important area for research. Several informal investigations indicate that such environments are no more dangerous than traditional playgrounds (Nicholson 1974; Vance 1977). The American Adventure Play Association (Vance 1977) received complete information from fourteen agencies with adventure playgrounds in five states. The number of injuries was "about the same" or "fewer" than at conventional playgrounds. Officials in the Swedish Playground Society, the Scandinavian Playground Council, and the London Adventure Playground Association have reported to us that no injury resulting in permanent impairment or death has been reported on any of their adventure playgrounds.

Standards for Playground Safety

Steps are being taken to improve the safety of children's playgrounds. At least one country (Swedish Council for Children's Play 1976) has established a set of safety standards for the installation and maintenance of playground equipment, while England, Canada, and the United States appear to be moving in a similar direction.

Presently, there are no mandatory standards for the manufacture of playground equipment in the United States. At least two manufacturers (Miracle and Game Time) are operating under a set of voluntary standards developed by industry in conjunction with the Consumer Product Safety Commission (1973). Despite many limitations, these standards laid the foundation for a more comprehensive set of proposed standards developed by the National Recreation and Park Association (1976), under an agreement with the CPSC. The major thrusts of these standards are as follows:

1. Equipment designed for a specific age group shall be so labeled, and it shall be designed with an understanding of developmental characteristics of that specific age group.

2. The materials used in constructing playground equipment shall be durable, structurally sound, and stable following assembly and

installation, and shall be assembled using connecting and covering devices (bolts, hooks, rings, etc.) that shall not open during specified tests.

Suggested PLayground Equipment Maintenance Safety Checklist

Item	Look For . . .
Structure	Bending, warping, cracking, loosening, breaking, etc.
Surface finish	No protective coating, rust, other corrosion, cracks, splinters, harmful preservatives or paint, etc.
Hardware	Missing, bent, broken, loosened, open hooks, etc.
Edges	Sharp points or edges, protruding bolts, or other protrusions, etc.
Pinch or Crush Points	Exposed mechanisms, junctures of moving components, etc.
Mechanical Devices and Other Moving Parts	Worn bearings, lubrication needed, missing protective covers, etc.
Guard or Hand Rails	Missing, bent, broken, loosened, etc.
Ladders and Steps	Missing rungs or steps, broken, loosened, etc.
Swing seats	Missing, damaged, loosened, sharp corners, etc.
Footings	Exposed, cracked, loose in ground, etc.
Protective Surfacing under Equipment	Compacted, displaced to ineffective level, does not extend to potential impact area, unsanitary, poor drainage, etc.

Reprinted, by permission, from *Proposed Safety Standards for Public Playground Equipment* by the National Recreation and Park Association.

3. Equipment shall be free of sharp edges, dangerous protrusions (including exposed ends of bolts), points where children's extremities could be pinched or crushed, and openings or angles that could trap part of the child's body.

4. Moving equipment such as swings and merry-go-rounds shall not exceed certain impact and velocity limits described in the standards.

5. Falls from equipment will be controlled by increasing the degree of enclosure of the surface as the height of the structure increases (4 to 8 feet: railings; 8 to 12 feet: protective barrier; over 12 feet: totally enclosed).

6. Slide exits and inclines, side protection on the slide surface, ladder and stairway inclines, and slide heights will be regulated by the standards.

7. A statement recommending appropriate surfacing materials must be included in all equipment catalogs and with all installation instructions for new equipment.

8. Manufacturers will be required to furnish complete instructions for the installation and maintenance of the equipment they sell. These instructions shall include a facsimile of the checklist in the table.

9. Recommended minimum space requirements for varying pieces of equipment are outlined in the standards.

Making Children Safe for Playgrounds

It is neither possible nor desirable to create a totally safe playground. Children would find such an environment sterile and uninviting. Challenging tasks that require some degree of risk-taking are an important ingredient of children's play. We can, however, eliminate the unnecessary hazards on playgrounds and help prepare children to deal sensibly and safely with the challenges the outdoor environment provides.

What can be done to "make children safe" for the playgrounds on which they play? One important step is to teach children the proper and safe uses of the playground equipment available to them. There is a reciprocal relationship between the amount of preparation children receive in using playgrounds and the amount of playground protection necessary for safe use (Wilkinson and Lockhart 1976). As the preparation for safety increases, the necessity for protection decreases.

Teachers can take an active role in understanding and facilitating children's outdoor play. Skillful, sensitive adults make a difference in the safe play of children. They can provide the following support to help children develop important skills for safe outdoor play:

Cooperative planning. Discussions of playground safety during group time are effective ways for children to identify safety needs for themselves. Important ideas and insights can be gathered from the children, and a workable list of "Safety Hints for the Playground" can be developed. Such activity also contributes to language, reading, evaluation, and decision making.

Adult-child interaction. Adults must take an active role if children are to be made safe for playgrounds. The time spent outdoors cannot be considered a break time for teachers, but rather a new and exciting setting for stimulating children's learning and development. The kinds of direction and guidance traditionally given children indoors are often appropriate outdoors as well. Adult-child interaction should take place naturally and informally as children move about the playground and engage in the play of their choice. Through informal comments and modeling by a teacher or child, the safe use of equipment can be demonstrated. Stopping a child momentarily to discuss a better way to climb the steps to the slide or the problems of running too near the swings is usually all that is needed to shape safe behavior.

Capabilities and limitations. Another aspect of making children safe for the playground is to help them realize their own capabilities and limitations. For many young children, the preschool setting is their first extended exposure to the equipment found on playgrounds. They need adult guidance in determining their own levels of competence. Words of encouragement and praise along with comfort and support when needed can help children strengthen knowledge of their own capabilities.

Challenge and interest. A wide array of challenges provides needed diversity on playgrounds and encourages safe play outdoors. A stimulating mix of different kinds of equipment is needed to keep children's interests high and to help prevent misuse of equipment. Using a basic concept from adventure playgrounds, children should have boards, sawhorses, cable spools, old tires, boxes, blocks, lumber, ladders, and so on to build creatively the structures needed in their play.

Developmental needs. Providing an outdoor play environment with equipment designed for use at increasing levels of complexity also makes good sense. We are constantly reminded that children vary in their levels of development. In terms of outdoor play, this means that children will have different climbing abilities, running skills, balancing skills, coordination, and strength. The play environment then is equipped and arranged to present graduated challenges appropriate to the skills of all children playing there. In addition, the equipment should be sufficiently varied to allow children to engage in all of the cognitive forms of play (exercise, dramatic, construction, and games with rules), to develop social skills through interaction with peers, and to allow for quiet solitude and reflection.

Time to play. Providing the finest play environment is of no consequence unless children are allowed time to play there. Extraordinary perceptual-motor skills are exhibited by children on some of the finest adventure playgrounds of Europe and the United States. On these sites children spend up to four hours per day in environments rich in challenge, complexity, and variety. Full-time play leaders, animals, and gardening further enrich experiences.

Wise teachers view the outdoor environment as a natural extension of the indoor environment. Each of these environments provides for unique experiences not readily available in the other. Indoor space tends to restrict noise, movement, and types of equipment, while the outdoor environment allows almost unlimited sound and movement and greater freedom with raw materials such as water, dirt, construction materials, and large play structures. Consequently, the types of play occurring in the outdoor environment are significantly different from those types occurring indoors (Henniger 1977). Both spaces are needed for a complete play/learning environment.

Summary and Conclusions

Conventional American playgrounds are hazardous and ill-suited for the developmental needs of children. Such play environments are now being rebuilt or replaced by more exciting creative or adventure playgrounds.

Many serious and fatal injuries on playgrounds can be eliminated by attention to two major factors: (1) reducing or eliminating hazards such as hard fall surfaces and poorly manufactured, installed, and maintained equipment, and (2) assisting children in learning to play safely.

Standards for the manufacture of play equipment are now being developed, but the major responsibility for safety lies with adults who work daily with children. Adults' roles are varied and complex, ranging from informal personal interaction with children to assistance in the design and use of exciting, varied, challenging play environments.

There is little argument that playgrounds created by adults and children working together are more stimulating and developmentally appropriate than conventional ones. The claim that creative or adventure playgrounds are more hazardous than conventional playgrounds is unsubstantiated.

References

Bureau of Product Safety. *Public Playground Equipment.* Washington, D.C.: Food and Drug Administration, September 12, 1972.

Consumer Product Safety Commission. *Hazard Analysis—Playground Equipment.* Washington, D.C.: Consumer Product Safety Commission, 1975.

Consumer Product Safety Commission. *Proposed Technical Requirements for Heavy Duty Playground Equipment Regulations.* Washington, D.C.: Consumer Product Safety Commission, 1973.

Desbordes, L. G., 1976: personal communication.

Frost, J. L. "The American Playground Movement." *Childhood Education* 54, no. 4 (1978): 176-182.

Frost, J. L., and Campbell, S. D. "Play and Equipment Choices of Conserving and Preconserving Children on Two Types of Playgrounds." Unpublished paper, The University of Texas at Austin, 1977.

Frost, J. L., and Klein, B. L. *Children's Play and Playgrounds.* Boston: Allyn and Bacon, forthcoming.

Hayward, D.; Rothenburg, M.; and Beasley, R. "Children's Play and Urban Playground Environments: A Comparison of Traditional, Contemporary and Adventure Playground Types." *Environment and Behavior* 6, no. 2 (1974): 131-168.

Henniger, M. L. "Free Play Behaviors of Nursery School Children in an Indoor and Outdoor Environment." Doctoral dissertation, The University of Texas at Austin, 1977.

International Playground Association. "Children's Playgrounds." *Newsletter* 6 (1977): 8-12.

McConnell, W. H.; Parks, J. T.; and Knapp, L. W. *Public Playground Equipment.* Iowa City: University of Iowa, College of Medicine, 1973.

National Electronic Injury Surveillance System (NEISS). *NEISS Data Highlights* 5, no. 1 (1977).

National Recreation and Park Association. *Proposed Safety Standards for Public Playground Equipment.* Arlington, Va: National Recreation and Park Association, 1976.

National Recreation and Park Association. "Summary of In-Depth Accident Studies Received from 1/9/74 to 6/17/75." Arlington, Va.: National Recreation and Park Association, 1975. Mimeographed.

Nicholson, M. *Adventure Playgrounds.* London: The National Playing Fields Association, 1974.

Swedish Council on Children's Play. *Annual Report.* Stockholm: Swedish Council on Children's Play, 1975-76.

Vance, B. "The President's Message." *American Adventure Play Association News* 1, no. 4 (Fall 1977): 1.

Vernon, E. A. "A Survey of Preprimary and Primary Outdoor Learning Centers/Playgrounds in Texas Public Schools." Doctoral dissertation, The University of Texas at Austin, 1976.

Wilkinson, P. F., and Lockhart, R. *Safety in Children's Formal Play Environments.* Ontario, Canada: Ontario Ministry of Culture and Recreation, 1976.

Sharing Your Impressions

1. Recall the safety problems you've seen at public playgrounds.
2. Suggest some rules for children's playground behavior.
3. How would you train parents to serve as aides on the school playground?
4. Make some guesses about why Adventure Playgrounds have not become popular in the United States.
5. Compare the relative safety conditions for children on a creative playground, Adventure Playground, and traditional playground.
6. How does the playground equipment your child uses compare with the equipment you played on?
7. Invent a better role for teachers assigned to recess duty on the school playground.
8. What things do you recall handicapped children doing at community and school playgrounds?

22

Playground Design with a Motive in Mind

Albert J. Rutledge

As if to outflavor Howard Johnson's, the list of playground structures has grown seemingly endless: animal figures, sculptures, space rockets, pirate lairs, and Lincoln log modules now stand beside the more traditional slides, swings and seesaws. A question necessarily arises: Which of these structures are the best?

Park and recreation planners in search of the answer might first ponder a more overriding query: Why do children play? Thoughts on that question guided the selection process in prior times, when it was supposed that kids played in order to burn up surplus energy. "Play needs" were equated with a number of motor exercises, and the playground was envisioned as a place where children could go to slide, swing, climb, jump, and otherwise acceptably purge the ferment from their systems. The common playground piece emerged as a contrivance which could accommodate one basic exercise; the "traditional playground" became an assortment of these one-dimensional contrivances distributed about in isolation from one another.

From *Parks and Recreation*, February 1975, *10*, 20-22, 43-44. Copyright 1975 by the National Recreation and Park Association. Reprinted by permission.

Research shows that the typical child uses these traditional playgrounds on an average of about 15 minutes at a time and plays on each structure for fractionally less time. It could be argued that such brief encounters are all that is necessary to spend the energy that bubbles within the typical healthy child. On the other hand, the brevity of play could just as well bear witness to youngsters' boredom with the stuff. A recent theory on the nature of play advanced by psychologist Michael Ellis makes the latter explanation seem more likely.

Ellis theorizes that play is an *arousal-seeking behavior* and that *children play for the stimulation they receive,* not just to burn up energy. Nor, apparently, do they play to become physically fit, socially skilled, conceptually aware, or historically attuned, however coincidentally those objectives might be achieved and no matter how advisable their pursuit might seem in the eyes of adults. Play is, then, an end in itself.

Ellis suggests that in order for the playground to be a stimulating environment, it should be capable of "eliciting new responses from the child as he plays and that these responses should increase in complexity as play proceeds."

It is the lack of complexity—the inability of an apparatus to offer something of an order beyond its most obvious, basic functions—which is the primary deficiency of the traditional slide, swing, and seesaw. The same relative simplicity of components and general layout casts suspicion upon a host of contemporary alternatives to the traditional equipment, including cutesy cartoon characters, intellectualized abstract forms, romanticized Dodge City streetscapes, and even many of the packages available from our friendly hewn timber people.

Choosing Structures

Which structure is better than another? Ellis advises that when faced with a choice of play pieces or layouts, planners should select that which (1) allows the child to manipulate it in the greatest variety of ways; (2) allows for the most cooperation between children (other kids being a great source of stimulation); and (3) inhibits the child the least.

These are the guidelines which have been put to work in a number of playgrounds designed and built by students and faculty in the Department of Landscape Architecture at the University of Illinois in Champaign-Urbana. The criteria have also been expanded by department researchers to adapt to their observations on what seem to be the normal habits of children at play. For example, observations of children darting about playgrounds indicated that play is an impulsive activity, quite frequently occurring in random patterns. So it was theorized that play pieces should be woven into *systems* as opposed to the still most popular fashion of spotting structures about hither and yon.

Linkages with systems provide "complexity as play proceeds" by maximizing the number and variety of play circuits. In addition, a system can be constructed to stimulate children even as their capabilities change over time: sliding poles can be made mountable from varying heights, for example, and bridges—which can be traversed, jumped, or dangled from—made approachable from a ramp, by hopping from brace to brace, or by pulling a rope. Even elements usually looked upon as merely structural can be part of the system: struts can be notched for climbing, cross pieces broadened for "fence walking," and wall members caused to alternatively rise and fall for giant stepping.

Kids Like Cubbyholes

University researchers also observed that children are attracted to enclosed spaces, their play more likely than not proceeding in places unintended for their presence—under a slide, an arching shrub border, or even a bench reserved for adults. Through a jog here, a recess there, and varying platform levels, enclosures can be incorporated into a system and can then serve as role-game features (a jail, a house, or boat) or secure territories for sedentary play (sand piling), socializing, respite, or whatever else whimsey might suggest.

Through such use combinations, opportunities for play invention are enhanced. It is no secret that children see possibilities in things other than what adults might expect or intend them to see. Also, multiuse units enable the accommodation of a small army of kids in a relatively small amount of space.

What are the reactions of the users, the kids themselves? Hours of observations have attested to the popularity of the systems built at the University of Illinois. A comparative investigation was conducted over a number of weeks, minimizing the influence of mere novelty. Scores of third-graders were taken to two playgrounds, both similar in size and number of structures, yet differing in that one was a "complex" system and the other a "simple" assortment of typical swings, slides, spring horses, and roundabouts. The kids were asked to express their preferences on the entire site, individual structures, and the kinds of play allowed. The results were compared against time-lapse movie coverage of the play. Preference expressions and actual usage coincided—the complex playground was overwhelmingly favored.

Conclusions

The structures described here are not perfect; nor is a play system the only vehicle for stimulating children at play. No design is without flaws or room for improvement. Indeed, the development of totally new concepts of equal or more value is infinitely possible, especially those which would provide for a higher degree of manipulation. Developing such concepts is no mean task. For unlike the liberties which supervision affords the "adventure playground" of loose scrap materials, the ungoverned nature of open public play sites demands structural soundness.

Absolutes, therefore, remain to be discovered. In the meantime, an application of the Ellis guidelines embellished by observations of children at play can go a long way towards helping planners decide which playground structures will best suit their needs.

Sharing Your Impressions

1. Describe the type of playground you would prefer for your child.
2. Why do you suppose there isn't greater use of the playground space and equipment in urban parks?
3. Speculate about the relationship between playground design and vandalism of playgrounds.
4. How do you feel about the play space currently available to your child?
5. Compare the benefits of a complex system playground with those of a simple playground.
6. Suggest some guidelines for choosing public playground equipment.
7. Recall the places you most enjoyed playing as a child.
8. In what ways is your local parks and recreation department responding to the play needs of handicapped children and adults?

23

Loose on the Playground

Richard Louv

A kid named Stuart crawled into a cardboard barrel, cushioned himself carefully with pillows and styrofoam and rolled down a steep hill until he crashed into a jumble of old tires. He staggered out of

From *Human Behavior*, May 1978, 7(5), 18–21, 23–25. Copyright © 1978 *Human Behavior* Magazine. Reprinted by permission.

the barrel and yelled, "That's radical!" Around him, a shantytown was rising like a Rube Goldberg pipedream. Multistoried forts were mushrooming from the packed clay; kids, like ants, were scrambling in and out of them, brandishing hammers and saws. Close by, small dark objects that only vaguely resembled children were hurtling down a 30-foot mudslide. At the center of the commotion were two ponds surrounded by shrubs. On the bank of one of them, a boy sat quietly fishing; at the other pond, kids had labored for weeks to sink enough tires under the surface to build an underwater bridge. The sole purpose of their effort was to fool adults who lived in the houses up on the ridge: when the kids crossed the pond atop their underwater bridge, it looked like they were walking on water.

If these escapades sound as if they've been lifted from the adventures of Tom Sawyer and Huck Finn, they are the more remarkable for having transpired on playgrounds in upper-middle-class suburbs. These are no ordinary playgrounds, with obligatory metal-frame swing-and-slide sets. They are "adventure playgrounds" that invite children to build forts out of donated scrap lumber; string up rope swings; and construct mud slides, tunnels, lakes, dams and rafts. Supervision is limited to one play leader, who guards rather than leads the children. The kids are encouraged to create and destroy their own play areas.

The theory is that children, more than adults, know what type of play children like best. Adventure playgrounds are proposed as an antidote to TV and the vanishing of open space in urban areas. The proponents warn that the present generation of children cannot cope with schoolwork without a high degree of supervision; that their creativity and self-reliance are being blunted; and that they are always waiting for someone in authority to point the way. Adventure playgrounds have sprung up in 18 cities, from Los Angeles to Minneapolis. Where they are presented as clear alternatives to traditional playgrounds or neighborhood parks, adventure playgrounds are drawing enthusiastic crowds of children who usually have chosen the street over traditional play areas.

"Playgrounds in the United States died about 1940," one recreation and leisure studies professor claimed recently. "We just haven't gotten around to burying them yet." Plenty of evidence is around to back up that contention. Seymour M. Gold, professor of environmental planning at the University of California at Davis and one of the nation's leading experts on park usage, has been writing recently in professional journals about a newly detected phenomenon: the nonuse of urban parks. Gold writes, "In a projected era of scarce resources and competing needs for public programs, the survival of many urban park systems is at stake. . . . Some observers have already predicted the demise of these systems because they do not serve the needs of people."

The essential assumptions on which park planners have relied are now up for grabs: Dianna Dunn, professor and coordinator of the University of Arizona's recreation department, says, "At this point in time we can't document that urban parks and recreation areas contribute *anything* to the quality of urban life. That doesn't mean parks are a total failure, but if a billion dollars were dropped on Phoenix today, earmarked for recreation, we simply wouldn't know how to spend it, if improving the quality of life was our objective. People in our profession are painfully aware of this, and they're worried."

The picture Gold paints of urban parks is essentially an empty canvas. He and other professionals describe thousands of flat, joyless parks shunned by children in favor of the street or the natural areas that have thus far escaped the bulldozer. As for traditional playground equipment—such as slides, swing sets and cement turtles—most recreation experts agree that children tend to use the equipment a few times, then grow bored with it. Clare Cooper-Marcus, associate professor in the College of Environmental Design at the University of California, points out, "Once children have figured out the normal uses of play equipment, they start creating their own risks, like climbing up the slide, swinging on the poles, anything to break up the static nature of the apparatus."

By 1980, more than 70 percent of Americans will live in 125 metropolitan areas with populations of 250,000 or more. Gold predicts that a number of related social trends—including decreasing income levels, increasing unemployment and inflation—will "add to the demand for simple, low-cost activities close to home. Transportation problems are at the heart of the matter," says Gold. "Reduced speed limits, increasing traffic congestion, the termination of freeway construction programs, escalating gasoline costs and the threat of gasoline rationing will further discourage people from using regional and remote parks." The burden will be on neighborhood parks and playgrounds.

In the face of this forecast, there is a growing mood of excitement among recreation specialists and community activists who are seeking alternatives to the standard park and play areas. Gold calls this trend the "greening" of American play.

"The best playground is one designed by a child," asserts Larry Naake, executive director of the California Park and Recreation Society. "The next best playground is one designed by an adult, with the possibility for children to create their own areas within it." This approach, he reports, is gaining credibility. In much of the San Francisco Bay Area, neighbors and children build parks from scratch, using the donated talents of local architects, engineers and landscapers. "Citizens go out and work on their own neighborhood parks on weekends. They construct the parks from scratch with donated material. Vandalism has decreased significantly. The people who built the park are now its protectors; it's their turf." Nearly 40 such neighborhood parks have been developed in the Bay Area.

At least one school—Washington Elementary in Berkeley—has torn up half an acre of asphalt playground and replaced it with shrubs, boulders and places to dig and explore.

The majority of experiments are superficial, such as painting asphalt playgrounds bright colors or incorporating expensive wood structures. But the most radical alternative—the relatively inexpensive adventure playground—has been quietly spreading throughout the United States.

The adventure playground concept has been around for a long time. The first one was designed in Denmark in 1943 by landscape architect Prof. C. T. Sorensen, who observed that children were ignoring the standard playgrounds he had designed in Copenhagen. Instead, the children were playing in construction sites and junk yards; so Sorensen designed a "junk yard" playground. The idea quickly spread to Britain, where city blocks bombed during World War II were fenced off and given over to the children, who built up from the rubble. There are now more than 200 adventure playgrounds in Britain alone, and hundreds more throughout Europe.

The first U.S. adventure playground was constructed in Minneapolis in 1950, but it was not until Robin Moore, a student at MIT (now creator of the Washington School yard experiment), constructed an adventure playground for his master's thesis that the concept began to receive attention from recreation experts. During the last three years, though, the greatest American growth has occurred, especially as the proponents have learned to deal with the standard neighborhood objection to "unsightliness" by building high fences or berms around the play areas.

Of the 18 existing playgrounds, the most adventuresome is in Huntington Beach, California. Built on the site of an old quarry, it is a child's paradise, with a 30-foot mudslide; lakes for fishing and swimming; rope bridges spanning the water; and shacks, forts and treehouses. It frequently draws in excess of 500 children each day.

But the most revolutionary adventure playground thus far is in Irvine, California. Whereas other adventure playgrounds have been created in response to pressure from citizens' groups, the Irvine playground is the first to have been conceived, budgeted and built by a municipality as an integral part of the city's recreation plan.

According to Bill Vance, president of the American Adventure

Play Association, the Irvine project represents his association's dream: to create enough acceptance among municipal recreation officials that the adventure playgrounds become standard fare, just like baseball diamonds. An exmarine and a recreation instructor at California State University at Long Beach, Vance is an unlikely social revolutionary. But, to Vance, the Irvine precedent is a radical departure in a professional field known for stodginess and bureaucratic caution. Vance sees adventure playgrounds as important and inexpensive social programs that, if popularized, could help improve a host of problems: drugs, boredom, dependency, crime and the ennui of a generation alienated from woods and streams and weaned by television. "My vision is to have adventure playgrounds within reach of every urban child," says Vance. Can you imagine, he asks, any social program having the impact of adventure playgrounds, at the cost?

Steve Simms, in his early 20s, served as the play leader for the Huntington Beach adventure playground and now the one at Irvine. He is clearly a man who has found a mission. A majority of his leisure hours are spent driving through Irvine, hunting for scrap. "Sometimes I wear a suit when I'm out hunting; I go to lumber companies, building contractors and hardware stores to talk businesspeople into giving us donations. It's never a problem finding enough junk, but it's a constant effort, because the kids are always redeveloping their turf."

Every year, the youngsters are encouraged to destroy their forts; sometimes they'll develop ingenious demolition methods. "The telephone company donates giant wooden spools. The kids will roll those things up to the top of the hill and let them hurtle back down the incline and crash into the shacks; it's legitimate destruction, and it prepares them for Future Shock: what goes up must come down—creation begins again." One of the psychological twists Simms has discovered is that children lose interest if they have to rebuild the shacks with the same old junk; what they want is new junk. "The key factor in a successful program is to keep the junk moving. When I pull up in my truck with a load of new scrap, the kids swarm over the truck immediately. A lot of the kids who go nuts over junk are affluent kids, who have everything they want at home."

Often, the children are out scouting the neighborhood themselves. Does Simms ever receive "hot" lumber? "I never reveal my sources," he says and laughs.

Unlike most playgrounds, adventure playgrounds endure few expenses because of vandalism. Says Simms, "The kids grumble a bit, then rebuild." While most midwestern adventure playgrounds are open only in the summer, California's are open all year round. "Every morning," reports Simms, "the kids are at the gate waiting for me."

Sometimes he organizes overnight camping so the children can experience their forts after dark. Unlike the Boy or Girl Scouts, though, there is no effort to formalize the camping.

The typical response from adults who visit an adventure playground is one of surprise and delight. "We have a real problem," says Simms, "with adults who want to get in here and play and build things for the kids. We tell 'em to go build their own forts somewhere else." He points to a ladder that has parallel rungs. "See that? That was built by an adult. If a kid had built it, the rungs would have been crooked." It is precisely that crookedness that makes adventure playgrounds so visually stimulating. Some of the multileveled forts are 15 feet high with tubes through which to slide, tunnels from one compartment to another, ropes strung from one fort to another, across which children hurtle on makeshift tram cars. And everywhere are the signs: Keep Out; Josh Mullen's Junk Fort; No Girls; No Boys; This Unit For Lease; Darth Vader Lives; God Bless This Mess.

"We've documented that in British adventure playgrounds, signs aren't nearly as popular," says Vance. "Maybe this reflects the American penchant for rules."

Paul Burton, the adventure playground leader at Huntington Beach, tells a story about a boy nicknamed "Tiger," who responded in his own way to some local political friction regarding the adventure playground concept. "Tiger spent a whole day painting the words SAVE ARE FORT on every structure in the playground. On his own shack, he painted SAVE OUR FORT. When I asked him why he spelled the word *our* correctly, Tiger explained, "That's theirs. This is mine." Adds Burton, "It made perfect sense."

The play leaders agree that, while the children endure normal squabbles, the competitive fights are limited as long as there is enough junk to go around. "We try to stay out of the way as much as possible," says Simms. "Usually the kids find their own ways of dealing with the conflicts. I've had mothers bring their children to me and tell me, Steve, Johnny has a problem getting along with other kids; can you encourage him? But I don't have to do much in those situations. Sooner or later some other kid will pick up a heavy board, and suddenly Johnny is part of a group effort, to build—not to compete."

Possibly because the forts are torn down every year, territorial disputes are kept to a minimum. "At Huntington Beach's adventure playground," says Simms, "the high-rent district is lakefront property, and there's some competition for it. But some kids get sick of the urban blight, so they move out to the suburbs." Simms points to a pile of mud and sticks separated from the rest of the shacks. "Arnold moved out there. Worked fine until it rained."

The most important factor in keeping disputes to a minimum, though, is the constant creation of new distractions. Somebody always comes up with a new invention that grabs the others' imaginations.

Huntington Beach's most popular activity is the 30-foot mudslide. "We've never had a complaint from parents about dirty kids," Burton points out. "They come shrinkable and returnable. One woman drove up one day in her Mercedes and put three kids (covered completely with wet mud) in the back seat and drove off. We did get one complaint, from a charter bus company that was transporting kids in and had to put up with mud on the way back; so we started hosing the kids down before they went home."

Not all the activities are so messy. At one of the adventure playgrounds, the youngsters decided they wanted to know what time it was, so they built a sundial out of sticks and an old tire. "Told time fine," says Vance, "until Arnold Miller came along and kicked the tire."

Last Christmas, one child painted elaborate, beautifully intricate Christmas trees on the sides of forts. "If he'd done that on a conventional playground," says Vance, "it would have been considered graffiti."

The play leaders agree that, along with older children helping younger ones, children are basically self-regulating. The younger ones slide down those hills that they feel comfortable braving, while the older children take greater risks.

Risk, in fact, is the core of the issue, for both proponents and opponents of adventure playgrounds. "Fire is a good example," says Vance. "We encourage fire on adventure playgrounds—under supervision. We belive that kids are naturally fascinated with fire and should be exposed to it, safely, instead of out behind the garage. During the eight years we've encouraged fires, there has not been one serious fire-related injury. But when I make presentations to park or school administrators, the mention of fire will send them up the wall . . . or out of the room."

Vance believes that the greatest lessons come through taking risks, stretching physical or mental capabilities into unknown turf: "Billy Edwards, for instance, at age five, is one of our youngest participants at Huntington Beach. One day he caught a fish in one of the ponds; he was determined he was going to eat it. So he walked all the way home, trundled back with a huge frying pan and cooked his fish over an open fire. We all stood around watching him eat it. When he was done we asked, 'How was it?' 'Terrible,' he answered, 'but I sure am glad I done it.'"

The idea of loose nails, open fires, rope swings and heavy lumber sends many parents (and, to a greater extent, administrators) into nervous tremors. But adventure playground enthusiasts point to such sports as Little League baseball or Pop Warner football, in which kids are seriously injured every year. They also point to standard playground equipment that is inevitably adapted by the child to his or her need for risk.

While no serious injuries have resulted from adventure playgrounds, an abundance of minor wounds—especially puncture wounds—have. But play leaders have learned to adapt; at one adventure playground, children are required to collect three bent nails for each nail they receive. The practice has reduced the puncture rate by half. Regular inspection teams view each fort to ensure safety.

Still, liability is the greatest hindrance to adventure playgrounds, even though the Adventure Play Association's comparisons show about the same accident ratio as traditional parks. All but one of the existing adventure playgrounds are provided liability insurance protection by the municipalities' regular carriers, with no additional premiums. Even so, many cities continue to fear the liability problem. To avoid the skyrocketing cost of liability insurance, many municipalities have moved toward self-insurance. By using risk managers—city employees who make sure every city operation is as dangerfree as possible—the city is consequently able to drop liability insurance. As cities adopt self-insurance, some recreation experts fear the chances for adventure playgrounds and other experiments will be further limited.

One way around the liability problem is to encourage private entrepreneurs to pick up the insurance tab and the profits of an experimental program. Ironically, this technique has allowed a high-risk form of recreation to prosper; skateboard parks have started to multiply all over the country, and several of them enjoy municipal contracts. "Sadly, you could never find a private businessman who would invest in an adventure playground," says one park superintendent who tried and failed to establish an adventure playground. "There just wouldn't be any profit in it for him." So the liability system continues to encourage highly competitive, high-risk, highly structured recreation such as skateboard parks, but discourages noncompetitive, creative, low-profit, minimally supervised adventure playgrounds.

Carroll Berner, a San Diego real estate businessperson, was once one of the entrepreneurs pushing skateboard parks, but he dropped out of the race. "I started wondering how good these kinds of sports were for children. At a skateboard park a child is completely structured and is under constant surveillance." Berner wonders if the nature of this play is preparing children to accept constant surveillance as a fact of life.

"We need supervised play *and* the adventure playground concept. As a society, we've got to get back to the idea that each person has to assume some risk. When I was a child and had a problem, I had fields and woods where I could be alone and think. The kids on the block where I live today don't have that. The real tragedy is, I don't think they know what they're missing."

Some observers see this trend toward structured, competitive play as a nonconspirational "hidden agenda" of social control. It used to be, say the hidden agenda theorists, that accidental adventure playgrounds existed: vacant lots, woods, empty fields. But as the accidental playgrounds have disappeared, the effectiveness of mass behavior modification has increased proportionately.

One recent study created ripples of nervousness in recreation corners—and in the national press: Mary Duncan, an associate professor of recreation at California State University at San Diego, lived periodically for several months in the slums of Tijuana, Mexico. After observing Tijuana's children, who play in canyons filled with rubble, scrap lumber and sometimes raw sewage, Duncan concluded that the Mexican children played more creatively than did middle-class children in the United States. "Why was it," she asks, "that I had to journey to the poorest slums of Tijuana to rediscover children who, as a norm rather than as an exception, created their own play?"

Professionals such as Duncan project a subtly frightening future, based on their own view of disappearing free-spirited play and increased social control of play. Indeed, as children, most of the government officials and educators interviewed for this article ran and hid and dug and built in wild areas. It may be difficult for adults who enjoyed that kind of independence to understand an urban generation that has not.

Extensive research has suggested a strong connection between playfulness, creativity and mental health. Psychiatrist Erik Erikson, for instance, conducted a 30-year followup on his patients and determined that the people most happy were those who maintained a sense of playfulness at the center of their lives.

"If you project ahead a few years," says Duncan, "can you imagine a generation of adults who never learned to make their own choices regarding play, and to whom play means competition, following someone else's rules and having to fulfill society's expectations?"

Of course, one person's play is another's regimentation. The problem with all of this is the definition of play, which remains elusive. The supporters of adventure playgrounds define child's play as, roughly, lacking in adult-prescribed structure; fantasy making rather than fantasy feeding; and self-regulated risk taking. Another definition of play, though, assumes that it must prepare a child for the world by providing a laboratory for roles later assumed as adults, roles grounded in rationality. Monkey see, monkey do.

The adventure playground concept is rooted deep in the assumption, too, that the American child's play is becoming sterile. But Brian Sutton-Smith, professor of education, folklore and communication at the University of Pennsylvania, an internationally respected expert on children's play, does not accept the assumption. "True, TV, the disappearance of open space and the emphasis on organized sports have had an effect, but you have to consider the counterforces of increased permissiveness of make-believe in the home. You can't consider today's regimentation without looking at much more stringent methods of regimentation in the past." Sutton-Smith points to the proportionate decrease during the last few years in the sales of physical activity toys, such as tricycles, in favor of "symbolic activities" such as card games, strategy games and electronic manipulation games.

"I'm sympathetic to what Mary Duncan and the others are saying about the sterility of modern child's play," he says, "but I think it's a partial truth. True, there has been a reduction of experience of physical autonomy in natural environments, but you have to look at it historically. Children in the 19th century, whose main concern with the natural environment was to survive it, were not especially imaginative with it. Not until the 20th century was a generation caught between rural and urban areas but exposed to libraries and media. Only then did children become imaginative with the woods and streams."

Similarly, Sutton-Smith questions Duncan's views on the creativity of Tijuana slum kids compared to American children. "True, children there are more self-reliant and better with their hands. But you can't separate child's play from the adult society. Tijuana is an artisan society; the United States is technological." Sutton-Smith believes some of the proponents of adventure playgrounds may be stacking the apparent evidence in their favor, simply because "they're living out their own folklore of what childhood should be," even while childhood has already changed to fit modern society. Sutton-Smith alludes to several studies he says have shown an increasing difference of opinion *within families* as to what constitutes play. "In effect, there is *less* standardization because more activities now qualify as play."

"Still, we are all discontented with parks and playgrounds. I'd favor play centers which allow people-oriented play, like theater, painting, writing, instead of only the object-oriented adventure playgrounds. People are the best models for kids, not bits of wood." Sutton-Smith, despite his reservations, remains a solid supporter of adventure playgrounds. "Any improvement is welcome."

Whether fort building is out-of-fashion folklore is merely an academic question to Clare Cooper-Marcus, one of the staunchest supporters of adventure playgrounds: "I've been asking my students for years to recount their most important childhood memories; and almost without exception they remember forts as the most important element." One way Cooper-Marcus encourages park or school officials to consider adventure playgrounds, in fact, is to have them draw their own childhood environments. With few exceptions, the professionals draw forts and treehouses. And none of them draw parks or playgrounds.

"Even my students, though, future recreation officials who know in their hearts that this kind of play is needed by children, are increasingly concerned with the liability problems. Parenthetically, I think this has something to do with the different medical systems in the United States and Britain. In Britain, if a child breaks a leg, it doesn't cripple the family, due to socialized medicine," she adds.

Cooper-Marcus is also concerned that American adventure playgrounds have so far been enjoyed primarily by children who are white, upper-middle-class, suburban and male. Only 10 to 15 percent are girls, compared with the 50:50 girl-boy ratio at British adventure playgrounds. She attributes the American imbalance to a "more sexist society." And she proposes that more adventure playgrounds be introduced in low-income, highrise, inner-city regions. "Curiously, only one American adventure playground is in the inner city. The movement seems to be a WASP phenomenon, so far." (Vance reports considerable resistance in low-income areas: "Residents tell me what they want is the concrete turtles and the asphalt playgrounds; they've got enough shanties and trash already. They tell me to go back to suburbia, where kids are really needy.")

After writing about adventure playgrounds in professional journals for the last 10 years, Cooper-Marcus, a Britisher, is excited that the concept is finally catching on in America. "They definitely represent the most important playground innovation on the horizon, but it's disturbing to me that they're still on the horizon—40 years after they were accepted in Europe.

"We're all hungry for some unstructured play, though. Not far from my Berkeley office are the mud flats of Emeryville, where, for years, adults have been sneaking across a fence and sculpting magnificent structures out of driftwood and junk. Maybe we're all starting to realize that central heating and good schools aren't the only important priorities. The opportunities to be messy, creative, to build our dreams, are just as important. Whether we're adults or children."

The American fetish for order and cleanliness, though, is a high hurdle. Mary Duncan tells this story: "After a newspaper article had appeared regarding my work in Tijuana, I was talking with an associate of mine at her home. She was agreeing with me that children's play opportunities have become sterile. Then, in midsentence, she disappeared into the backyard, where she scolded her children for playing with a refrigerator packing crate. They were making a fort out of it."

Sharing Your Impressions

1. What qualities do you feel a play leader should have in order to function well in the Adventure Playground setting?
2. How do you suppose urban crowding can influence children's play?
3. What do you remember about the relationship between big and little kids on the playground when you were growing up?
4. Describe some ways an Adventure Playground can benefit handicapped children.
5. Outline the steps that would be necessary to get an Adventure Playground underway.
6. How do you feel about permitting children to have control over their play space?
7. In what ways does a play leader contribute to child development?

Chapter 9

Selection of Playthings

24

How to Choose Toys

T. Berry Brazelton

When the earliest crises of infancy are over—colicky crying, feeding difficulties and so on—parents of three- and four-month-old infants begin to worry about the kinds of toys they should be providing for their babies. One young woman whose husband is a struggling student put into words the thinking of many mothers of babies in this age group: "I realize that I should buy the newest and best toys to provide stimulation for my baby. I want to give him the best chance to learn how to play *early* so he'll be able to keep up with other children his age. We can't afford too many toys, but on the other hand, if it's worth it to push Grant's development, we certainly will find the money somewhere. Many of my friends already have bought educational toys, and I feel we should too, if as much research as they say has been put into them."

When I asked Mrs. Richards why she and her husband didn't make a cradle toy of squares of colored cardboard to string across Grant's crib so that he could learn to reach for them while he lay in his bed in the mornings, she said, "But my friends buy more complicated toys with many different sizes and shapes. If we just used squares, wouldn't Grant miss out on learning about other shapes?"

As Mrs. Richards talked I became pretty upset. My immediate reaction to her statement was anger at the pressure she felt to respond to the advertising of toy manufacturers. But as I began to think it over I realized that the manufacturers themselves were responding to a trend that society was creating.

The suggestion that there is a *need* for educational toys is coming from child experts. For a number of years psychologists have been pushing toward earlier cognitive, or intellectual, stimulation, and the implication has been that parents must provide their infants with toys that will "help them learn how to learn." Implicit in this kind of pressure is that children won't learn enough by themselves, that young parents today cannot offer enough stimulation for their tiny babies, that their affectionate play and caring do not provide children with enough necessary building blocks for the future. Implicit too is that parents must

From *Redbook Magazine,* November 1974, *144*(1), 29–30, 33. Reprinted by permission of the author.

be told by experts and toy manufacturers what their baby needs to draw her or him on from one stage of development to the next.

The competitive nature of our society puts added pressure on young parents. Not only do they feel they must keep up with everyone around them and with all the latest information in the field of child development, but also they feel that unless they do, their baby may lose a foothold in our society's competitive race.

Of course, I don't agree with this kind of thinking and I don't like the pressure it puts on parents. I am saddened to realize how undermined young mothers and fathers must feel who cannot trust their own instinctive reactions to playing with their baby and who feel they must be told how to teach a four-month-old to compete in our world. After talking with Mrs. Richards I had to realize that young parents today are getting a real brainwashing about the importance of early cognitive development.

Research has been widely quoted that seems to establish the importance of providing children with early cognitive stimulation. But this research has been done with groups of really deprived children. For the most part these children were in institutions that were unable to provide the person-to-person contact they needed. And even when parents were available, they often were too deprived and disorganized themselves to be able to see the needs of their babies, too desolate to provide even simple homemade toys.

When researchers came into such environments to carry out their studies, the effect of their efforts was to organize the disorganization, to fill the emptiness. As a result of the caring attitudes brought by the researchers, as much as because of the toys they offered, the environment could provide a new kind of responsiveness that filled the children's desperate need. It's no wonder that they thrived!

But the conditions of deprivation that were improved by toys and stimulation were not present in Grant's case. His family cared about him, played with him and provided him with all he needed, both emotionally and cognitively. Certainly he didn't need complex toys to supplement any deficiency. And I felt that Mrs. Richards would be wasting her money and devaluing her own good parenting by thinking she ought to provide them.

What little extra stimulation Grant might have used certainly could be provided by a set of multicolored cardboard squares! And the main thing the simple homemade toy would represent was a chance to play alone when his parents, who cared a lot and were available to him most of his day, needed time to themselves. He could learn to master his own new skills and to feel the excitement of self-mastery—a feeling that is the base of all learning. What kind of toy he learns this from may be of relatively little importance in an environment that offers as much as Grant's does in care and affection.

Through play, children learn about themselves as well as about the world around them. They may learn about their intellectual competence in one kind of play, about their emotional competence in another and about motor skills in another—or they may combine all three kinds of learning in one afternoon of play. But the seriousness of the goal—learning about oneself and how to grow up in an adult world—certainly cannot be ignored.

As two children play beside each other they learn how a peer sees other men and women of the culture. They imitate one parent and discard parts of his behavior, and then imitate the other and decide *in play* what aspects of each parent they want as a permanent part of their own personality. Their peers are a good testing ground for the new behaviors before they are fully accepted. As the play becomes more involved and the children begin to act out more-aggressive behavior, it is easy to see that this kind of role playing and testing of self is serious business.

One of my colleagues, Daniel G. Freedman, at the University of Chicago, demonstrated the serious aspect of play with little boys. After being introduced to my four-year-old and his friend of the same age he asked, "Which of you is stronger?" Both children replied simultaneously, "I am," and locked in each other's arms to prove it. When neither prevailed they began to climb high on the jungle gym and then to run up and down the street, each in an effort to outdo the other. Finally exhausted, they came back to us, having worn themselves out trying to answer the question.

If one accepts learning about oneself and about the world as a goal for play, what role do toys serve? Wouldn't children learn more about themselves if they had to make their own toys? Certainly the ingenuity of a child's imagination is demonstrated even when adults don't provide toys. Babies left in a cradle under a tree will reach up for leaves to bat at with clumsy fists. They will watch a bee buzz around the cradle when no mobile has been offered.

In one of the less affluent societies I have visited, where no ready-made toys were available, I remember watching a group of three-year-old children play with the substitutes they themselves had constructed. A forked stick holding a smaller stick became a mother and baby and a tall stick represented the father.

Certainly it seems to me that when children make their own toys, or when parents help their children do so, it always produces the most gratifying results. Still, Elaine Gurion, who teaches mothers how to make ingenious toys from recycled materials at the Boston Children's Museum, has told me that she finds painfully few mothers who dare compare their homemade efforts to manufactured toys. If this is true, we certainly are not fostering one of the most valuable aspects of toys for small children—that they can represent a form of communication. Toys that are made by parents immediately become invested with all the magic that parents have to offer their children.

This is not to say that commercial toys have no value—they certainly do! First of all, many of them can offer a child a kind of excitement and complexity that homemade toys sometimes cannot. And then, of course, most of them have been designed according to rigid standards of safety.

At the same time, in a society as complex as ours commercial toys can become important adjuncts for learning. And most important, they may serve a major role in providing and reinforcing communication with others—peers, siblings and parents. This role is a valuable one, and one with which we can afford to be honestly concerned.

For example, many toys have labels and instruction booklets that tell parents how to play with the child with the toy. This may sound pretty condescending, yet as a distractible father I have experienced the value of an instruction booklet that came with a racing toy. The booklet described ways to race the toy, from which I could find enough complexity to satisfy me, and yet there was enough simplicity in its wording to give my children an understanding of how to "gang up on and beat Daddy." We relied on its instructions as ways of testing each other, of conquering our internal struggles as a family, of stirring up new roles for and new competition with each other, of having fun with each other at many levels.

I do not feel that labels or instructions are a substitute for interpersonal exploration. But I can see that a busy parent may want them to help him decide which toy will reward him and his small child simultaneously, so that the result of a period of play together will be one of communicating with and learning about the other.

I would hope that toys would increase the chances for periods of play—however short—between a busy parent and his parent-hungry child. Too many of us feel guilty that we haven't time for our children—when it may not be quantity, but quality, of time with them that we have as a goal. Can toys make such bridges for us? If they can, they are worth the effort for all of us.

One young father expressed his own involvement in an "educational toy" that was accompanied by a brochure explaining the stage of development of his year-old baby. He said, "Janet may not be learning much by stacking those colored blocks on top of one another in the right sequence, but I am. When I see her pick up one, compare it to another and discard it for the next one in sequence, I get a real charge! I feel like I've created a genius and that she's learning by herself all the things I'd like to be able to teach her. And I've done it! I could sit and watch her by the hour."

I asked him how much the brochure had added to this pleasure. He replied that probably he never would have known how to look at his baby's play or what to see without these guidelines on her stage of development.

I'm not sure I agree with this father's estimate of the brochure's importance, and I have seen parents overuse the knowledge they have gained from such things in an effort to push the child's development along, but I am sure that the cementing of the parent-child relationship is the most important ingredient in this episode. How much cement the toy manufacturer has provided may be open to question, but the fact that such a potential exists is indisputable.

But there are other issues that are not really so clear. For example, can toys be so rigidly structured with advice and labels that they are no longer any fun? If labels tell children what to expect, and parents buy them for their "fit" with the child's stage of development and temperament, couldn't we inadvertently be cutting out the factor of surprise and exploration and creating a dullness that might lead to boredom? Couldn't we thereby be encouraging parents to believe that such products offered enough stimulation, and thus to abdicate their roles in play with their babies? Couldn't toys in our culture become substitutes for play with people?

How do we see to it that the toy manufacturers and child experts do not intimidate mothers and fathers so that they buy expensive and unnecessary products, and how do we at the same time reinforce parents' natural authority in filling their children's needs?

The manufacturers are spending vast sums on good research, but paradoxically this laudable effort, whose end is, of course, business success, is not all that is required. It seems to me that some kind of multidisciplinary advisory group ought to be formed so that there can be more formal communication between the manufacturers and the psychologists, pediatricians, government representatives and consumer advocates. The knowledge about toys and their influence on children's development that could be assimilated in this way might be extremely important.

I think the most important goal of the toy manufacturers, of the parental groups and of the professionals who might become interested in this venture would be to encourage parents to use toys to have more fun with their children. I am all for that!

Sharing Your Impressions

1. Describe how the pressures for early educational development have influenced children's play.
2. Suggest some ways in which toy manufacturers could help parents and children benefit more from play.
3. How do you feel about the advertising of toys on television?
4. Why do you suppose some toys appeal to children for a long while, and others do not?
5. What sources of guidance can parents turn to when choosing playthings?
6. Recall some of your favorite play activities as a child and as a teenager.
7. How do you decide what toys or games to buy for your children?

25

Toys That Reach and Teach Kids of All Ages

Brian Sutton-Smith

Imagine growing up without toys. Surely, if there were none they would have to be invented, which, of course, is how toys first came into being. Fashioned to represent miniature replicas of objects or people in the grown-up's world, toys have provided children in all societies with the means of learning about the world and preparing themselves, through play, to function in adult roles later on in life.

Toys give a child the experience of mastery and help him to learn new responses, and thus to grow. I base this belief on findings in play therapy over many years, and also on several recent experimental studies, which demonstrate that children who are shown how to play in make-believe ways subsequently do better on creativity tests than children who have not had the same training.

If we apply these principles to toys, we would expect that the first thing that happens when a child receives a toy is that he explores it and finds out what he can do with it. All this is very serious work for him. It's the same thing you and I do when we get a new "toy" for the first time—say, a pair of skis, a new piano, or electric saw. Our first activities are always mastery activities—that is, we find out how to use the new object. Later, when we are fully familiar with the devices, we begin

From *Parents Magazine,* June 1975, *50*(6), 30, 31, 62. Copyright © 1975 Parents Magazine Enterprises. Reprinted from *Parents* by permission and by permission of the author.

to impose our desires on them, to make them do what we want them to do. In other words, we try out novel responses with our new "toys." And that is the second thing a child does, too. He puts his own ideas into effect. A block which was, at first, just something to be stacked and thrown, later becomes a ship or an airplane.

Having mastered the toy's nature, the child can then use it to express his own nature. That is what play is. It takes him beyond the way things are, into the way things might be. That is why we often think that play is unimportant. It deals only in possibilities, not in actualities. But out of these possibilities come all the innovations in society. Innovative people (scientists, artists, thinkers) are those who play a lot in their heads. They are always considering the way things might be.

We all know that some toys are for infants and some for toddlers, some for children and some for adolescents. So it would follow that there is a curriculum of toys. I like to call the world of toys and entertainment the second educational system. The first educational system is, of course, the parent-child relationship. The third system is formal schooling. As we discover more about which toys are truly "educational," it is my belief that there will be toy libraries in every school and community. There are some already. In these libraries toys will be sorted by age level and by function. Some will be for motor learning (tricycles), some for intellectual learning (puzzles), some for social learning (strategy games). Furthermore, they will be arranged to allow for both mastery and novelty. Thus an ideal toy would have the following qualities:

1. It would be a *realistic model* of some aspect of the world.
2. It would be a *working model* that could be managed by the child.
3. It would be an *assembled model* that could be disassembled and recomposed by the child.
4. It would provide parts that could be assembled into alternative models by the child.

These are the steps from playfulness to mastery. Obviously not all toys can be used in all these ways. Most dolls fit only the first two stages, but those plastic human figures with the organs inside represent at least stage three. Blocks and Plasticine don't really begin until stage three or four. Some people think that the unstructured toys (steps three and four) are better than the structured toys (steps one and two). But that is only a partial truth. You can't even carry out steps three or four unless you already understand steps one and two. There is research to show that when children are first beginning to understand something, they play more if they get a realistic toy. Thus an eighteen-month-old, who is just beginning to understand mothering and babies, plays more with a realistic than a nonrealistic doll. However, a year later the child will play more with the less realistic doll. So for every new function, there is always a time when realism helps. I would need a realistic model of the universe to help me understand it because I am not an astronomer. But the astronomer has gone way beyond that, and he can play with the universe in terms of mathematical symbols.

Parents are the first resource for children's play and learning. Parent-child play is tremendously important because it teaches the infant the delights of surprise, anticipation, and climax. By playing "This little piggy went to market" with a six-month-old, "peek-a-boo" with a ten-month-old, the emotional excitement of the theater is first brought into the baby's life. Later the child will initiate these games with his parents and others, and become a master, himself, of the arts of surprise and climax.

Parents can and should join in their children's toy play, too. First, watch how your child plays with a toy, then play with it yourself. Don't tell the child what to do; show what can be done through your own play. But don't do advanced things the child can't manage. Play in a way that is a little bit ahead of where the child is, so he can progress by copying you. However, don't make toys a substitute for human interaction.

What Kinds of Toys Are Appropriate at Different Ages?

A baby needs toys that do something when he does something to them. Then he searches for the ways in which he can make his playthings do different things. Trying to find out what makes things happen is an early form of reasoning. He is learning that his own explorations can make a difference. He discovers that rattles make different sounds depending ont he way he holds them. The baby mirror reflects different things according to the angle or hand in which he holds it. The musical mobile makes sounds if he shakes his crib. Squeeze toys squeak if he presses them hard enough.

A toddler or a preschooler can do more and can react more to what happens after he has made his first move. The toddler truck can be pushed by hand, it can run by itself, it can bang into blocks. A child experiments with velocity and direction playing with his truck either with or without its load of blocks. He stacks blocks into towers of ever greater precariousness which may or may not come tumbling down. A toddler can feed his teddy bear and put it to bed. Parents still fill their little girls' rooms predominantly with babies and dolls, whereas they give their sons many more varied toys that help them believe in and understand how to manipulate the object world around them. Girls should not be denied these advantages. Both sexes during the preschool years can gain from play with model houses, stores, gas stations, hamburger stands, along with blocks, toy cars and miniature people—all allow the child a great variety of world control. A young child is strongly concerned with his own sense of power so that the opportunity to control models of the adult world gives the player a sense of mastery.

Then there are all the art materials, crayons, clay, Plasticine, paints, and paper and scissors, which are among the best of all activities, because they encourage the child's innovation and creativity.

Children from six years onward enjoy board and card games. These games are all exercises in decision-making and in dealing with success and failure; with luck and deprivation. These are important elements in the character of modern man.

This is the age for doctor kits, tea sets, the doll's house, band sets, stamps, paint sets, more complex trucks and trains, Frisbees, roller skates and construction models. By and large, it is my opinion that one should not give toy guns to children. Ours is a violent world and such self-denial can serve as a symbol to politicians that we want the world to change. We want gun control and armament reduction.

As adolescence approaches all the usual sports equipment, model construction sets, art equipment, more abstract board and card games (chess, checkers, poker, word games) are appropriate. Indoor sports games such as Ping-Pong, darts, miniature hockey tables are popular. There are craft activities: sculpture sets, flower sets, jewelry, tool chests. Some girls like to collect stuffed animals or have shelves of dressed miniature dolls.

The adolescent is also capable of making his own games and own toys. While this is not the way things usually have been, it is an emerging trend in our culture. Those who have had parents who played with them and made up play with them (puppets, acting, stories, jokes), and then have gone to schools where they learn some of their subjects through games (called game simulation), become increasingly sophisticated in making up their own games. Adolescents have modeled academic interests such as international affairs or economics after their favorite board games, complete with boards, dice, pieces, players, and so on. A most valuable trend in the future would be to have adolescents plan and construct the toys, games, and activities that they think are appropriate to children of different age levels. It seems important that in an innovative society, more children should have the experience of being innovative themselves. Learning to make toys rather than just playing with those already available, or to make up games rather than just to play the familiar well-practiced games, is a sure path to such innovation.

Sharing Your Impressions

1. How do children benefit differently from playing with structured and unstructured toys?
2. What is your definition of the ideal toy?
3. Why do you suppose young players are so concerned with mastery and power?
4. State your opinion about the need for including toys in school budgets.
5. Compare the toys of your childhood with those you purchase for your children.
6. What considerations would you recommend to someone purchasing toys for girls? Boys?
7. Identify some activities that are suitable for peer play across a wide age range.

Chapter 10

The Exceptional Players

26

Integrating Handicapped and Nonhandicapped Preschool Children: Effects on Social Play

Catherine Devoney, Michael Guralnick, and Helen Rubin

We have long regarded the play of young children with fascination, but only recently have we begun to systematically explore its functions and development. This interest was sparked by both the remarkable increase in our sensitivity to the preschool years and the exciting possibility of being able to alter significantly the course of cognitive growth through early intervention programs. As a result, many investigators have come to the conclusion that involvement in sociodramatic play can have a very favorable effect on the social, emotional and intellectual development of the young child (Slobin, 1964; Singer, 1973; Smilansky, 1968).

Additional systematic explorations of this issue have focused on the kinds of conditions that facilitate various types of play and their relationship to cognitive and social development. For example, Freyberg (1973), in support of Smilansky's work (1968), successfully trained five-year-old disadvantaged children to play more imaginatively in only eight twenty-minute sessions. Initially, the experimenter modeled various imaginative play scenes and then gradually encouraged the children to engage in similar activities as the training period progressed. As she notes, "The enhanced fantasy play proved also to be associated with greater verbal communication, longer and more complex sentence usage, more sensitive responding to the cues of other children, more apparent spontaneity, more creative use of play material, more inventiveness and originality, more labelling and increased attention span. There were also considerably more positive expressions of emotion in the trained than the untrained group" (Freyberg, 1973).

Similarly, Dansky and Silverman (1973), drawing upon Piaget's discussions (1962) regarding play and creativity, demonstrated that free play with objects produced an increase in associative fluency. Techniques based on reinforcement principles (Bandura, 1969) have also

From *Childhood Education*, April/May 1974, *50*, 360–64. Reprinted by permission of the authors and the Association for Childhood Education International, 3615 Wisconsin Avenue, N.W., Washington, D.C. Copyright © 1974 by the Association.

been successful in increasing the play behavior of young children. Generally, the delivery of social reinforcement, usually in the form of adult attention and praise, is carefully programmed to follow instances of appropriate play (Allen, Hart, Buell, Harris, and Wolf, 1964; Hart, Reynolds, Baer, Brawley, and Harris, 1968). These procedures for play development have worked well with children who are adjusting successfully in other respects as well as with children with severe learning and behavioral problems (Guralnick and Kravik, 1973; Whitman, Mercurio, and Caponigri, 1970).

In spite of these efforts, we need to learn a great deal more about those conditions that foster the development of play behavior in young children, especially if those children are handicapped. The present article describes our efforts to increase the social play of a varied group of handicapped preschool children. It will be seen that after repeated but generally unsuccessful attempts to promote social interactions, using many of the procedures outlined above, we were able to effect marked positive changes through introducing of nonhandicapped preschool children and providing structured activities.

Method and Results

Seven handicapped children enrolled in a private preschool program were involved in this study. The range of handicaps was quite large, from children with little or no functional speech to children with considerable verbal skills. In addition, many of the children manifested various behavioral problems such as hyperactivity or excessive passivity.

Initially, we tried to structure the play situation in a manner designed to increase the likelihood of play interactions and to reinforce with praise and attention any approximations to increased and more highly developed play. However, although these techniques of modifying antecedent environmental conditions (Keogh, Miller, and LeBlanc, 1973) and consequent events (Baer and Wolf, 1968) have worked for other populations, no changes were detected here. Accordingly, an agreement was reached with a preschool class of nonhandicapped children that occupied the room next door to send five of their children three times a week during the free-play period. Our purpose here was to attempt to use the nonhandicapped children to prompt our youngsters to engage in more advanced and frequent play and to have them, rather than the teachers, provide the positive consequences that attend this type of activity.

Children were rated on a time sampling basis on a social play scale ranging from autistic and isolate play to cooperative play, with a rating of six being the highest. Ratings were carried out by a teacher with the occasional introduction of an additional person to check reliability.

During baseline conditions, the seven handicapped children were permitted to play as usual. As Figure 1 indicates, the average play rating stabilized at about three (parallel play). During the next phase, referred to as "intervention," the nonhandicapped children were introduced into the situation. As indicated in the figure, social play did improve, although not very substantially, and stabilized at the level indicated on the graph. In the final phase, when the teacher directly intervened by structuring the play for the combined group of children, a noticeable increase in play occurred. It should be recalled that when the teacher structured the situation with only handicapped children only small positive changes resulted.

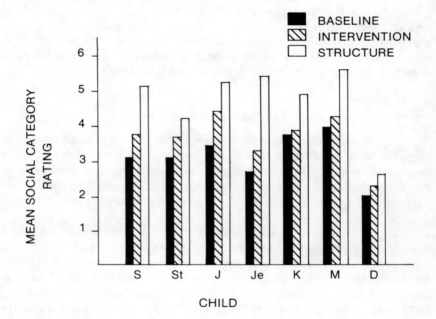

FIGURE 1.   The effects of the three conditions
on the social behavior of each child.

Figure 2 illustrates the same sequence of events, with the dependent variable being the percent of time spent in the two highest social categories. Viewed this way, the marked effects of structuring the play situation with both nonhandicapped and handicapped children can be seen quite clearly. Note that, after structuring, five of seven children spent almost 75 percent or more of their time engaging in associative or cooperative play. The two children for whom these gains did not occur were the only nonverbal children in the class.

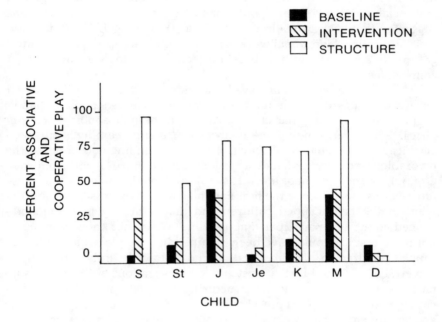

FIGURE 2.   The effects of the three conditions
on the associative and cooperative play of each child.

Our attempts here were designed to increase the frequency of social interactions in the direction of cooperative play. However, unexpectedly, during the intervention phase, important and dramatic changes occurred that do not appear on the graphs. Specifically, as we noted, although changes were not very substantial during this period for most children, the teachers observed that during other free-play periods throughout the day the handicapped children not only interacted with each other more, but the play itself took the same form as the play modeled by the nonhandicapped preschoolers. This play is much more sophisticated and organized than any our handicapped children had ever evidenced.

Discussion

The results of this investigation suggest that nonhandicapped preschool children can serve as effective models for play behavior and produce a substantial and rapid increase in both the quantity and quality of play in handicapped children. We have not determined here whether these increases produced concomitant positive changes in the cognitive and social-emotional spheres, but work with disadvantaged children has suggested that such gains do tend to occur (Freyberg, 1973; Smilansky, 1968). Of course, additional work is needed, utilizing appropriate control groups or applying multiple-baseline techniques, to warrant stronger conclusions.

These results may have important implications for the current discussions regarding the integration of handicapped and nonhandicapped children in regular classes. Although the philosophical and empirical issues surrounding the concept of "mainstreaming" still need clarification (Reynolds and Davis, 1971), our findings do point to the favorable effects on the handicapped children that can result from such grouping at the preschool level. It should be noted, however, that these interactions took place in the familiar and supportive classroom environment of the handicapped children and that relatively few nonhandicapped youngsters participated at one time. We do not know whether or not these results would have been obtained had we placed a few handicapped children in a normal setting and followed similar procedures. Nevertheless, should further systematic investigations of this effect support these findings and if the structuring of situations designed to encourage nonhandicapped preschool peers to model appropriate language and emotional behaviors also turns out to have similar effects on the handicapped children, then the merits of carefully planned integration procedures can be argued from a more objective perspective. Moreover, quite apart from the issue of mainstreaming, but perhaps of greater significance, we can at least state on empirical grounds that we have a useful instructional technique at our disposal.

References

Allen, K. E.; B. M. Hart; J. S. Buell; F. R. Harris; & M. M. Wolf. "Effects of Social Reinforcement on Isolate Behavior of a Nursery School Child." *Child Development 35* (1964): 511–18.

Baer, D. M., & M. M. Wolf. "The Reinforcement Contingency in Preschool and Remedial Education." In *Early Education: Current Theory, Research and Action,* R. D. Hess and D. M. Baer, Eds. Chicago: Aldine, 1968.

Bandura, A. *Principles of Behavior Modification.* New York: Holt, Rinehart & Winston, 1969.

Dansky, J. L. & I. W. Silverman. "Effects of Play on Associative Fluency in Preschool-aged Children." *Developmental Psychology 9* (1973): 38–43.

Freyberg, J. T. "Increasing the Imaginative Play of Urban Disadvantaged Kindergarten Children Through Systematic Training." In *The Child's World of Make-believe*, J. L. Singer. New York: Academic Press, 1973. P. 132. Reprinted with permission.

Guralnick, M. J. & M. A. Kravik. "Reinforcement Procedures and Social Behavior in a Group Context with Severely Retarded Children." *Psychological Reports 32* (1973): 295–301.

Hart, B. M.; N. J. Reynolds; D. M. Baer; E. R. Brawley; & F. R. Harris. "Effects of Contingent and Non-contingent Social Reinforcement on the Cooperative Play of a Preschool Child." *Journal of Applied Behavior Analysis 1* (1968): 73–76.

Keogh, W. J.; R. M. Miller; & J. M. LeBlanc. "The Effects of Antecedent Stimuli upon a Preschool Child's Peer Interaction." Paper presented at biennial meeting of The Society for Research in Child Development, Philadelphia, Pennsylvania, 1973.

Piaget, J. *Play, Dreams, and Imitation in Childhood.* New York: Norton, 1962.

Reynolds, M. C., & M. D. Davis. *Exceptional Children in Regular Classrooms.* Minneapolis: Department of Audio-Visual Extension, University of Minnesota, 1971.

Singer, J. L. *The Child's World of Make-believe.* New York: Academic Press, 1973.

Slobin, D. I. "The Fruits of the First Season: A Discussion of the Role of Play in Childhood." *Journal of Humanistic Psychology 4* (1964): 59–79.

Smilansky, S. *The Effects of Sociodramatic Play on Disadvantaged Preschool Children.* New York: Wiley, 1968.

WhitmanT. L.; J. R. Mercurio; & V. Caponigri. "Development of Social Responses in Two Severely Retarded Children." *Journal of Applied Behavior Analysis 3* (1970): 133–28.

Sharing Your Impressions

1. How do you suppose nonhandicapped children benefit from play with handicapped peers?
2. Recall the way handicapped children were treated by other kids when you were growing up.
3. Identify some sports handicapped persons are participating in now that were unavailable to handicapped people when you were growing up.
4. What kinds of play would be appropriate for integrating handicapped and nonhandicapped children during elementary school? High school?
5. How do you feel about being around mentally retarded persons?
6. Give some reasons why handicapped children need to play with nonhandicapped children.
7. How does play compare with other methods for achieving the integration of handicapped and nonhandicapped children?

27

Facilitating the Play Process
with LD Children

Eleanor Irwin and Mary Frank

The Scene: a special classroom for learning-disabled children, one week before Christmas. The Action: 16 youngsters jumping and shouting, excitedly trying to hit a colorful papier-mâché piñata hanging in the middle of the room. With a whack, a well-aimed blow hits the mark and candy spills everywhere. After the contents are happily divided and the room returns to normal, the children look up eagerly and ask, "Now can we play?"

Obviously, "play" wears many faces and comes in many disguises. The piñata party described above was "play" yet the children did not consider it to be a substitute for their usual "free-play" time. For them, the latter was sacrosanct, and not even a piñata party could take its place.

For all children, play is important; for children with learning disabilities, however, play may be especially valuable. For such youngsters, play can provide a natural setting for the possible remediation of specific deficits, such as those that involve language, visual and auditory perception, gross- and fine-motor deficits, short attention span, hyperactivity, and distractibility.

Play and Social Skills

While there has been a substantial amount of research devoted to the diagnostic and remediation problems of learning-disabled children, relatively little attention has been paid to their social and interpersonal development. Several studies have suggested that these children have difficulty in social relationships, being less popular with peers, parents, and teachers than their nondisabled classmates. In several studies, Tanis S. Bryan has investigated peer popularity among learning-disabled children and their controls in the middle grades. She found that learning-disabled children, particularly white or female children, are not accepted, but rejected, by their classmates. While such children interacted with others as much as a comparison group, they

From *Academic Therapy*, Summer 1977, *12*(4), 435–443. Reprinted by permission of the authors and Academic Therapy Publications, San Rafael, California.

were twice as likely to be ignored by teachers and peers when they initiated conversations. In her study, replicated one year later with similar results, Bryan found that learning-disabled children received a significantly greater number of votes on social rejection and fewer votes on social attraction than did a group of comparison children. She states:

> It is possible that whatever factors lead a child to have a learning disability might also affect a child's social learning. Deficits in attention, language, or perception might hinder the child in detecting critical cues or making inferences about people just as they appear to hinder the child in the acquisition of academic information. In short, the findings may support the premise that lack of peer popularity is not a question of intelligence, labeling or expectancy, but rather another symptom of learning disabilities.[1]

Bryan concludes that there is a need for educational programs which have social-affective components as well as cognitive-achievement goals.

Such studies indicate that learning-disabled children may need help in acquiring social skills, just as they need help in academic areas. It is important for parents and teachers to be sensitive to the quality of the play and interaction of such children, and, if necessary, take concentrated preventive measures to help remediate social deficits during the early years.

Importance of Play

Recent research on play with "normal" as well as disadvantaged children underscores the importance of play and suggests ways in which adults can facilitate imaginative play. Renewed interest in play by educators, psychologists, and child development specialists has reiterated the fundamental importance of play, intertwined as it is with the growing child's sense of identity.

Gregory P. Stone has suggested that play, especially make-believe play, represents an important factor in the process of individuation:

> "Play" has several meanings, among which *drama* must be included; and drama is fundamental for the child's development of a conception of self as an object different from but related to other objects—the development of an *identity*. To establish a separate identity . . . the child must literally get outside himself and apprehend himself from some other perspective. Drama provides a prime vehicle for this. By taking the role of another, the child gains a reflected view of himself as different from but related to that other.[2]

Jean Piaget's pioneering work, positing play as an aspect of intelligence, called attention to the important relationship between play and cognitive functioning.[3] Calling play "assimilation over accommodation," Piaget considers that the make-believe "play" of children is an indispensable step in cognitive development, made possible by the symbolizing function of language and speech.

Others have also studied the multiple relationships between play, playfulness, creativity, and learning. Jerome Singer's research, for example, has indicated that children and adults who have rich fantasy lives also show greater ego control and increased ability to wait, tolerate delay, and endure frustration.[4] He believes that play and the imaginative capacity are enhanced by close relationships with adults, privacy, and the opportunity to experience a wide variety of toys and materials. Similarly, J. Nina Lieberman's research with kindergarten children has shown that the more playful children in her study were also better at creative tasks and showed greater ability to solve problems.[5] Brian Sutton-Smith's work has demonstrated the value of play in helping children adopt an "as if" attitude.[6] He believes that play, games, and cognitive development may be functionally related.

Play and Language Skills

Play, in addition to helping define a sense of self and aiding cognitive development and emotional growth in children, also facilitates the acquisition of speech and language skills. In the course of their play, children argue, discuss, explore, plot, and talk together; "playing" with words, images and concepts, thereby enriching their language skills.

Research with disadvantaged, speech-handicapped, and emotionally-disturbed children has indicated that children can make significant gains in speech and language skills following experiences in spontaneous dramatic play.[7]

In her study of disadvantaged children, Sara Smilansky identified a number of play skills which are important for dramatic play with peers:

1. *Imitative role play* in which the child undertakes a make-believe role, and expresses it in imitative action and/or verbalization.
2. *Make-believe in regard to objects* in which movements or verbal declarations are substituted for real objects.
3. *Make-believe in regard to actions and situations* in which verbal descriptions are substituted for actions and situations.
4. *Persistence* in that the child plays for at least ten minutes.
5. *Interaction* in that at least two players are engaged in a play episode.
6. *Verbal communication* in which there is some verbal interaction related to the play.

According to Smilansky, each of these skills is essential for the development of play and can serve as guidelines for the development of dramatic play skills.

Correlation of Play and Research

Research with disadvantaged children has greatly increased our knowledge of the play of learning-disabled children. As the sociological, psychological, and biological impact of poverty continues to be the focus of numerous studies, its devastating effects on the development of children are unmistakable. Reviewing research in this area, Daniel Hallihan and William Cruickshank have commented that brain damage is far more prevalent among deprived children than had been previously believed.[8] They state, "Many of the learning, perceptual, and motor characteristics commonly ascribed to these children are, in fact, identical to the classic symptoms of cerebral dysfunction."

Similar findings have emerged in studies of abused children. Brandt Stelle writes, "A small but significant number of children who were abused or neglected in their earliest years suffered organic brain damage due either to head trauma or to malnutrition during critical growth periods. As a result they had perceptual deficits, diminished IQ, and significant delay in language development."[9] The research on the play of such children is of interest because, behaviorally, their play often resembles that of the learning-disabled child (i.e., it is characterized by hyperactivity, impulsivity, etc.). In short, their play is "different."

The "Play Tutor"

Dana Feitelson and Gail Ross, working with deprived children in Israel as well as in this country, found that these youngsters could be taught play skills in individual sessions with a "play tutor" whose sole task was to play with the child, stimulating and encouraging his play ideas.[10] This research led them to stress the importance of the adult in teaching play skills and modeling play behaviors. Similar research has been reported by Smilansky and others.

Since these disadvantaged children frequently begin school with built-in deficits that mitigate against success in socialization and play experiences, adults need to become aware of ways in which such children can be helped to engage in more satisfying play, both alone and with others. The teacher may be doubly important, not only as a model for play, but also because children need to have a basic, accepting relationship with an adult before they can feel secure enough to play with others. Some young children have not had this kind of basic acceptance in the past. As a result, remediation in play may mean that the teacher must first serve as a model of identification for the child before the child is able to learn the play skill and generalize it in his play with others.

This important research work has gradually altered the perception of the teacher's role from one of nonintervention to one of intervention for a specific purpose (i.e., to teach missing play skills and promote thematic play). Teacher intervention can be accomplished in a variety of ways. First, make a thorough assessment of each child's developmental level of play through carefully recorded observations over a period of time.[11] Then, identify his motor, visual, auditory, and language skills through educational diagnostic testing and speech and language evaluations. Once the teacher has this baseline, she can determine which abilities are intact and which ones are in need of remediation. She can then plan interventions and goals that will raise the level of play and socialization and, at the same time, remediate specific deficits.

Case Histories

In order to illustrate more specifically how the teacher can sensitively observe and plan interventions, the following examples are cited:

John: A child who needs help controlling his hyperactivity. Six-year-old John was bright-eyed and active, perhaps *too* active! While not destructive of property or hurtful to others, John's play was characterized by a lack of organization and impulsivity. In one free-play period, for example, he continuously moved from one play situation to another, without elaborating upon any one activity. At the block corner, he stacked the wood pieces in a seemingly random fashion, without paying any attention to size, shape, or function. When the blocks tumbled in a heap, John drifted away, his attention caught by two boys building boats at the woodwork table. Observing them, John commented to no one in particular, "I'm gonna build me a boat." Then, with great energy, he took a large piece of wood and began to pound a nail into the top. Bending the nail, he muttered, "This ain't workin'." John aimed one final blow at the bent nail, disgustedly threw the wood down, and gave up, discouraged. He again circled the room. John was "hyperactive" and could not independently organize or inhibit his impulses.

To engage in play in a satisfying way, children need ego control, a kind of internal structuring which they gain in identification with others. Because of organic impairment, the hyperactive child lacks such controls, which must therefore be substituted externally, through constraints from the environment or support from the teacher (i.e., in helping him to sequence his activities, become organized in play, interact with others, etc.). When this external support is provided, and when appropriate behaviors are recognized and rewards given, the child has the opportunity to internalize these controls, and thus "build in" what he lacks.

Jane: A child who needs help elaborating play and moving from solitary to interactive play. Jane, like John, had difficulty elaborating her ideas into thematic play. Observing her over a period of time, the teacher noted that six-year-old Jane rarely engaged in play with another child, preferring instead to passively sit alone with her doll in the corner, or to watch others play. Jane was visually oriented and seemed to enjoy sitting by herself and watching others. In assessing Jane's behavior, it seemed feasible to first help her elaborate and develop themes around her play ideas, and then help her move from solitary to interactive play with others. Accordingly, the teacher first offered herself as a "play model" for brief five-minute periods. Joining Jane in the corner, the teacher said, "Hello, how's your baby?" thus directing attention to the doll that hung limply in Jane's right hand. The child's response triggered an "as if" dialogue, as teacher and child play-acted together, pretending to be two parents discussing their children. When the teacher left after a few minutes, Jane was able to continue with her play, trying to fix the diaper around the doll. In time, with these kinds of experiences, Jane gained the ability to elaborate her ideas into play themes, which usually revolved around mother-baby play.

Once Jane was able to sustain dramatic play for a brief period, the teacher attempted to help Jane move from solitary dramatic play to sociodramatic play with another child. For example, one day the teacher suggested that they find a store clerk to buy some new clothes for the baby. Tentatively, and then more surely, Jane responded. With help from her teacher, she began to give up her isolated play, eventually joining others in hospital, store, and firehouse play themes. She still kept a somewhat peripheral position in group play and was usually a follower. Yet, she was able to respond and interact with others in a role.

In helping Jane to elaborate play themes, the teacher was following suggestions made by Smilansky in regard to intervention from *inside* the play (as a co-player) or *outside* the play (giving ideas for further play activities, such as suggesting that they go to the store). Intervening from *outside* the play enables the teacher to make suggestions to the child about the play content, establish contact between two players, or simply give suggestions to facilitate further play.

Intervening from *inside* the play requires the teacher to take a role as a co-player, as the teacher did when she pretended to be another mother with Jane. Again, the purpose of the teacher's active involvement is to provide a play model and facilitate the play to help the child gain the missing play skill. Such intervention should be as short as possible, and, once the intervention has achieved its purpose, the teacher should withdraw from the play and once again become an observer.

Danny: A child who needs help in planning. Children frequently have ideas about play themes, but cannot get themselves organized in order to think through the play sequences. To help such children, the teacher might have a "preplay" planning time, during which the children's ideas can be discussed. For example, Danny loved to play doctor, but was frequently rejected by his peers because his play was so disorganized. Unable to sequentially integrate visual-motor, visual-memory, spatial, and auditory experiences, Danny played in a very haphazard way which annoyed his classmates and provoked rejection. Noting this, the teacher became more active with him, helping him decide what kinds of things he wanted to do and how to carry his ideas through to completion. When Danny said he wanted to play doctor, the teacher asked him what kind of doctor he wanted to be (foot doctor, head doctor, throat doctor, etc.). When Danny responded that he would like to be a bone doctor, his teacher talked to him about the things a bone doctor did (i.e., measuring, bandaging, and giving medicine). As might be suspected, Danny himself had had many experiences with a bone doctor, but he still found it hard to remember what the doctor did. By doing this, Danny's teacher helped him preplan and prerehearse how "doctor play" might be carried out, thus giving him an opportunity to "try on" the play experience. Such preplay-planning can help a child integrate the bits and pieces of an experience into a more comprehensible whole. Therefore, Danny now had an "internal program" which he could utilize during the play time.

Robert: A child who needs help in sensory integration. Some learning-disabled children need multiple sensory experiences in order to learn. Robert, for example, had visual-memory and visual-spatial problems. Remembering simple facts, such as his address or the color of the family car, presented great difficulties for him. He was often unable to say whether the family car had two wheels or four wheels, and he had equal difficulty designating the front from the back of the car. Because Robert especially liked firemen themes, the teacher took the class to the firehouse which was several blocks from the school. There, they eagerly inspected the fire engine, looking, touching, hearing, feeling, and even smelling it. They listened to the fire whistle, felt the shiny brass bell, and tried on a fireman's hat. Returning to the classroom, the teacher and children reviewed the trip, wrote about it, drew pictures, and played "fireman." With an imaginary fireman's hat perched on his head, Robert gleefully clanged the bell, grabbed his pretend hose, and made loud "whoosh" noises as he put out the fire. While this kind of learning experience contributes to the education of any child, for some learning-disabled children, it is not a luxury but a necessity for true integration. This kind of exploring and investigating on a multisensory level can help Robert and others like him understand and integrate what they learn.

Richard: A child who needs help with communication but who is still able to serve as a "play tutor" to others. Many children know exactly what they want to do and how to do it despite real communication problems. Richard was such a child. Often, he seemed to clearly understand what was going on but was severely handicapped in being able to communicate verbally with others. Despite his handicaps, however, Richard did not need an adult as a "play tutor," because he was able to employ his imaginative capacities to find nonverbal, gestural ways to share his ideas with his peers. He especially liked playing doctor, perhaps not only because he had experienced a number of hospitalizations himself, but also because it placed him in a controlling position. As doctor, he could do to others what had been done to him. Through gestures and the use of materials, he made himself understood to others, both giving and taking in the play experience. When Peter needed a cast, for example, Richard very cleverly used a roll of paper to make one, much to Peter's delight. When, in the course of an examination, Peter indicated that there was something wrong with his knee, Richard used a potato masher to test the knee reflexes. Enchanted, Peter called the others to see the new equipment and, from that point on, the potato masher became part of their "doctor" gear. Observing Richard's play, the teacher noted that in spite of his speech handicaps, he functioned as a "play tutor" to the other children and clearly did not need her help.

Summary

This article suggests that learning-disabled children need help in learning social skills and play skills, just as they need help in academic areas. Research on disadvantaged children, which outlines some ways in which teachers can help facilitate the play of children, seems to have applicability to learning-disabled children as well. Both groups often show the same behavioral characteristics (i.e., hyperactivity, impulsivity, and lack of ability to sequence and integrate bits and pieces of information into larger segments). This article also suggests that teachers should carefully note the play of learning-disabled children, establish a baseline of their assets as well as their deficits, and sensitively and selectively intervene in their dramatic play, along carefully prescribed lines, in order to function as a play model, and thus teach play skills. A regularly scheduled play time, in which children are helped to learn how to play, may be necessary to facilitate self-awareness and to promote more positive ways of interacting with others.

Notes

1. S. Tanis Bryan, "Peer Popularity of Learning Disabled Children," *Journal of Learning Disabilities* 7:10 (1974): 31–35.
2. Gregory P. Stone, "The Play of Little Children," in R. E. Herron and B. Sutton-Smith (eds.), *Child's Play* (New York: John Wiley and Sons, 1971): 4–14.
3. Jean Piaget, *Play, Dreams, and Imitation of Reality* (New York: Academic Press, 1973).
4. Jerome Singer, *The Child's World of Make-Believe* (New York: Academic Press, 1973).
5. J. Nina Lieberman, "Playfulness and Divergent Thinking: An Investigation of Their Relationship at the Kindergarten Level," *Journal of Genetic Psychology* 107 (1965): 219–224.
6. Brian Sutton-Smith, "The Role of Play in Cognitive Development," in Herron and Sutton-Smith, *op.cit.*: 252–260.
7. Sara Smilansky, *The Effects of Sociodramatic Play on Disadvantaged Pre-School Children* (New York: John Wiley and Sons, 1968); Eleanor C. Irwin and Betty Jane McWilliams, "Play Therapy for Children with Cleft Palates," *Children Today* 3:3 (May-June 1974): 18–22; Eleanor C. Irwin *et al.*, "Assessment of Drama Therapy in a Child Guidance Setting," *Group Psychotherapy and Psychodrama* 25:3 (October 1972): 105–116.
8. Daniel Hallihan and William Cruickshank, *Psychological Foundations of Learning Disabilities* (Englewood Cliffs, New Jersey: Prentice-Hall, 1973).
9. Brandt F. Stelle, "Working with Abusive Parents: A Psychiatrist's View," *Children Today* 4:3 (May-June 1975): 3–5, 44.
10. Dana Feitelson and Gail S. Ross, "The Neglected Factor—Play," *Human Development* 16:3 (1973): 202–223.
11. D. H. Cohen and V. Stern, *Observing and Recording Children's Play* (New York: Columbia University Press, 1968); L. M. Rasken, W. J. Taylor, and F. G. Kerckhoff, "The Teacher as Observer for Assessment: A Guideline," *Young Children* 30:5 (July 1975): 330–344.

Sharing Your Impressions

1. How does the play-tutor method compare with other means of overcoming the deficits of learning-disabled children?
2. Speculate about why normal children tend to reject learning-disabled peers.

3. Compare the way learning-disabled children play with the way other boys and girls play.
4. Suggest some ways for parents to facilitate the learning-disabled child's play with neighborhood peers.
5. Recall your childhood feelings about playing with peers who were doing poorly in school.
6. Give your opinion about the value of Special Olympics.
7. Describe the teacher's role as model of play for the learning disabled.

Chapter 11

Education for Leisure

28

Education for Leisure in the Elementary School

C. Hugh Gardner and Sandra V. Gardner

Education for leisure should bring about desirable changes involving attitudes, knowledge, skills, and ultimately, behavior. If the teaching effort is meaningful, it must lead to participation. In an adequate program, leisure training is fused into the entire curriculum program. Such preparation involves children in focusing on the human dimensions of leisure, in dealing with their own feeling level responses to leisure, and finally in determining their own mode of expression in the world of leisure. Keeping this in mind, let's explore examples of some curriculum areas where leisure can be diffused.

Correlating Leisure and Career Education

Leisure education and career education go hand in hand. Work roles for some are often leisure activities for others. Truck farmers make a living from the soil, but many individuals enjoy gardening as a leisure activity. Photography is a hobby for many, yet professional photography serves as the occupational role of others. Participation in sports is the profession of a few, but recreation for the masses.

The work of some involves helping others utilize their leisure time. Included here are such occupations as life guards, national park rangers, waitresses and cooks in restaurants, musicians—the list is endless. Other workers are involved with producing or repairing items used primarily for leisure. Examples of these would include employment in the manufacture or repair of sporting goods, toys, and stereo equipment. When these types of careers are studied, the interrelationship they have with leisure should be covered. In other words, one is not "good" while the other is "wasteful," but they are interdependent and necessary in the lifestyles of our culture.

An understanding of how recreation is important to our

From *Journal of Physical Education and Recreation*, March 1976, 47(3), 21–22. Copyright 1976 by the American Alliance for Health, Physical Education and Recreation. Reprinted by permission.

economy is necessary. What items do the children have at home that are used primarily for leisure? What would happen if no one bought any leisure items anymore? What would happen if all movie theaters, bowling alleys, restaurants, golf courses, and travel agencies had to close because no one felt right about using them? Pursuing these ideas can further children's awareness and understanding of leisure roles.

Resource persons brought in to discuss their careers can also be questioned about how they like to spend their free time, how their interests got started, and how much time they devote to these activities. This can be furthered by questioning parents, teachers, and neighbors about their leisure time activities.

Basic to career education and its partner, leisure education, is self-concept development. Children should see their leisure as a part of their life—as an extension of themselves. They should be clear as to what it is in themselves they want to express—what they want to develop in themselves, how and what they want to contribute to a leisure role. Each child should be the one who makes a leisure choice and sets goals on the basis of that which is deemed important.

Aspects of a child's personality can be brought to light through such activities as "me" pictures. Children cut out pictures of things they specifically feel good about, and mount them, together with their name, written the favorite way, on a large paper. Since children's concepts of themselves are ever-changing, this activity can be repeated at different grade levels.

Physical Education

The physical education program in the elementary school is all important in building skills and attitudes about leisure. Children's feelings about recreational competence are being developed in the lower grades. Children need practice in building muscular skills and coordination; they need to learn specific rules of games and team sports; they need to realize how important physical fitness is to organic well-being. Development of positive mental attitudes toward sportsmanship and group cooperation are imperative. When possible, a physical education teacher trained in elementary physical education should be a member of the regular school staff. This will give the children more expert help in developing the needed skills and attitudes. Children should have experience with spectator sports, and should have opportunities to watch their schoolmates perform. Contrasting active and passive roles of leisure is valuable to children in choosing free time activities.

Arts, Crafts, and Leisure Education

Artistic pursuits at the elementary level must be broad and varied. There should be specific training in skills and techniques as well as numerous opportunities for creative self-expression. Many mediums should be introduced, and children should be encouraged to pursue further those mediums they enjoy using most.

Children should be encouraged to bring in craft projects or art forms created by adult acquaintances. This sharing will create an awareness of how adults find enjoyment and leisure opportunities through artistic pursuits. Parents with a particular talent might be involved as resource people for projects that the teacher feels inadequately prepared to teach.

Art is the interpretation of feeling and experience. In showing children prints of famous pictures, it is good to include a few facts about the artist and what he may have had in mind when he painted the picture, but children's thinking should be stimulated and their observations and interpretations shared.

Music and Leisure

Music appreciation as a form of education for leisure has a definite place in the elementary school. Music appreciation has often been used as a quiet, restful time following an activity which demanded active involvement. But have children been made aware of this? Do they associate this with the way their parents often listen to soothing music after concentrated mental or physical work?

Teachers can quickly list music that they think should be included in an appreciation program. But have teachers given pupils a chance to share the music *they* feel strongly about? By the upper elementary grades contemporary music is important to children and should be included in the curriculum.

Vocal and instrumental music will have more meaning if children are introduced to it in an effective manner. One elementary principal developed vocal and instrumental musical participation through bi-monthly "jam sessions" on Friday afternoons. Accompanied by guitar, piano, or other instruments, the children sang old favorites as well as popular songs like "Leroy Brown" and "Locomotion." Boys' and girls' glee clubs were formed at the upper elementary level, as well as a girls' dance group and a guitar instructional program. These groups performed at assemblies, PTA meetings, and community functions. They became involved in writing their own music and did several commercials on a local radio station. Parents who were talented and trained in these fields volunteered their services. This type of program developed a deep self-satisfaction which led to a greater appreciation of all forms of music.

Integrating Leisure with Other Curriculum Areas

A conscious framework for leisure can be integrated into each of the subject matter areas. Language arts should include reading for pleasure and an introduction to poetry. Some will enjoy creative writing as a leisure type activity.

Correspondence with pen pals may further an interest in other countries and a desire for travel. Some children may find letter writing an enjoyable leisure occupation in itself. But the necessary ingredient is that the child is aware of his feelings about these activities and how they can affect his use of leisure.

As a contrast to verbal communication, a child can take slides or snapshots and tell a story through the pictures. Rewarding experiences with photography lead to creative self expression and can be utilized in a variety of subject matter areas.

Comparisons made between the use of educational TV programs at school and the use of TV in the home can help children understand themselves. Do they learn anything from the shows they watch at home? What are their favorite kinds of shows? Why do they choose these? Since TV has become a major leisure activity, a conscious awareness of how much time is spent viewing it might be enlightening to the child. A balance between this passive form of recreation and more active forms is important. Too many passive activities can be bad for the health, as everyone needs a certain amount of exercise. Similar kinds of ideas can be fostered about movies.

Most children have some time during the school day when they can choose an independent activity. If they finish their seatwork assignments before others, possibly they can draw, read a book, work a puzzle, listen at the listening station, or use a learning center. Make them aware of their choices. Do they choose the same activity most of the time, or do they like variety? Do they feel they have used their free time wisely or is it wasted? What one child may consider a waste of time may not necessarily be considered that way by another. Lead children to explore the reasons they feel as they do. In this way, their knowledge of themselves as individuals will be expanded.

There is a great need to develop an interest in and favorable attitudes toward the service areas as possible leisure pursuits. Too many adults view involvement on church committees, taking an office in a club, or collecting for a charity as work, and consequently avoid doing these types of things whenever possible. Student participation in collecting money for UNICEF at Halloween or working with the Junior Red Cross should be encouraged. Elect class officers in the upper elementary grades and provide guidance to the class as they delegate certain responsibilities to each officer. Changing officers quarterly will allow more students a leadership opportunity. Publicity projects, such as making posters to advertise a school carnival, produce a feeling of involvement and self-fulfillment.

Summary

Since the ultimate purpose of a program in education for leisure is to develop attitudes and behavior toward leisure marked by good selection of recreational pursuits, the school must serve as a laboratory situation. Schools need not add new subject matter to their already crowded schedule. Rather, leisure is built into the existing curriculum.

Our society is full of dynamic change. Leisure pursuits of today may not be the same as those twenty years from now, but by establishing good attitudes toward leisure in our youth, teachers will have laid a groundwork that can be built upon. Children will have developed a sense of individual identity and self-worth and will be in a much better position to adapt themselves to an ever changing lifestyle.

Sharing Your Impressions

1. How do you suppose homework affects a child's learning about leisure?
2. How were you taught to think of the relation between work and leisure?
3. How much of the schooltime schedule should be devoted to education for leisure? Explain your opinion.
4. What do you see as the most desirable changes likely to occur in education for leisure?
5. Make some guesses about how sex-role misconceptions can hinder education for leisure.
6. What do you think of the proposal that all boys and girls should receive training in relaxation techniques?
7. Identify some aspects of family-vacation planning in which children should participate.

29

Leisure Education for a State of Mind

James Christensen and Rick Crandall

The continuing increase in time for leisure makes education for leisure an important area of public concern. Its goal is to help people realize the full potential of their leisure. To date, what little education for leisure has been available has been provided by professionals in areas such as park and recreation and physical education. With the increasing importance of education for leisure, professionals in these and other areas must seek to improve their ability to educate the public in this area.

When asked to define leisure, people generally give three kinds of responses. They define leisure in terms of (1) nonwork activities, (2) time free from work, or (3) state of mind. Any emphasis on either activities or time usually defines leisure in opposition to work. An emphasis on state of mind focuses on subjective variables.

Formal theories of leisure contain the same general dimensions as popular definitions, defining leisure along two dimensions. The first dimension is defined in terms of work: the less an activity is like work, the more it is considered leisure. The second dimension is constraint vs. freedom: the more an activity is freely chosen the more it is considered leisure. More recently, some theorists have defined leisure solely in terms of perceived freedom, intrinsic motivation, enjoyment, or other subjective variables relating to the state of mind of a person.

Existing education for leisure for both professionals and the general public has emphasized the nonwork or activity aspects of leisure rather than the more subjective aspects such as freedom and internal motivation. Most universities and public leisure providers such as park districts offer excellent courses designed to teach "nonwork" skills to students and the general public. These are a valuable first step for leisure professionals and the general public to better utilize leisure, but there is little effort to provide leisure education emphasizing a state of mind by helping people to increase their sense of freedom and enjoyment from their leisure.

A complete approach to education for leisure must help people deal with subjective aspects of leisure such as freedom and enjoyment. This is the area which needs the most development. People today

From *Journal of Physical Education and Recreation*, March 1976, *47*(3), 10. Copyright 1976 by the American Alliance for Health, Physical Education and Recreation. Reprinted by permission.

have become relatively free from religious, social, and economic constraints in most areas of their lives, but handling this increased freedom is a problem for many.

Inability to deal with freedom is especially relevant for leisure defined in terms of a state of mind. We need to educate people to use their leisure to increase their ability for self-development rather than to seek new dependencies.

Education for leisure has not taken this approach in the past. It has emphasized products such as activities and skill development. As a result people work at leisure as time to be filled. Individuals faced with increased free time often substitute a blind pursuit of popular activities for the opportunity for self-development through leisure. Education for leisure emphasizing leisure as a state of mind would focus on leisure as a process rather than as a product. Leisure as a process emphasizes the use of leisure for continual self-development; free time and leisure activities become part of an ongoing process, not products themselves.

Modern education for leisure must expand beyond the acquisition of nonwork skills to the development of individualism. This will require increasing attention to understanding the subjective meaning of leisure for individuals. Increased understanding of basic motivational and behavioral processes will also be important for providing the best leisure education. The use of basic research for the social sciences and trends toward multidisciplinary leisure studies departments will lead the way in this direction.

In order to deal with the important area of leisure education, diverse approaches will be important. In addition to the past emphasis on skills and activities, leisure education must educate people toward a leisure state of mind. Only then will the real potential of education for leisure be realized.

Sharing Your Impressions

1. How do you feel about the way leisure time is used by your children? Your spouse? Yourself?
2. What childrearing changes do you anticipate in a society with lots of leisure time?
3. Describe the leisure activities you pursue for the purpose of self-development.
4. Compare the amount of leisure you have with that of your parents when they were the same age.
5. Many families watch television together. What sorts of questions could parents ask children that would enrich this mutual experience?

6.   Identify the advantages of perceiving leisure as a process rather than a product.
7.   In your opinion, how should parents' view of their educational responsibility change in a society with greater access to leisure time?

30

Work, Leisure, and Identity

Robert D. Strom

Parents and teachers have always expressed concern about the self concept of adolescents. So long as their own identity was closely linked to a job, grownups could reasonably assume that teenagers would find a sense of purpose once they entered the labor market. But does it still turn out that way? Industrial sociology studies have shown that the monotonous tasks being created by automation have caused an increasing number of job holders to begin to find their major life interests outside their jobs. The idea that all people need jobs to feel good about themselves and that job holding brings satisfaction is erroneous. When people say "Thank God it's Friday," what do they mean? Do they mean that they achieve so much pleasure and extract so much significance and self-fulfillment from their jobs that the sheer ecstasy of it all cannot be sustained for more than five days at a time? Or do they mean that their jobs lack importance for them, fail to satisfy their need for potency and force them to look to the weekend for fulfillment? Do they mean that it would be nice not to have to hold their jobs but that the need for income and social status demands it? The inner turmoil of millions of workers does not signify that they are lazy or that constructive achievement doesn't interest them. It does mean that alienation from the job is becoming common. In a leisure society, the incidence of such behavior is destined to rise as industry shifts to the four-day week and people can give more attention to other interests.

"Thank God It's Thursday"

More than 700 U.S. companies currently have all or most of their workers on a four-day week, and at least 1000 other companies are contemplating such a shift. In 1976, the nation's largest employer, the federal government, began a three-year experiment with four-day work

From *The High School Journal*, May 1978, *61*(8), 393–401. Copyright 1978 by The University of North Carolina Press. Reprinted by permission.

weeks and other flexible work schedules for nearly 3 million employees. Municipal employees in Atlanta, Long Beach, Phoenix and other cities made the transition several years ago. A dozen companies, including Metropolitan Life Insurance, have gone even further, assigning some of their workers a three-day work week. Some political and labor leaders are suggesting that perhaps the single best way to reduce unemployment is to redistribute existing work. It is estimated that if we all move to a 35-hour work week, the resulting creation of jobs would employ six million more people.

In a leisure society, for the first time in history, most of people's time would belong to them, and they could live far away from the city of their employment. However, confidence in the leisure society seems to be declining as its arrival draws near. Previous generations believed that a relatively jobless economy would introduce greater contentment than ever before, but only 23% of the people polled in a recent national survey assume that labor-union proposals for a four-day week and three-month annual vacation will result in happier homes. Evidence from industrial sociology supports this popular doubt by indicating that a shorter work day does not necessarily increase family interaction or ensure other forms of constructive activity. Many physicians have stopped prescribing holidays and vacations for tense and anxious patients, because leisure could bring disaster rather than relief. Suicides, depressions and other self-disabling behavior increase over weekends and holidays, when inner conflicts can no longer be repressed by the rigors of routine. In many cases leisure appears to generate domestic conflict or withdrawal.

Coping with free time is a problem for teenagers too. Mindful that our youngsters are easily bored, many of us anticipate difficulties during the summertime, when school is not in session. Accordingly, we plan a schedule of activities for our sons and daughters that will take up nearly their entire summer. This same recognition of the probable consequences of boredom is used by city officials in defending their proposed summer budgets. Thus, the parks-and-recreation departments of most cities may be expected to argue that, unless they are properly funded, the resulting cutback in youth programs will enlarge the delinquency problem for the police. In effect this amounts to an admission that such programs don't teach people to rely on themselves in coping with extended leisure.

Rising Aspirations

Given these circumstances, parents are naturally ambivalent about how to counsel children. They realize that many jobs may not offer a sense of purpose and yet—leisure is considered an impractical realm for seeking identity. The resulting advice for sons and daughters is to pursue high marks at school so it will be possible to enter some profession that seemingly guarantees social status and personal satisfaction. That many adolescents are led to embrace unrealistic career goals was made evident more than a decade ago by Project Talent, the first national census of aptitudes and abilities involving 440,000 high school students. More recently, the 1977 National Survey of Children illustrates how the pressure for academic achievement begins even earlier than high school. Some 2,200 boys˙and girls aged 7 to 11, who represent 18 million youngsters, were chosen to participate along with 1700 of their parents. When asked about academic goals for their children, the Black parent sample revealed higher aspirations than White parents. We know that parents' expectations are communicated to their children from the reports by more than three-quarters of the Black children and about two-thirds of the White children that their mothers wanted them to be "one of the best students in class." Essentially the same findings were obtained by General Mills in their 1977 nationwide study of American families with children under 13.

The expression of lofty goals is commendable, and all children should be urged·to do their best at school. However, disappointment is inevitable when neither the parents nor the child can accept the truth about the child's actual level of achievement as compared to other students. Although the students in the survey represented a broad range of intelligence, nearly 30% of them were described by their parents and themselves as "one of the best students in class." Only 5% were seen by both parties as below the middle of the class. Finally, while less than 4% of the students considered themselves to be near the bottom of the class, not even 2% of the parents were willing to acknowledge that this was a proper estimate of their child's class standing.

A variety of research sources combine to suggest that, besides having an inflated impression of their ability, a large number of students also lack sufficient information about the world of work. These obstacles to career selection have serious implications. To correct the situation, the United States Office of Education began in 1973 to design career curricula for use at all grade levels. The basic purpose of career education is to acquaint children with the range of occupational choices, the nature of available jobs, and the satisfactions they offer. The hope is that students' exposure throughout the schooling process to the benefits and demands of various kinds of work will result in more realistic career decisions. It would be premature to evaluate the impact of career education during its still formative stage, but the enlarging scope of this kind of education is promising. As career education develops, the long-range plan is to include nonvocational objectives, those important aspects of a person's life that are not linked to employment. With this broader definition of career, encompassing parenthood training and the development of lifelong hobbies, we can anticipate that students' chances for mental health and maturity will improve.

The Two Cultures

I wish to propose a way for more teenagers to achieve identity, an alternative by which favorable self impression can be sustained during adult life even if one's employment is boring and routine. Let's begin by reminding ourselves that the school has two cultures—one expressive and the other instrumental.

The instrumental culture is made up of those activities that lead to the skills, knowledge, and values that are stated as goals of schooling. A student participates in the instrumental culture for the sake of obtaining or achieving something outside of and beyond the process of study and learning—to be promoted, to be praised by the family, to get a diploma, to become a doctor or an engineer. The school consists in part of a set of instrumental procedures that produce an individual who is a reader, mathematician, or master of a foreign language. On the other hand, the expressive culture at school includes those activities that students take part in for the sake of the activity. Intramural athletics, art, music and so on are all part of the expressive culture.

Although the expressive culture sometimes involves the learning of knowledge and skills, these outcomes are generally not as important as they are in the instrumental culture. Youngsters can enjoy singing in the chorus, working with clay, or playing volleyball without acquiring much knowledge or skill. The criterion of success is not so much how well they can do as it is how much they enjoy doing it. To be sure, the instrumental culture sometimes has expressive impact—for instance, when a student learns to enjoy reading or performing science experiments or doing algebra and will do these things for their own sake. Conversely, there is an instrumental undertone to most expressive activities. But students usually distinguish the expressive from the instrumental culture. Since most students can succeed in the expressive culture, where there is not such rigorous and explicit competition, it follows that this realm is especially good for teaching values. In this context some youngsters can learn to appreciate school, to become committed to learning, to value successful participation in the expressive as well as in the instrumental culture. Then, too, even the parents with little formal education can take part in the expressive aspects of school without embarrassment.

There are various combinations of success and failure in the expressive and instrumental cultures of the school. The social and intellectual development of a student depend on his or her particular combination of successes. A high level of success in both cultures is characteristic of the good student who also finds satisfaction as a social leader. A high instrumental/low expressive combination describes the bookworm who is socially invisible but does well at scholarly pursuits. A low instrumental/high expressive combination defines the mediocre student who is still able to obtain satisfaction at school because of participation in extracurricular activities. There are young people whose interest in athletics or band is the only incentive for staying in school. It is foolish to tell such persons that unless they maintain a "B" average on the instrumental side they can no longer take part in the expressive realm. Finally, a low instrumental/low expressive combination represents the students who can find no satisfaction or reward in the school. Often these youngsters decide to quit formal education as early as legally possible.

Through a creative use of the expressive culture, the school can become a place of satisfaction for more children, and it can teach certain values more effectively as well as improve performance within the instrumental culture. A dramatic illustration of these possibilities was recorded a few years ago in New York City. The setting was Junior High School 43, located in a slum section of Harlem. About 50% of the student body were Black, and nearly 40% were Puerto Rican. The most successful half from the entire school population of 1400 were selected to participate in the Higher Horizons project. These students had a median IQ of 95 and were, on the average, a year and a half below grade level in reading and mathematics. Instead of increasing the amount of time these students spent on math or reading by eliminating the so-called "frill" areas of education, an opposite approach was taken. That is, a number of motivating influences from the expressive culture were introduced to increase satisfaction with school and desire for learning. The boys and girls were brought to sporting events, concerts and movies. They went to parks and museums and on sightseeing trips.

Follow-up studies showed that the project members who entered senior high school graduated in substantially greater numbers than had those from the same junior high school in pre-project years. Furthermore, 168 of the graduates went on to an institution of higher education, compared with 47 from the three classes preceding the experiment. It seems that the expressive activities gave rise to some important value changes in the experimental group that in turn led to improved performance in the instrumental culture. Findings like these ought to cause more of us to take the extracurricular, the nonacademic, the expressive aspects of schooling far more seriously than we do. That students in higher education sense this need is made obvious by their increasing enrollment in noncredit classes such as belly dancing, bicycle care and repair, blackjack, indoor gardening, Hatha yoga, non-loom weaving, occult science, self-hypnosis, photography, macrame, beginning water color and Scottish country dancing.

A Hierarchy of Needs

We turn now to what models can do for the young who admire them and choose to act as they do. Models are in a unique position for influencing others to adopt a life-style balanced between instrumental and expressive involvement. The necessity of such a balance for each of us can be demonstrated in terms of mental health.

Human beings have three innate needs, all of which demand satisfaction. As shown in the diagram, our highest need is for identity, the opposite of anonymity. Below identity is stimulation, the opposite of boredom. Security is the lowest need; if it is unfulfilled, the result is anxiety. Our society may be without precedent in enabling the largest proportion of a society's people to achieve security and the smallest fraction ever to attain identity. This massive failure to ensure our highest need can be explained in part by unemployment due to automation, by the nature of jobs in large, impersonal organizations, by unfair competition in schools and by life in overcrowded neighborhoods. Whatever the reasons, identity has eluded millions of anonymous beings for whom there is no rank, no territory, and no sense of significance.

Hierarchy of Needs	*Consequences If Unsatisfied*
Identity	Anonymity
↑	
Stimulation	Boredom
↑	
Security	Anxiety

Achievement of security and release from anxiety presents us with boredom, the psychological process least appreciated by social planners. We are only beginning to see something of the chaos that a bored society can produce. Of course, massive boredom could not exist if we were other than a technological people with little chance to preserve identity. The knowledge that we have influence and are respected is the appeal of identity. Among animals this need is met by territory or social rank. But for ourselves, imprisoned by affluence and anonymity, stimulation appears to offer the only escape from boredom. It is more than coincidental that shock and sensation have arrived at the same time in most industrial countries. The frustration of boredom triggers a high growth rate for pornographic pictures, fantasy drug trips, adolescent sexual adventures, casual adultery among the married, nudity on the stage and screen, petty theft by affluent burglars, topless and bottomless attractions, music to assault the senses, violence for kicks and street vocabulary by literary figures. All these and other nuances provide stimulation for the members of bored societies who have nowhere else to go to escape boredom.

In certain of the economically poor nations, people must settle for the security-anonymity combination. But in the United States we are committed to enabling individuals to achieve identity. We need not give up this goal, but there may be good reasons for reconsidering the path to identity. During recent years the prevailing view has been that, in order for more people to feel they are important persons, we must create an increasing number of awards, trophies and titles. Although this approach has in some cases met the need for recognition, in other cases it has made the quest for recognition insatiable. I believe that there is a more promising alternative. We can make identity possible for a greater number of people by removing the barriers to their involvement in the expressive culture. Our government has begun to support this view and is serving notice that girls will no longer be denied access to team sports. Title IX of the Elementary and Secondary Act also calls for making instrumental music available to students who seldom participated in the past because parents could not afford it. These and other legislative efforts to reduce the scope of sex and economic discrimination are commendable. But even laws that guarantee equal opportunity will not greatly increase participation in the expressive culture so long as youngsters are led to exclude themselves. And this is precisely what happens when they are taught to regard the outstanding performers of an activity as the only ones who deserve to participate.

The use of a restrictive standard for determining who is worthy to participate begins early. It can be observed among the very young in little-league sports. Similarly, within the classroom, teachers feel obliged to "find out what the student is good at and encourage tasks calling for that particular strength." In effect, the message is that everyone ought to limit themselves to those leisure pursuits in which they excel. It follows that, unless students are identified as having extraordinary talent in athletics, music, or art, they should withdraw, because the quality of their performance will not support a favorable self-impression. Under these conditions it is no wonder that many children reluctantly conclude "I like spending time in this way, but I'm not good enough to continue." Thus they give up certain activities that could have provided them with life-long satisfaction.

Adults often experience the same pressure to subordinate enjoying an activity to achieving competence in it. To illustrate, four "good" golfers are waiting behind the first tee for the couple ahead to begin play. As it happens, the couple are not avid golfers, so each of them drives the opening shot just a short distance. The waiting foursome then wonder aloud "What are they doing here?" as if to say that the only people who belong on the golf course are highly skilled players. The less serious persons who want to play for fun ought to reconsider and become spectators. As spectators they can watch the expert few and perhaps in the process experience at least a vicarious sense of identity.

It has taken a while to learn an important lesson, but we now know that in the future identity cannot be reserved for persons of uncommon achievement. Adult models have a special obligation to bring about the necessary transition. Parents who are anxious about the occupational futures of sons or daughters may not recognize the need for a balance of academic and expressive activities. Consequently, they often urge the school to reduce or give up expressive offerings. In turn, when teachers are held accountable for scholastic attainment only, other important aspects of a student's personal development are neglected. By encouraging all students to participate in the expressive culture for fun, we can help them develop self-esteem and avoid boredom.

References

Asher, Jules, "Flexi-Time, Four Day Weeks," *American Psychological Association Monitor 6,* 1975, pp. 4, 5.

Flanagan, John, *A National Inventory of Aptitudes and Abilities,* Pittsburgh: University of Pittsburgh, Project Talents Bulletin, 4, 1965.

Hamilton, Andrew, "Career Education Working Model," *American Education,* December 1975, pp. 22–25.

National Panel on High Schools and Adolescent Education. *The Education of Adolescents, Summary, Conclusions and Recommendations.* Submitted to the U.S. Office of Education and Department of Health, Education and Welfare, Washington, D.C., U.S. Government Printing Office, 1975.

Strom, Robert, *Growing Together: Parent and Child Development,* Monterey: Brooks/Cole, 1978, 300 pp.

_____. *Parent and Child in Fiction,* Monterey: Brooks/Cole, 1977, 271 pp.

_____. "Too Busy To Play," *Child Education, 54,* 2. November/December 1977.

Temple University Institute for Survey Research. *National Survey of Children: Preliminary Results*, New York: Foundation For Child Development, 1977, 21 pp.

Yankelovich, Daniel, *Raising Children In A Changing Society*, Minneapolis: General Mills, 1977, 146 pp.

Sharing Your Impressions

1.   Comment on the extent to which boredom affects the people you know.
2.   How do you feel about taking art, music, or physical education out of the curriculum in elementary school? High school?
3.   To what extent do you decide how your children use their leisure time?
4.   In what ways do you suppose school practices will change to fit the emerging leisure society?
5.   If a child does not have much ability in a certain sport, how can he or she participate without feeling inadequate?
6.   In your opinion, what constitutes a successful vacation?
7.   Compare the satisfactions your job provides with the satisfactions you receive from leisure activities.

4619